The Public Management and Leadership ser

Series Editor: Paul 't Hart, Utrecht University and Netherlands Sch

Public management and, more recently, public leadership have over several decades emerged as increasingly central elements in the study and practice of governance, public administration and public policy.

Around them have developed important new strands of research, debate, education and professional formation. And these in turn have informed a wide range of initiatives in many parts of the world to 'modernize', 'reform', 'innovate', 'de-bureaucratize' and 'professionalize' existing institutions and practices.

The Public Management and Leadership series aims to provide a set of key texts to meet the changing needs of the growing range of graduate, post-experience and other courses in this area as well as concise and accessible reading for busy practitioners.

Genuinely international in scope and conception; accessible in style and presentation; and drawing on empirical information and illustrations from a wide variety of jurisdictions and policy sectors, each title offers an authoritative review of the state of theory and practice in its respective field, and will identify the key challenges and the most promising conceptual and practical tools to tackle them.

The Public Management and Leadership series

<u>Series Editor: Paul 't Hart,</u> Utrecht University and Netherlands School of Government

Published:

John Alford and Janine O'Flynn
Rethinking Public Service Delivery: Managing with External Providers

Martin Lodge and Kai Wegrich
Managing Regulation: Regulatory Analysis, Politics and Policy

Forthcoming:

Richard Mulgan
Making Open Government Work: Accountability, Transparency and Public Management

Mirko Noordegraaf
Perspectives on Public Management

John Uhr
Ethical Public Leadership

In Preparation:

Understanding Public Leadership

The Public Management and Leadership Series
Series Standing Order ISBN 978–0230–23657–8 hardback
Series Standing Order ISBN 978–0230–23658–5 paperback

(outside North America only)

You can receive future titles in this series as they are published by placing a standing order. Please contact your bookseller or, in case of difficulty, write to us at the address below with your name and address, the title of the series and the ISBN quoted above.

Customer Services Department, Macmillan Distribution Ltd
Houndmills, Basingstoke, Hampshire RG21 6XS, England, UK

Thanks for shopping with us.
Kindest Regards, Customer Care

RETURNING GOODS

Please re-pack, in the original packaging if possible, and send back to us at the address below. **Caution!** Don't cover up the barcode (on original packaging) as it helps us to process your return.

We will email you when we have processed your return.

---✂--

PLEASE complete and include this section with your goods.

Your Name: _____

Your Order Number _____

Reason for return _____

Select: Refund my order ☐   **Replace my order** ☐

(Please note, if we are unable to replace the item it will be refunded.)

Return to:

---✂--

RETURNS
Unit 22, Horcott Industrial Estate
Horcott Road
FAIRFORD
GL7 4BX

Managing Regulation

Regulatory Analysis, Politics and Policy

Martin Lodge
and
Kai Wegrich

palgrave
macmillan

First published 2012 by
PALGRAVE MACMILLAN

Palgrave Macmillan in the UK is an imprint of Macmillan Publishers Limited,
registered in England, company number 785998, of Houndmills, Basingstoke,
Hampshire RG21 6XS.

Palgrave Macmillan in the US is a division of St Martin's Press LLC,
175 Fifth Avenue, New York, NY 10010.

Palgrave Macmillan is the global academic imprint of the above companies
and has companies and representatives throughout the world.

Palgrave® and Macmillan® are registered trademarks in the United States,
the United Kingdom, Europe and other countries

ISBN 978–0–230–29879–8 hardback
ISBN 978–0–230–29880–4 paperback

This book is printed on paper suitable for recycling and made from fully
managed and sustained forest sources. Logging, pulping and manufacturing
processes are expected to conform to the environmental regulations of the
country of origin.

A catalogue record for this book is available from the British Library.

A catalog record for this book is available from the Library of Congress.

10   9   8   7   6   5   4   3   2   1
21   20   19   18   17   16   15   14   13   12

Printed in Great Britain by the MPG Books Group Ltd.

Contents

List of Tables and Figures

Tables

Figures

Acknowledgements

The development and writing of a book such as this incurs many debts. Eckhart Schröter is responsible for introducing us to each other. We are grateful to our students at the London School of Economics and the Hertie School of Governance for being involuntary but enthusiastic providers of immediate 'customer feedback' on many ideas contained in this book. Some of the material was also tested in short courses in Libya and Brazil. These experiences suggested to us that this book's approach resonated with different audiences and settings. We are indebted to Chico Gaetani for his friendship and support, and to PRO-REG for facilitating our exchanges with Brazilian regulators. A special thank you to Luciana Vieira, Vanessa Almeida and Gustavo Foizer.

This book project greatly benefitted from the guidance and support of the series editor Paul 't Hart. Steven Kennedy is a legend in the world of political science publishing, and we are most grateful to him for his motivational leadership. The British Academy (SG41761) facilitated research activities that encouraged conversations about this book. The authors and publisher are grateful to John Braithwaite and Oxford University Press for allowing us to reproduce Figures 4.1 and 4.2.

Martin Lodge would like to especially thank the ESRC Centre for Analysis of Risk and Regulation at the LSE and colleagues on the MSc Regulation for a truly interdisciplinary setting for the study of Regulation. Gail McElroy gracefully listened to the latest developments in Amnesian regulation. Kai Wegrich would like to thank his former colleagues at the University of Potsdam, Werner Jann and Sylvia Veit, as well as the German 'better regulation' community, especially the Bertelsmann Foundation and the Normenkontrollrat. Leon, Mia and Maja Krüger earn a special thank you for their endurance while this book was being written – and so do Ralf Clasen, Alex Ratz and Andrés Walliser for their friendship and support.

Regulation is about life, but life is not only about regulation, so we would like to acknowledge the late Knut and Thomas Dörflein. We thank the tactical genius of Roy Hodgson and the late Ernst Happel for highly memorable moments (long before we started drafting this book). Our parents have always been generous in their support. Roger A. Lodge in particular deserves a special thank you for going through and commenting on all of the draft chapters.

However, in the end, we blame each other for all the mistakes and misinterpretations in this book.

London and Berlin   MARTIN LODGE
                                                              KAI WEGRICH

Introduction

Many countries in the early 21st century are wrestling with regulation. Continuous calls for a 'high quality regulation' agenda fill political chat show programmes. Regulation is said to be out-dated, poorly framed, too punitive and too prescriptive. Environmental groups complain that regulatory approaches are too loose. Public transport has witnessed major difficulties, while the media have voiced disquiet over the rise of a new type of 'monster dog' and the quality of care home oversight. Business interests are complaining about the lack of social order in general and are urging their national governments to consider alternatives to regulation in order to cut 'red tape'. Regulators have come under attack for being both too responsive to political demands and for acting too autonomously.

These debates have featured on the agenda of most developed and lesser developed countries over the past decade. This book explores these debates and considers the different options available for key aspects of what observers have described as the 'regulatory state'. You, the reader, will play a critical role throughout this book in developing the conversation about regulatory tools and approaches. In doing so, you will come across the key definitional and theoretical debates that have characterized regulation as a field of study and practice over the past three decades or so. Ultimately, we want you, the reader, to consider and decide how you would solve particular regulatory problems.

This book is about developing a regulatory analysis perspective. This means that it is not about offering a legal discussion, a consideration of applied or theoretical economic models, or the development of the latest ideas in price review methodologies. Instead, it is about taking a multi-disciplinary perspective to consider problems – and to explore systematically the ways in which different regulatory strategies can be used to solve problems. This book is neither about encouraging a prescriptive 'how to do it' approach nor about developing a philosophy that might suggest that all regulation is 'bad' or some approaches particularly 'good'. If the book wishes to communicate any messages, then they are twofold. First, exercise scepticism. It is unlikely that any one approach or instrument will provide a long-term solution that will not generate side-effects; most instruments require particular prerequisites to function. Second, consider the contestable nature of regulation: only by considering competing understandings of problems, different potential responses to these regulatory problems and the different underlying prerequisites are we able to have an informed conversation about regulation.

1

These two messages are not to be confused with a fatalist 'nothing works' perspective. We wish to generate a healthy understanding of debates and assumptions that are often left implicit in the advice by 'off the shelf' consultants or in the findings of academic works. We seek to offer an analytical tool-kit for thinking about regulatory problems and appropriate solutions; solutions that might be appropriate in one context (and point in time) but not in others.

The rest of this introduction sets out our wider agenda. First, it asks why it is important to consider regulation at this time: what aspects have changed that require a consideration of key debates on the regulatory agenda? Second, it explores in somewhat more detail what we regard as the central features of a 'regulatory analysis' approach. Third, we introduce our particular angle, namely a reliance on vignettes that draw on one fictional country, named Amnesia.

Why is regulation on the agenda now?

This book is for all those who are interested in the implications of regulation for public management and public policy. As noted, it is therefore about general principles and debates, and not about the latest artefacts and websites of consultants or the design of evaluation exercises in terms of econometric or other methodological choices. This book is about advancing the conversation regarding debates and challenges that confront the regulatory agenda. Without aiming to offer a comprehensive list, these challenges can be roughly separated into two broad areas:

The rise of the regulatory state

One of the most widely used claims has been that the past two or three decades have witnessed the 'rise' of the regulatory state (Majone 1994, 1997; Levi-Faur 2006). The implications of this claim are twofold. The first implication is a broad shift in the goals and objectives of public policy and administration. The age of the regulatory state is said to give priority to the use of legal means as a tool of public policy (thereby requiring third parties to comply and carry the cost of complying). This contrasts with an earlier age where the use of tax-based financial and organizational (i.e. state-owned production) devices were said to be more dominant. Such a reliance on regulation has been justified by an emphasis on the value of efficiency: policy is supposed to achieve outcomes with the least resource input, rather than trying to maximize the goals of fairness (through, for example, redistribution) or of redundancy (by creating gold-plated extra-capacity).

The second implication is that the administrative machinery of the state is said to have changed in response to economic and international forces. Most of all, this shift has involved, first, a growing reliance on private providers for the operation of public services. A second indictor has been the establishment of regulatory agencies tasked with the oversight of these activities. These agencies are usually organized to be autonomous from direct political involvement. The third indicator is a growing reliance on formalized or contractualized relationships between the different actors within a regulated domain. These changes, however diverse their implementation in various national contexts might have been (Lodge and Stirton 2006), have given rise to debates regarding the appropriate organization of the regulatory state, involving different ownership forms, the organizational set-up, legal powers and resourcing of regulatory agencies, and about the extent to which contractualized relationships can be properly enforced regardless of whether these contracts have been framed in highly precise or very broad language.

Building on these two implications, the language of regulation has spread across domains and across countries. Regulatory agencies have become a ubiquitous feature across countries in both northern and southern hemispheres. Two decades ago, observers were suggesting, for example, that 'regulation' did not resonate with the German administrative law tradition. Today, it would be difficult to argue that the regulation word had not become a common feature in German political and administrative discourse (Döhler and Wegrich 2010). Similarly, the language of regulation has also spread across domains, penetrating areas, such as sport, that had previously been largely autonomous in their organizational and controlling principles. Indeed, regulation *inside* government, whether this involves government overseeing public services, or the way in which particular ethics watchdogs or bean-counters monitor political and parliamentary activities, has been a further growth business over the past two decades or so. More generally, the language of regulation has penetrated traditional areas of policy-making and political life, such as environmental policy, thus changing the way practitioners and researchers think and talk about these issues.

An additional growth business has been the concern with regulatory quality or 'red tape'. While a concern with over-complex rules has been a long-standing feature in administrative reform advocacy (the 'red tape' campaign of the 19th century included the author Charles Dickens, for example), the interest with overseeing the activities of regulators and the curtailment of 'red tape' has been a prominent feature on government and international organization agendas for the past two decades. This interest reflected the wider development and spread of the regulatory agenda within national contexts: the central interest in regulation as a 'controlling device' that sought to harmonize behaviour conflicted with the growing specialization and fragmentation of regulatory activities across different domains. The 'better regulation' agenda, as exemplified by the procedural Regulatory Impact Assessment Tool, was to bring about a harmonization of regulatory behaviours by at least achieving decision-making consistency across regulatory domains (similar debates also flourished in the areas of risk regulation and enforcement).

The growing embeddedness of the regulatory state within the national 'policy' and 'administrative' landscape also allowed a growing interest in regulatory sources that were 'outside' the state. Regulation 'outside' the state included the considerable importance that private sources of regulation continued to play in the regulation of national activities. Similarly, there was a growing interest in transnational regulation, not just through the traditional intergovernmental channels, but more in terms of private and public–private settings. These, often private transnational initiatives had, in turn, a considerable impact on national states, raising issues of legitimacy and accountability.

The growing sense of crisis in regulation

Despite the sense of a growing embeddedness of the ideas of the regulatory state and of regulation as a central steering device to address policy problems, the early years of the 21st century also pointed to considerable evidence of a process of 'dis-embedding'. This did not mean that regulation was likely to become unimportant (control and oversight, after all, have been part of state activities since ancient times). However, it meant that the key ideas of regulation became increasingly confused and contested. Again, we can identify a number of factors that facilitated this process of dis-embedding.

One key factor was, unsurprisingly, the financial crisis in which the problem of private debt and the risk of bank defaults quickly turned into a sovereign debt crisis and an argument about the problem-solving capacity of national states and communities of states. As such, the situation of the early 2010s resembled that of the 1970s: then the argument was made that the old economic policy approaches had failed and that political systems, especially those in Western Europe, were unlikely to maintain competitiveness and therefore were on an inevitable downward path. The reforms associated with the regulatory state (privatization, liberalization and internationalization) were arguably a (surprising) response to these concerns with the 1970s. However, at the time of writing, it was not clear what the consequences of the financial crisis will be for the area of regulation.

The financial crisis pointed to the fundamental problems that were associated with a regulatory strategy that believed that private organizations were not just willing, but also capable of managing risk. Furthermore, the financial crisis highlighted the problems for regulators in devising regulatory regimes able to deal with systematic rather than merely individual organizational behaviour. The ability to understand the interconnected nature of markets and products is inherently limited.

However, there was a growing realization that requiring similar regulatory responses to risk might have facilitated the 'safety' of an individual firm, but overall caused a deterioration in terms of systemic risk (similar to the idea that monocultural agricultural production might offer efficiency gains but is more likely to be prone to disastrous contagious diseases) (Haldane and May 2011). Questions were therefore asked how regulators could encourage a sophisticated pluralization of corporate responses to regulation that would lead to overall systemic 'stability'. Finally, the financial crisis and the concerns over the sustainability of public finances also raised the question about how well-resourced regulators ought to be and how demands for 'more' oversight could be addressed with dwindling revenues and a reluctance among politicians to provide regulators with sufficient resources.

More broadly, the conventional wisdom that had characterized regulatory thinking at the advent of the 21st century was also in crisis. This was largely due to disappointment effects. In the field of development, a decade or so of institutional reforms in regulation ended with the realization that the regulatory design had not necessarily had an immediate and direct effect on industrial performance and development goals, especially where politicians, regulators and businesses paid little attention to formal provisions. Elsewhere, the demand for 'regulators' as part of formal conditionality requirements (such as accession to the European Union) was not necessarily met with a commitment towards respecting these new 'offices' or even in equipping them to fulfil their tasks. More generally, there was a growing realization that the 'orthodox' understandings of legal enforcement that characterized large developed countries were difficult to 'transport' into the settings of small, if not micro-states.

In developed contexts there was a similar questioning of the capacity of market-based solutions (i.e. those associated with regulatory state arrangements). For example, it was questioned whether volatile energy markets were able to provide the kind of investment 'climate' that would facilitate a shift towards renewable sources of energy generation. This challenged the self-conceptions of regulators as being mostly interested in competition and efficiency.

Finally, there was also a continuing sense of regulatory failure. Failures were prominent throughout the late 20th and early 21st century, in food safety (BSE in the 1990s and early 2000s, E.coli outbreaks across different countries throughout the Noughties), oil platforms (Piper Alpha in 1990, Deepwater Horizon in 2010), nuclear safety (Fukushima in 2011), maritime safety of oil tankers (Exxon Valdez in 1989, Erika in 1999 and Prestige in 2002), or financial markets (Barings in 1995, the financial crisis post-2008, with the UK Financial Services Authority, regarded as the most innovative 'light touch' regulator in the world, witnessing one of the very few runs on retail bank deposits on its own turf). These highlighted that traditional concerns in regulation – how to encourage 'in-depth' regulatory inspections, how to manage relationships between regulators and industry, how to detect whether a firm is motivated and capable of complying with regulatory requirements, how to combine political demands for more 'industry awareness' with political demands for less regulatory 'closeness' to industry – remained unresolved.

In other words, the field of regulation had witnessed considerable evolution. There was a growing awareness about the limitations of particular strategies that only a decade earlier had been widely praised as offering superior problem-solving solutions. As a result, debates regarding regulation have remained central to practitioner and academic debates across fields traditionally associated with regulation (law, economics, public administration/political science, social policy and sociology) and reflecting on those debates is a central task for the field of public management.

Such debates have increasingly moved regulation outside the national domain towards an increasing penetration of national regulatory activities by transnational processes, whether through the presence of international standards or through the increasing prominence of national regulatory processes (and verification) in facilitating international economic relationships. At the same time, the intellectual crisis in regulation (in particular, the crisis of the initially much trumpeted reform concepts that were supposed to be internationally diffused and applied) has led to a likely 're-nationalization' of regulatory conversations as those international 'diffusion' organizations become increasingly challenged because of the limited effectiveness of their tools and approaches.

Why a focus on regulatory analysis?

The processes of embedding and dis-embedding have gone hand in hand with a process of an increasing specialization and fragmentation of regulatory processes. There is also a risk of an increasing decoupling of regulatory discussions between countries, either because of the increasing extent of the regulatory agenda (which means that only the select few are able to enjoy regulatory conversations in the OECD's Paris-HQ) or because of a reluctance to consider international and cross-domain experiences given the *felt* uniqueness of one's own domain or field of interest. This book tries to counter this trend of specialization, differentiation and fragmentation by offering a 'regulatory analysis' perspective.

So what is a 'regulatory analysis' perspective? The 'analysis' word is inspired by a number of sources. One inspiration is the field of 'policy analysis' (the transdisciplinary field that emerged in the post-World War II period in the United States under Harold Laswell, but one that could arguably be traced back to the cameral sciences or *Policeywissenschaft* that characterized the pre-liberal era across German states). The ambition in the field of policy analysis was to advance the systematic understanding of various approaches that could be deployed to address a given problem or to achieve a certain set of objectives. An emphasis on 'analysis' is both *analytical*, we are interested in why certain approaches might be selected and why they evolve in particular ways, and *prescriptive*, we are interested in what is involved in considering the improvement of regulation in its different components. As we are interested in problems and potential solutions, we are less interested in explaining political and regulatory decision-making processes, or the way in which individual pieces of regulation have been formulated in late-night sittings only to be ignored by firms and inspectors alike. Rather, we are interested in considering sometimes complementary, sometimes rival approaches to particular problems that are typical for regulatory decision making, regardless of level of government.

A related interest has been that of 'administrative analysis'. This term was employed by Christopher Hood (1986) to focus attention on the importance of the 'administrative factor' rather than on the policy-specific considerations that dominated debates. Indeed, he defined administrative analysis as 'the ability to think and argue systematically about alternative ways of providing public services' (Hood 1986: ix). In other words, the importance of organization, drafting rules and how to enforce them is central to the work of those who conduct policy-related work – and a focus on administrative analysis points to the necessity to consider the plurality of options when it comes to general matters that affect the structure, organization and operation of public services. The emphasis is *not* to be an expert in child protection, prisons, food safety or railways, or in terms of economic analysis, budgeting or human resources, but to be able to analyze problems in a transparent and systemic way by going back to the 'basics' of the core underlying problems, to be able to offer informed, cross-cutting experience and questions and to perform a 'challenge function' to those 'conventional wisdoms' that often dominate standard operating procedures in particular domains.

Similarly, a regulatory analysis perspective seeks to encourage cross-cutting, or cross-domain conversations and challenge functions. Too often debates in regulation are conducted in ways that resemble the chanting of particular international reform slogans without much consideration of the underlying mechanisms. Alternatively, debates are not conducted at all, as regulators claim that cross-domain experiences are irrelevant and that their own conduct reflects either the 'state of the art' or reflects the 'art of the possible' because of political and industry demands. Such realities are important, as is noted below. However, regulatory analysis is about seeking to develop creative and systematic means to consider regulatory problems.

Regulatory analysis combines interests that have characterized earlier policy analysis and administrative analysis perspectives. An interest in the formulation of standards and their implementation has been a traditional concern of policy analysis. However, over time, the interest has turned more into a concern with outcomes at the expense of a consideration of the administrative factor. At the same time, administrative analysis has arguably become mostly interested in the processes of administration per se, thereby giving insufficient interest to the actual policy problem. Regulatory analysis requires both a focus on the 'administrative factor', but it also requires a good understanding of the different ways the actual problem is being defined.

More broadly, a regulatory analysis perspective seeks to enhance a general 'thinking like a regulator' perspective. Much of the discussion on regulation – indeed much of the popularity of the term 'regulation' in international reform discourse – is based on the view of regulation as a technocratic and apolitical process. Once regulatory settings are established, things are assumed to be under control and operating in regular ways. The word 'regulation' itself seems to imply a cool-headed and technical approach towards steering that seems to be able to detach itself from all political constraints. As a consequence, some regulators were accused of having a misguided 'Platonic' view of regulation, mistaking legal procedures and powers as sole and 'pure' authority within a context in which political realities needed to be considered and not intentionally ignored. Others saw the emergence of regulation as the promise of the growth of far-reaching (in terms of depth and breadth) means of exercising control (see Moran 2003 for different perspectives on regulation).

A regulatory analysis perspective, in contrast, accepts that any regulatory intervention – whether it is through a reliance on self-regulation or through the most traditional state-based 'command and control' type regime – is likely to be facing trade-offs and side-effects. Inspectors might be overwhelmed by the demands placed on them. Hostile 'target populations' counter-learn to avoid regulatory interventions. Companies are incapable of monitoring their subsidiaries. Regulation takes place in 'living systems' and regulatory decisions are inherently of a political nature, often taking place in highly politicized contexts.

These potential limitations of any regulatory strategy need to be openly considered, especially in view of alternative approaches. Learning from other domains or countries is not, when taking a regulatory analysis perspective, about the 'copying' of what appears to be successful elsewhere. Rather it is about asking the question: what underlying mechanisms make this particular approach achieve desirable results? Such an 'extrapolation' view (Bardach 2004; Barzelay 2007) has shaped contemporary thinking in the wider public management and public policy setting, and it is an essential ingredient of regulatory analysis as well.

In short, thinking like a regulator – from the perspective of regulatory analysis – is about (a) the analysis of the underlying problem, (b) the consideration of different regulatory options, (c) the open conversation about these different options, (d) the acknowledgement of inherent side-effects, trade-offs and inevitable unintended and unexpected consequences, and (e) the realization that regulation takes places in a setting that involves political and other interests and requires support from these arenas. The last point does not mean that 'regulation' in terms of formal approaches does not matter and that everything is merely a matter of negotiation and discussion. Instead, it implies that 'thinking like a regulator' is about accepting the context and constraints in which one operates and is also about how to overcome particular constraints in creative and constructive ways.

Looking at Amnesia's regulatory problems

We introduce each chapter with a particular vignette. These involve regulatory problems in Amnesia. Amnesia is, of course, no real country (although we hope that by the end of the book readers may wish to apply for imaginary citizenship, join special social networking sites, or set up an Amnesia in a virtual 'second life' and test ideas about regulatory analysis there). This book has been written both for the individual reader who is interested in debates in the field of regulation, and for a seminar setting, in order to introduce literatures and to encourage debates in the classroom. Being a visitor to Amnesia concentrates attention on the essential aspects of the regulatory problem without distracting the reader by particular institutional and political contexts that 'real' cases would introduce (for example, the presence of a particularly unhelpful minister, or the implicit assumptions characterizing intergovernmental relations in a particular country, or the reputation of a particular agency). We do so with an international readership in mind. Focusing on particular jurisdictions would require students to acquire a background understanding of that particular country, which, in our view, would not facilitate the development of a regulatory analysis perspective. It would also age the material in this book too quickly.

The vignettes seek to encourage readers – on their own or in groups – to consider what kind of regulatory strategy they would advocate before moving on to reading the chapter (and possibly also any further literature). Each chapter considers different options to the particular chapter's problem and discusses advantages and disadvantages. Readers may wish to consider their own country as an example of Amnesia. They may equally wish to ask how particular constitutional or developmental settings might influence the way they develop particular regulatory strategies. In short, Amnesia is an 'open case'. It can be treated as a developed or lesser developed country, it can be considered as a very small, medium-sized or large country, it might be considered as a unitary or federal state, or as a presidential or parliamentary democracy (or even as a non-liberal democratic system, although our vignettes draw on contexts that are liberal democracies).

The vignettes draw on 'real life' cases from a range of countries (with some artistic licence). We have chosen to use vignettes from different domains to highlight that regulatory analysis is not about environmental, utility, health and safety, or social regulatory activity in particular, but rather that many important questions can be raised by looking across domains. For those readers working in particular regulatory fields, these vignettes are to encourage a consideration of their own experience *outside* their particular domain. Of course, when considering these vignettes in group settings, readers from different backgrounds may wish to consider their own experience. The vignettes and the discussion in the chapters are to establish the groundwork for such a 'regulatory conversation'. In the end, we can only be 'regulatory analysts' if we are able to share particular terminology across different areas and are thereby able to understand as well as influence conversations in particular regulatory domains.

This book cannot claim to be anything but an introduction to a select field of regulatory debates. The originality lies in the way it introduces and discusses the different cases and literatures. This book therefore differs from other introductions to the field of regulation (especially Ogus 1994; Morgan and Yeung 2007; Baldwin *et al.* 2012) or more general 'state of the art' overviews (see Baldwin *et al.* 2010). This book is purposefully selective in its treatment of particular regulatory fields and it seeks to develop the regulatory analysis perspective throughout the chapters.

Overview

Having established the regulatory analysis perspective and introduced the overall ambition of this book, it is now time to provide a brief guide to the rest of the volume. The next chapter introduces the field of regulation, in particular dealing with different definitions of the *regulation* word, and also with the traditional normative justifications that have underpinned regulatory interventions. The discussion then moves to considerations of theories (Chapter 2) before progressing to the fundamental components of regulatory regimes, namely standard-setting (Chapter 3), enforcement (Chapter 4), and the consideration of so-called 'alternatives to regulation' (Chapter 5).

The book then proceeds to the discussion of particular regulatory concerns, namely regulation *inside* government (Chapter 6), questions regarding which level of government regulatory activity should be allocated to and how international should be operated (Chapter 7), before we consider particular issues that have been at the heart of infrastructure regulation, namely the design of overall regulatory regimes, including regulatory agencies (Chapter 8), and, in particular franchising and concessions (Chapter 9).

We then consider different options that have been developed to advance the 'high-quality regulation' or 'better regulation' agenda (Chapter 10), focusing both on instruments and organization. In Chapter 11, we move to the discussion of risk regulation, that is, the way in which regulatory regimes have been developed to deal with particular types of risks or threats. We conclude this volume with the question 'What is good regulation?' (Chapter 12), where we discuss the key components that are said to make for 'good regulation', and consider the types of challenges that regulatory analysis faces.

Welcome, then, to Amnesia.

Chapter 1

What is Regulation?

Business associations in many countries complain that the 'regulatory burden is too high'. Regulation is seen as an obstacle to economic growth, because regulation is a cost factor and because bureaucratic regulation impedes innovation. The Amnesian business association is seeking advice from consultancies to substantiate this claim.

What kind of examples from the world of regulation should these consultancies list to justify the claim that the 'regulatory burden' is too high?

What is a regulatory burden?

What examples would we expect to emerge? For some, the regulatory burden is created by 'bad' rules. Examples would include complex rules that, it is argued, stifle innovation or any form of discretion. Some industries complain about the prescriptiveness of rules that force companies and organizations, such as polluting industries or nursing homes, to invest in technologies that, they maintain, offer hardly any benefits, or whose benefits could be achieved much more cheaply. Other industries are concerned about legal uncertainty, given the poor drafting of regulations. The telecommunications industry is complaining about 'out of date' and 'steam age' regulation that pre-dates the digital era. The construction industry, in the meantime, is critical of the high price and low quality of cement that it blames on the exclusive import licence granted to the (recently privatized) 'Amnesian Concrete Monopoly'.

Others would focus on the way in which inspectors and regulatory agencies go about their business: accusations here include the seemingly arbitrary way in which regulators enforce regulation. Some inspectors are seen to be lenient and flexible, others excessively punitive or relying on protocols and documents to an extreme extent. Complaints are also made about the lack of expertise among regulators and the way in which governments have failed to resource regulators properly, causing problems in export business as customers in export markets do not trust the quality of Amnesia's products. Other industries complain about the high charges levied by regulatory bodies.

Another set of protests about Amnesia's regulatory burden concerns the costs of completing inspection and monitoring reports. Tax forms are seen as long, complex, and highly detailed, forcing, especially small firms, to spend considerable time and effort completing paperwork that, they suggest, threatens their economic livelihood. Firms also complain about having to report similar information to different regulatory agencies in different formats. Other industries object to alleged inconsistencies between various regulatory regimes. For example, provisions in air pollution regulation are said to be far more lenient than those regarding water pollution, with the different inspectors for air and water quality requiring different kinds of (often inconsistent) responses to the objective of environmental health.

Finally, there are also complaints about a 'level playing field'. Industries moan about inconsistent regulation across domains. For example, Amnesia's manufacturing industries complain about the much more lenient regulatory standards that apply to their competitors in neighbouring Dezertia. The financial industry argues that Amnesia's financial regulation is not sufficiently 'light touch' to attract international business, and threatens that it will have to relocate should the 'regulatory burden' not be significantly reduced. Similarly, small supermarkets are objecting to a lack of a level-playing field when facing the much bigger out-of-town hypermarkets whose licences grant them more lenient opening-hours.

These examples point to the numerous ways in which regulation matters to everyday private and corporate life. Regulation matters to individuals, to public organizations, such as nursing homes, schools or prisons, and to private organizations, such as large manufacturers, small restaurants and supermarkets. Regulation is therefore not just about rules that apply to private business. For some, the above might appear as typical examples of lobbying (and griping) by actors that seek to benefit from reform; for others, they point to the inherent problems affecting all state activities, namely their over-prescriptive nature. Whatever their motivation, these examples of regulatory burden suggest that regulation involves three key aspects: *Reg regime perspective*

First, *standard-setting*, or the 'rule' itself. These are the aspects of regulation that set out the direction of the regulation, namely its target, its objectives and the way in which these objectives are to be followed. Standard-setting also includes the choice of 'agents' to conduct regulatory activities, for example, whether regulation is operated through a 'state'-based regulatory agency or through self-regulatory bodies, and through what kind of regulatory strategy (i.e. 'command and control' or 'management-based standards').

Second, *behaviour-modification*, or the way in which rules are complied with and enforced. As noted above, enforcement plays a critical role in making 'rules happen'. In other words, it matters how compliance is achieved, whether, for example, compliance relies on advice and persuasion, or on the threat of punishment, such as the threat to close down facilities found to be in contravention of regulatory requirements.

Third, *information-gathering*; systems of regulation require elements of 'detection', as otherwise regulators would not know whether their standards 'make sense' and are being complied with. Any basis on which to enforce regulation would be absent. Therefore, the way in which regulators inspect and monitor activities, requiring regulatees to provide information (similar to tax self-assessment forms) and how frequently, is clearly at the heart of regulatory activities.

The three aspects are separate, but their functioning is interdependent: without a standard, we do not know what should be enforced or monitored, without any detection regarding activities 'on the ground', standards are meaningless and attempts at achieving compliance will be more or less random. Equally, without the ability to ensure compliance and modify behaviour, no change in behaviour is likely to occur, especially if this is not in the self-interest of the regulatee. Therefore, we need to consider regulation from a 'regulatory regime' perspective (Hood *et al.* 2001): regulation is inherently about the functioning of standard-setting, behaviour-modification, and information-gathering. We explore these different components in subsequent chapters in more depth. However, any discussion of 'regulation' needs to consider all three components and should not focus on one component alone. In addition, any discussion of 'regulatory failure' or 'regulatory burden' needs to examine whether the diagnosed 'burden' or 'failure' focuses on any one single component of a regulatory regime, or whether it relates to aspects of the interaction between different components. For example, one of the key complaints in contemporary regulation is the inconsistency that arises from standards that have been agreed at the supranational level (EU environmental standards, for example) and are then transposed into national regulation by national regulators, enforced by one set of local inspectors and monitored by another. A regulatory regime perspective therefore requires us to dig deeper into the word 'regulation' and to question why a particular regulatory regime looks the way it does.

A regulatory regime perspective, however, does not tell us what the limits of regulation are (and consequently what the limits of this book are). If regulation has no boundaries, then regulation might be said to be a meaningless concept (we need to know what is 'inside' and 'outside' our field of interest). Equally, if regulation is only about 'making people do what they may not wish to do otherwise', then the regulation word could be replaced by the word 'power'. If so, we might as well have written a book about power.

Such definitional problems arise in particular if one takes the field of regulation to define *all forms* of social and economic influence. According to a 'governmentality' influenced (or Foucaultian) view, states and markets are inherently power-related and constructed settings that place some actors in a position of power over others. This includes the way in which societies are encouraged (or controlled) to 'self-control' their behaviours. For example, we find regulation when looking at the patterns of behaviour that govern family lives and gender relations, class-rooms (i.e. students sitting in a seminar room reading this book might be seen to be regulated) and mental institutions. Sources of regulation are, according to this perspective, not necessarily a result of hierarchical rela-tionships. Regulatory authority is said to lie within a 'decentred' (inter-national) society with actors 'auto-correcting' themselves according to the logic of contemporary governing (in the current era, this might be the self-adoption of the norms characterizing a dominantly 'neoliberal' system, i.e. individuals willingly accept having to behave according to the logic of the 'market') (see Foucault 1991; Dean 1999; Rose 1999; Power 2007; Miller and Rose 2008).

Other, similarly extensive definitions would argue that regulatory power is to be found not just in the formal representations of regulation, that is, government offices and regulatory authorities, but in all 'controlling' devices, such as property rights, international relations and other means that stabilize particular modes of (capitalist) production (see Jessop 1997; Boyer and Saillard 2002/1995). This is a most exten-sive definition of regulation that builds on the French *Régulation* school. This approach represents an attempt to understand, in quasi-Marxist fashion, the interaction between types of state 'modes of control' that stabilize and facilitate capitalist systems of production (for example, rules regarding the allocation of radio wavelengths facilitating interference-free radio broadcasting, something that a 'free' market may not be able to achieve). In addition, this extensive definition of what regulation might include also highlights the importance of seeing chang-ing forms of control as reflecting changes within the economy, such as changes from mass-industrial (Fordist) to service-oriented type of economies (post-Fordist).

Such an extensive definition of what regulation 'is' may be seen to be too extensive, especially when contrasting this with the examples of the 'regulatory burden' provided at the outset of this chapter. A far more narrow definition would regard regulation as a *specified set of legal commands*. This would limit the study of regulation to legal measures (as set out by government ministries and regulatory agencies). In the purest sense, this definition would limit regulation to those rules that emerge in response to broader legislative measures, for example, when a food safety regulator specifies particular rules regarding meat hygiene. In a somewhat wider sense, this definition would also include legislation (i.e. the legislation setting out the powers of the regulatory agency in food). Regulation, then, would include all forms of legal authority.

Whereas the former definition might be seen as being too wide, this second definition is arguably rather limited. It does not include, for example, those regulatory measures that have no backing in 'law' (such as self-regulation). It also is unable to accommodate the fact that formal rules and provisions are set within a system of informal understandings. In other words, regulation is inherently about what economists would call, 'incomplete contracts' in which there is considerable uncertainty. This uncertainty is filtered and 'regulated' by taken-for-granted norms and understandings. For example, regulatory standards may set out what to do in the case of a certain set of incidents, but it is almost certain that these standards will not account for all incidents and behaviours. Similarly, how a regulatory inspector interacts with regulatees is unlikely to be defined by formal standards, but will be a matter of understandings, past history and wider interaction patterns within the regulatory domain.

To account for such limitations, we treat regulation in the broad sense of all forms of *intentional use of authority* by state and non-state actors to affect a different party (see Black 2002a). This involves all three regulatory regime components (standard-setting, information-gathering and behaviour-modification). Authority includes the use of formal legal force as well as informal understandings and conventions. Such a definition is therefore wider than one that is focused on legal commands, but is also more restrictive in that it requires *intention* rather than a mere pointing to all forms of potential control that might exist within society or the economy.

Who regulates?

Our definition of regulation, the 'intentional use of authority that affects the behaviour of a different party' (Black 2002a: 19), includes public and private actors as the source of regulation. This contrasts with the possibly most well-known definition of regulation, namely Philip Selznick's understanding of regulation as a 'sustained and focussed control exercised by a public agency over activities that are valued by a community' (Selznick 1985: 363). That definition was (legitimately) formulated to demarcate boundaries of regulation research by concentrating on the activities of 'public agencies'. However, for a number of reasons such a definition is far too limited and arguably unhelpful, especially when taking a regulatory analysis perspective.

First, talking about 'public agency' might include a number of public bodies, such as ministerial departments and different kinds of non-ministerial bodies, such as regulatory agencies. However, it does not include the number of ways in which regulation can be organized through non-state bodies, for example, through self-regulation at the national or international level. It also assumes that a single agency is responsible for 'regulation' instead of the more likely scenario of a variety of bodies being responsible for all three regulatory regime components. In fact, much of the concern with regulatory burdens has usually little to do with the way single regulatory bodies go about their work. Instead, there is more concern about the cumulative and potentially inconsistent way in which different regulatory actors (state and non-state) understand their role.

Second, understanding regulation as 'sustained and focussed' control requires a focus on all three regulatory regime components. As the chapters in this volume show, considerable debates about how to exercise 'focussed and sustained control' exist, and such debates are further complicated by the need to see the different regime components in relation to each other.

Third, many regulatory activities involve transboundary issues and have international effects (Boin 2009). This might be less the case when considering the regulation of care homes, but it is most certainly the case in environmental protection standard-setting, the licensing of new food-stuffs, or the inspection of health and safety and hygiene standards for exporting industries. This, then, raises issues as to what constitutes the 'relevant' community. In particular, it raises questions as to the legitimacy and accountability of those regulatory regimes that are decided outside normal and mostly national processes of political legitimization. It also raises questions about regulation activities exercised by private agents that in some cases act with state blessing, but in other cases without direct legitimization by national states. Increasingly, private regulation also occurs in the regulation of state activities themselves. For example, private credit-rating agencies are widely regarded as undertaking regulatory functions in that they evaluate a state's creditworthiness.

Finally, Selznick's suggestion that regulation focuses on 'valued' activities is also highly problematic. Regulation is inherently a political process and it might be argued that any attempt at preference aggregation, at whatever level of government, is highly arbitrary and unlikely to reveal properly what is 'valued' within any community. Indeed, so-called capture theories would suggest that regulation inherently reflects concentrated and highly select interests rather than any broad 'community value' (see Chapter 2).

Problem of concentrated interests

In addition, the list of regulatory burdens also points to another key challenge that affects public management, namely the inherent contestation that underpins regulation. The list of complaints, noted above, suggests differences in what regulation is supposed to achieve: some want 'less' regulation, viewing the role of the state as inherently problematic in interfering with individual (social and economic life) and see 'light-handed' regulation as part of the 'competitive advantage' of any particular country. Other sceptics of regulation see any regulatory intervention as an outcome of biased political outcomes, or warn of the inevitable unintended consequences that any regulatory intervention will bring, often making things worse rather than better. Others see regulation and the state as essential in controlling against the potential 'excesses' of individual and corporate behaviour, especially in securing markets or in controlling for social and moral concerns (such as controls over alcohol consumption, the availability of abortion or the rules governing divorce). Thus, how regulatory burdens are ultimately understood and addressed depends on the way we understand the purpose of regulation to be. Throughout this volume, we emphasize the inherent contestability of regulation and explore the various dimensions of this contestability.

In short, thinking about regulation through a regulatory analysis lens emphasizes the importance of understanding the whole set of pluralities and instrumentalities that are in the regulatory toolbox. The public management of regulation therefore needs to consider and integrate this plurality of views on what regulatory regimes are supposed to be, why they exist and how they could be organized. Thinking about how to address a particular problem is an inherent part of the public manager's role, and reflecting about how to improve the overall quality of regulation is part of public management in general. Dynamics within regulatory systems are characterized by ever-greater domain-specificity (energy regulation, water regulation, biodiversity regulation, food safety). Such a process of ever-greater differentiation and specification requires a countervailing, more general public management-inspired regulatory analysis discussion to highlight that many of the problems and challenges that are encountered within regulatory domains are shared and can be addressed in a more informed way through cross-domain learning and the ability to communicate in the shared language of regulatory analysis.

Why regulate?

But what are the typical justifications as to why regulation exists? A focus on these justifications does not exclude a variety of motives for regulating. We will explore 'motives' in the next chapter as it relates to different theories of regulatory origin, behaviour and design. In this section, we briefly consider how regulatory activities have traditionally been justified (some may suggest that the below are 'normative' theories of regulation). These justifications can be summarized in two broad types of rationales, market-based and social solidarities.

Market-based rationales

As regulation comes with costs, if not burdens, and intervenes in markets, the most important justification (at least in the traditional economic thinking about regulation) is related to market failures, with the aim to achieve allocative efficiency. Market-based rationales are put forward to highlight that markets will not necessarily produce desirable solutions, as some markets are inherently imperfect. Markets may be absent, due to the presence of natural monopolies, negative externalities may exist (such as pollution) that require intervention, or information asymmetries may impede consumers from making well-informed choices in the market-place (for example, concerning their choice of food or pharmaceuticals). We consider these different market-failure based related rationales in turn.

Monopolies, limits of liberalized markets and natural monopolies

Monopolies are characterized by the presence of a single seller that controls the whole market. The products it sells know no close substitutes, so consumers cannot turn to alternative providers (for example, there are no real alternatives to cement, in contrast to butter where consumers might turn to margarine). In addition, market barriers exist that prevent entry by other firms. As is well-known, monopolists maximize profits by restricting their output and setting prices above marginal cost. The monopolist forgoes sales (it could extend sales and lower prices), but these 'lost' sales are compensated for by the higher revenues achieved from the higher sales price (the 'monopoly rent'). The results of a monopoly are reduced output, higher prices, a transfer of 'economic rents' from consumers to the monopolist and a 'deadweight loss' (the allocative inefficiency due to the loss of 'welfare' due to monopolistic 'artificial scarcity').

Introducing competition would reduce these imperfections. However, there exist traditional justifications for choosing to accept the 'imperfections' of a monopoly (we introduce them here without suggesting that they are plausible). For some, restricting access to goods through a monopoly might be a moral choice. For example, distributing alcohol or other kinds of drugs through a state-owned monopoly might be said to allow maximum control over pricing (reduce competitive pricing strategies), may reduce problems in overseeing retail hours, and facilitate the control of overall consumption patterns (and the type of alcohol being consumed). Similarly, monopolies have traditionally been justified by potential quality concerns. It has been argued that granting a monopoly to particular industries, such as cement, is justified to reduce the risk of a 'race to the bottom' that competitive markets might produce. In other words, if markets are allowed to exist, there would be a tendency to compete on price by reducing the quality of the product to such an extent that this would lead to negative consequences (i.e. in the case of cement, poorly constructed buildings).

In some situations, the introduction of competition (through legal means, structural solutions in the industry and suchlike) is not straight-forward. If we liberalize markets but a dominant provider remains, regulation may be justified to prevent this dominant provider (usually the incumbent) from using its position to exercise predatory pricing strategies which would allow the undercutting of the profitability of new entrants. Similarly, burdening 'legacy' providers with particular obligations while allowing new entrants to benefit from the existing infrastructure is likely to lead to calls for regulatory responses.

Furthermore, regulation of liberalized services is said to be required to address issues of *security of service* or *continuity of service*. If we believe that markets will provide an efficient allocation of resources, then it may be argued that such a constellation will have difficulty in providing for 'inefficient' 'surplus' or 'slack'. For example, private markets are unlikely to voluntarily provide stand-by spare capacity, so regulation may be required to facilitate the financing of this capacity (by offering subsidies, 'lighter' pricing constraints, or cross-payments from other industry actors). Equally, some services to remote areas may not be provided by private services (or only at extra cost, as private profit-seeking providers will only concentrate on profitable services) and therefore it may be argued that regulation should either force particular providers to offer these 'universal services' through internal cross-subsidization, or through the creation of a fund that compensates firms for the provision of such non-economic services.

Such concerns are also expressed when it comes to *price volatility*. For example, it has been argued that trading arrangements, a market-based alternative to 'normal' regulation, are only feasible if the trading price is sufficiently 'attractive'. As will be noted in Chapter 5, if the price for trading carbon is low, it is unlikely to provide sufficient incentives to alter behaviour (i.e. seeing 'carbon' as a valuable good). As a result, it has been argued that regulation should install price ceilings in order to reduce volatility and thereby offer market actors long-term 'stability' for planning purposes (for example, the solar industry is said to be keen on 'stable' and 'long-term' guarantees regarding feed-in tariffs so as to be able to offer an attractive proposition to potential customers).

In *natural monopoly* situations, the conditions for market entry do not exist, or are highly problematic. This affects industries with high fixed asset characteristics, for example, electricity transmission networks, railway tracks or water pipelines. In these cases, economies of scale exist that imply that the size of the relevant market can only be catered for by one single firm. Otherwise, one may end up with underused duplicate water pipelines, electricity networks, or railway stations and tracks. In such situations, redressing the monopoly position is not possible (even if it is desired). Therefore, regulation is required to deal with the setting of prices at near marginal cost in order to require the monopolist to operate under 'near-market' conditions. A further regulatory problem with natural monopolies is to identify their boundaries. One of the key arguments in favour of the vertical separation of infrastructure industries, for example, has been that this allows the introduction of competition in potentially competitive areas of the industry. However, often the ability to 'separate out' particular parts of an industry is dependent on the availability of technological devices.

A similar argument regarding the limits of markets has been made in the context of *scarce resources*. For example, it has been traditionally argued that rented accommodation should be price-controlled, as otherwise the low supply of rental accommodation would lead to price increases and uncertainty regarding the development of rents and make such accommodation unaffordable for so-called key workers, such as nurses, police, firefighters or teachers. The most famous example of rent control is New York State that introduced such controls in 1943, with most other US states and cities introducing rent controls during World War II to minimize the risk of 'profiteering' (earlier initiatives had taken place during World War I). The economic case in favour of such measures is that landlords are in a powerful position (both in terms of information asymmetries and transaction costs). Once tenants have moved in, the costs of seeking new accommodation and moving makes them open to 'exploitation' by the landlord. Rent control further supposedly protects tenants against landlords who may respond to demands for repairs by imposing substantial rent increases. Economic analysis has however largely suggested that these arguments lack evidence, that rent controls have reduced potential investment in accommodation (both in terms of quality and quantity; although subsequent alterations to rent control regimes have somewhat reduced the disincentives to invest by allowing rent rises at the beginning of a new rental agreement). Other accusations have been that rent control regimes were captured by landlords, thereby guaranteeing that rents were set at a high level, or that landlords escaped provisions by requiring extra-payments (such as asking for non-refundable deposits or payments for 'fittings').

Similar arguments about owners making profits through 'luck' or other circumstances outside their control have justified the use of so-called *windfall taxes*. For example, assuming that gas prices are linked to oil prices, it is argued that gas companies should not make extra profits from fast-rising oil prices. In other words, companies should not be allowed to benefit from developments that have nothing to do with their own efforts. Critics, however, argue that any windfall tax amounts to a dangerous encroachment on the principle of the sanctity of private ownership.

Information asymmetries

Effective choice in the marketplace can only exist if consumers have a degree of information about products. They need to know which provider offers a cheaper and/or better product (especially if they only rarely purchase a particular good or product). Consumers need to know what is 'inside' a foodstuff, such as a sausage, in order to make informed choices as to what kind of ingredients they wish to eat or drink. It is probable that consumers would like to know if the food they eat contains carcinogenic substances. It is also extremely costly for consumers to research the impact of particular pharmaceuticals themselves. In other words, as the famous work by George Akerlof (1970) on 'markets for lemons' suggested that (in relationship to used cars), without sufficient information, consumers are likely to make inferior choices and/or provide producers with an asymmetric power situation. It follows that in those situations where it can be argued that the cost to consumers of becoming informed is too high, regulation is required. Such information requirements include labelling requirements and the demand to publish comparative or, at least, comparable information.

Externalities

A further widely-made market-failure argument points to externalities. Externalities occur when consequences of the production of a particular service or good are not 'costed' within the production cost. In other words, the price of the good or service does not reflect the 'true' cost to society. One example of a 'negative' externality is pollution. If the price of air pollution (and CO_2 emissions) is not properly costed into the generation of fossil-fuel generated energy, too much of that form of energy will then be consumed. In contrast, the benefits for public hygiene of having access to water is a 'positive externality' that is not reflected in the individual consumption charges for water users. In both cases, one way to deal with this externality problem is through regulation, namely by requiring the internalizing of these 'costs' and 'benefits' into the internal cost-production function. Such externalities might also be of a long-term nature. For example, it is unlikely that the so-called discount rate for private investors will sufficiently reflect the problems or the benefits of particular investment decisions. In this case it is argued that the time-horizons of private markets are ill-adjusted to the kind of investment decisions where returns have to be measured in decades rather than in years.

Public goods and common pool resources

Finally, regulation is also said to be required in the case of public goods and other related type of goods. The most well-known example of a public good is a lighthouse: once it has been set up, it is impossible (or too costly) to exclude passing boats from 'consuming' (and benefiting from) the signal, nor does this consumption decrease the extent of benefit derived by other consumers (i.e. other boats do not suffer from a decline in signal, regardless of how many boats are receiving the lighthouse signal at any given time). The problem of public goods, therefore is that 'market mechanisms', that is, the ability to use price signals by being able to exclude people from consuming certain goods, do not function properly in these cases – and therefore it is unlikely that they would be provided for by private markets on their own. Another example of a public good is national defence or just 'fresh air'. In these cases, it is difficult to compel individuals to pay for a service that they can enjoy regardless of whether they pay or not (there is a 'free rider' problem). Regulation is said to be required to establish mechanisms that provide for payment for the generation of such public goods as they would not be provided for (or would be undersupplied) by private markets. Among the regulatory measures to facilitate these developments is to grant property rights (such as intellectual property and copyright laws), to provide for public subsidy, or to rely on their provision by government (and the compulsory requirement to pay tax).

Similar market failures occur in the case of so-called *common-pool resource goods* (Ostrom 1990). These goods are characterized by their non-excludability, but, in the case of these goods, their consumption does deplete the overall resource base. One well-known example is the so-called 'tragedy of the commons' (Hardin 1968) (i.e. with the inevitable result that collective decision-making leads to over-grazing). A 'real world' related problem is fish stock management: it is very difficult to exclude fishing boats from extracting fish from the sea (as property rights are difficult to assign and centralized control is difficult to enforce), with the end result that over-fishing is difficult to curtail (for discussion of potential solutions, see Chapter 7). The management of river pollution and the radio spectrum are further common pool resource problems, both of which require regulatory interventions to force potential users from interfering with and deteriorating the overall viability of the resource (pollution for downstream users of rivers, and interference in the radio spectrum).

Finally, regulatory devices may also be called for in the case of so-called *club goods* (i.e. goods where exclusion is possible, but where the consumption of the good, up to a point, is non-rivalrous). Examples of such club goods are parks and swimming pools. Such goods may be generated by private parties, but it might be argued that their public benefit calls for some regulatory intervention to manage access. For example, roads are a potential club good and we may regulate 'access' to roads (and their provision) either by allowing private consortia to provide roads and let them charge freely, we may encourage private provision, but guarantee minimum earnings, or we may provide such club goods through the use of the general (taxpayer-funded) budget, or through voluntary contributions (the Charlottenburg Palace Gardens in Berlin and the British Museum in London seek to encourage voluntary contributions for entry into their premises, for example).

Social solidarity-based rationales

One of the widespread accusations levelled against the above justifications for regulatory interventions (or expressed scepticism about the viability and utility of such intervention in addressing these problems) is not only that they seem to assume a 'benevolent' and cost-free government that regulates intelligently and carefully. It is moreover argued that the above arguments assume that in most cases markets offer appropriate problem-solving devices, and that regulation is only required to address market failures with the key debate then becoming one about discussing the acceptability and boundaries of particular phenomena and whether these constitute 'market failure'. Such a perspective is accused of ignoring the basic fact that markets and their regulation are historically grown phenomena that operate on the basis of traditional understandings, assumptions and formal rights. Markets are therefore unable to operate without regulation – they are not 'natural' phenomena but reflect historical and political constellations. Individual preferences, in addition, are not the result of 'free choice' but are based on the opportunities and constraints of the market place. As a consequence, a reliance on the 'markets' to allocate resources is as much a political decision as is a decision to grant welfare payments to any particular subgroup among a country's population.

More importantly, the above justifications are all of an economic nature, therefore paying too little attention to wider interests or justifications. Such justifications could, for example, be based on *social solidarity* (Prosser 1999, 2006, 2010; Feintuck 2010). According to such arguments, the regulation of key industries and other fields in life is fundamentally justified as it addresses key issues of citizenship: the regulation of infrastructure is not merely a matter of natural monopolies and universal services, it is fundamentally about the nature of citizenship and the wider welfare state.

These questions become particularly prominent when it comes to the regulation of services that affect particularly vulnerable customers where market 'choice' may not be all that straightforward. For example, questions as to how, for example, we wish to regulate nursing homes, often containing lonely and potentially extremely fragile (if not dementia-ridden) elderly people, prisons (with prisoners unable to 'choose' prisons as others are able to choose supermarkets), or social services (dealing with children who are deemed at risk from parental or other adult abuse), are less a matter of 'market failure', but centrally affect the kind of society in which we may wish to live. Establishing what social solidarity is and how to deal with potential conflicts between different views as to what this social solidarity supposedly constitutes is far from straightforward. Therefore, any discussion of regulatory regimes needs to acknowledge this inherent conflict between the most basic values that characterize human society. This inherent conflict is at the heart of regulation, but is often hidden in debates that, instead, utilize economic justifications.

The following chapters raise issues about the way we consider the way markets function (or fail): the extent to which we think the 'state' can provide for positive outcomes (or mostly regulatory failure), whether we believe that individuals and organizations are capable and willing to follow regulatory objectives or inherently to seek to cheat or avoid regulatory intent, and what interests should be considered in terms of regulatory objectives in the first place. However, how we decide on which values should be present in any debate regarding regulatory regimes is something that is inherently contested, and it is the role of public management to ensure that such value choices are made explicit in any regulatory debate.

Conclusion

This chapter has set out some of the groundwork for the following chapters. It had three key messages:

- Regulation is a phenomenon that includes three components: standard-setting (to provide for overall 'direction'), behaviour-modification tools (to provide for means of enforcement to change people's behaviour) and information-gathering (to allow for knowledge about what is 'happening'). Any discussion of regulation that focuses on one component alone needs to be explicit about such limitation as regulatory regimes can only achieve their intended effects if all three regime components operate in non-dysfunctional ways. Such a prerequisite becomes the more demanding, as the discussion on regulatory burdens has suggested, the more the various regulatory activities are distributed among different actors.
- Regulation is an intentional activity that seeks to alter the behaviour of another party. However, this does not mean that regulatory activity should be solely understood as an activity conducted by public regulatory agencies. Rather the regulatory toolbox provides for a number of techniques and alternatives that need to be considered.
- Regulation has traditionally been justified in market-failure terms. Such justifications have increasingly come under challenge, as analysis has suggested that market failure was not as prominent as believed, and that regulation often had political and interest group origins rather than a basis in economic analysis (see Chapter 2). Moreover, regulation is about competing values and therefore economic market failure arguments should not enjoy superiority over other types of arguments. Rather, regulation should be understood as an inherently

contested field of practice (and study) in which the right place for regulatory analysis is, first, to understand the plurality of competing options, and, second, to understand the prerequisites for one alternative to be able to offer a more persuasive or acceptable option than another.

Chapter 2

Theories of Regulation

Amnesia has not been able to avoid the financial crisis. The whole banking sector had to be nationalized after Amnesia's banks ran into severe financing problems. On one occasion, riots broke out when savers sought to withdraw their savings from one bank. Amnesia's regulatory institutions have been blamed for failing to spot the high-risk activities of its banks. Politicians are being blamed for their reluctance to intervene and allowing banks to expand so much that they became much larger than the rest of Amnesia's economy. To deal with the political fallout of the financial crisis, Amnesia has established a 'Truth Commission' to investigate the sources of regulatory failure. Why did regulation 'fail' and what lessons might be drawn from this experience?

What theoretical explanations exist that account for the failure of regulation? What can be learnt from these theories to avoid future repeats of such crises of regulation?

Four responses

So what has gone wrong? Why did countries across the developed world in particular witness bank meltdowns and accusations of regulatory failure? These questions have occupied academic and popular writing (Khademian 2009; FSA 2009, 2011; Posner 2009; Tett 2009; Lanchester 2010; Lodge and Wegrich 2010), and have also led to 'Truth Commissions' that sought to understand what had gone wrong. For example, Iceland installed its own 'Truth Commission' (Althingi 2010), Ireland established a banking inquiry (Honohan 2010; Regling and Watson 2010), while the United States' Senate inquiry failed to achieve a unified position (US Senate 2011). It is therefore not surprising that Amnesia's Truth Commission is similarly confronted with a range of views.

In particular, four prominent positions have emerged:

- Position 1: The problem with regulation is that it was captured by those interests that were supposed to be regulated. The relationship between regulators and regulatees has always been far too close with regulators regularly ending up in lucrative positions in regulated firms. Political control of regulators also hardly exists. Politicians do not want to upset powerful industry interests and want regulators to take

27

the blame when things go wrong. Regulators themselves will do their best to avoid any activity that could cost them their jobs. So, the best way to deal with regulatory problems such as the financial crisis is to trust in competition and not in regulation as this will just become a playground for special interests. Captured regulation only distorts true market forces and therefore leads to undesirable economic outcomes.

- Position 2: The problem with regulation is that there will always be unintended consequences. Any attempt to make banks take on greater capital reserves through regulation is likely to fail as it will push them towards even less regulated and more risky niche markets. This is because regulators cannot foresee future events and with the limited resources at their disposal cannot ensure that they will be prepared for all eventualities. Regulators will therefore always lag behind financial markets. In addition, most control regimes inevitably wear themselves out, as regulatees learn to 'play the system' and those that are opposed to the overall direction of the regulatory regime will seek to redirect regulatory efforts.

- Position 3: The problem with regulation has been that it was driven by a particular 'light-handed' ideology that assumed that regulatees would be interested in and capable of monitoring their own behaviour. This belief was entirely misplaced. The financial crisis has been caused by the inherent tendency of capitalist markets to undermine regulatory norms and to develop in 'boom and bust' ways. Furthermore, the financial crisis has shown that regulators are too fragmented and do not talk the same language. We therefore need a new politics of regulatory ideas that emphasizes the importance of addressing systemic market failure rather than one that is reluctant to intervene forcefully. It was universally agreed that governments should actively promote the expansion of the activities of Amnesian financial institutions to allow for an expansion of home ownership.

- Position 4: The problem with regulation has been one of poor institutional design. If only there had been closer attention to the design of regulatory institutions and instruments, there would have been less opportunity for things to go wrong. Most of all, this relates to the way in which regulatory agencies conduct their oversight activities and the way in which politicians are unable to change the overall regulatory regime as time goes by. The primary motive of politicians in setting up regulatory institutions has been to make sure that other people get the blame when things go wrong.

The Amnesian government is puzzled by these four positions (which, of course, partly overlap). All four agree that regulatory oversight failed, but they suggest different reasons for these failures. They also disagree about ways to prevent further regulatory failures. All four positions sound 'right' in practice, but the government wishes to know whether these positions also have a basis in regulatory 'theory'. So, the Amnesian government has asked its officials in the prime minister's policy unit for a background document that protocols the different perspectives and gives them an overview of the various theories of regulation. The rest of this chapter therefore offers an overview of those perspectives that would provide the foundations of the policy unit's background document.

From a Regulatory Analysis perspective we are interested in theories that offer explanations to three specific questions:

- How does regulation emerge, evolve and develop (origin)?
- How (and why) does regulation fail?
- How should regulatory institutions be designed?

Public Interest Theory is an account of normative justifications for regulatory intervention that also assumes that politicians and regulators are benevolent (they choose regulatory tools that address 'objective' failures). It does not tell us much about the ways in which regulation is created and implemented across all dimensions of the regulatory regime, that is, standard-setting, information-gathering and behaviour-modification (see Hood 1994; Noll 1989; Lodge 1999, 2002a). Regulation as a political process is not always benevolent, but a process where power and self-interest matter, where bureaucracies seek to defend their turf and politicians seek to advance their career prospects and enhance electoral success (however, see Levine and Forrence 1990; McLean 2004). Empirically, too, Public Interest Theory has problems in accounting for policy domains where considerable regulatory activity occurs without much evidence of an actual market failure. At best, therefore, the idea of a 'public interest theory' should be to offer an account that points to the goals that a regulatory programme *should* have and where one assumes that regulators seek to act in good faith (see Breyer 1982: 10).

The rest of this chapter introduces various theories in the light of the four positions outlined above. It does not seek to offer a conclusive account of why financial regulation failed, but accounts for the underlying assumptions and mechanisms that support the different theories. Looking at theories of regulation is not just about considering which theory, or theories, offers a persuasive account of particular events, but is also about strengthening our understanding of regulation by looking at contrasting positions.

Position 1: Regulation as a product of capture and interest group politics

The most prominent explanation for regulatory failure is capture. Broadly defined, capture suggests that regulators have failed to do their job because they have come too close to the interests of those they are supposed to regulate. Regulation therefore does not represent a 'universal' public interest but the immediate and special interests of a select industry. Accordingly, when translated into the case of the financial meltdown that has affected Amnesia's financial institutions, the argument is (as reflected at the outset) that regulators have been captured by financial institutions. There are two key different ideas that have both become known as capture theory (Bó 2006; Light 2010; Carrigan and Coglianese 2011; Thomas *et al.* 2011).

One variant of the capture theory follows a life-cycle argument (Bernstein 1955, also Huntington 1952, Kolko 1965). Accordingly, regulatory regimes are born in conditions of heightened public attention (for example, in the context of a banking failure), leading to the adoption of 'tough' regulatory measures to prevent any repeat occurrence. Over time, however, public and political attention wanes and shifts to other issues. As a result, the sole party interested in the activities of the regulator is the regulated industry which is strongly opposed to 'tough' regulation. Politicians, having lost interest (or the memory of why they were in favour of regulation in the first place) hear the demands of the industry and become hostile to the regulatory regime. The regulator therefore has a choice – face extinction or seek accommodation with the industry. Unsurprisingly, regulatory agencies are said to follow the latter path, leading to captured regulation. According to Bernstein, periods of youth where regulators operate with zeal but are regularly outclassed by better-resourced regulatees move into a period of maturity and, finally, old age, where agencies become more reactive and procedures become judicialized (see also Downs 1967, who highlights how young organizations 'mature' and thereby lose 'zealots' and 'climbers' as staff and turn into 'conservatives').

According to Stigler (1971), regulation is a result of capture at the point of origin: 'As a rule regulation is acquired by the industry and is designed and operated primarily for its benefit' (Stigler 1971: 3). At the heart of this argument is the utility maximizing (or strategic) politician-regulator who seeks re-election (and therefore seeks political support). The political benefits of regulating (and thereby pleasing a concentrated interest) are far higher than its costs, as the costs of regulation when dispersed across a diverse and large number of customers is negligible. For example, by restricting the import of particular foodstuffs due to 'safety provisions', domestic farmers are able to obtain considerable benefit, whereas the cost to consumers from higher food prices is arguably limited as food consumption is only a small part of total household expenditure. Thus, for politicians the benefits of regulating in favour of the concentrated industry are great as it is unlikely that voters will punish politicians for regulating (and increasing their costs).

The underlying theory follows Mancur Olson's 'logic of collective action' (Olson 1965). Small concentrated groups have an advantage over 'general' larger groups. Small groups are able to mobilize as mobilization is directly related to potential benefits received. In addition, small groups allow for the monitoring of participation and the sanctioning of non-participation. In contrast, large diffuse groups are prone to free-riding unless some other selective incentives are offered. Individual participation is not pivotal for the overall outcome (or is highly unlikely) and is difficult to monitor. Therefore, regulatory regimes are designed to meet the interests of the regulated industry, in particular the interest in limiting competition and fixing prices to extract 'monopoly rents'. Regulation is 'captured' by private interests. A similar argument was made by Sam Peltzman (1976); see also Keeler (1984). However, he argued that 'politician-regulators' were unlikely to ignore the interests of dispersed voters completely and, therefore, regulation would, at the margins, include special social provisions.

Does this mean that all regulation is inevitably a product of capture by interest groups, whether at the point of conception (Stigler, Peltzman) or over time (Bernstein)? If this were the case, the inevitable conclusion would be that all regulation was bound to fail and, therefore, should be avoided. Instead, 'true' markets based on competition-law principles should suffice. After all, it could be argued, it was the distortion of regulation that encouraged financial institutions to act with over-exuberance (i.e. they had become too big to fail because of regulation that guaranteed that they could not fail).

Empirically, it is hard to claim that all regulation is captured. For example, social, consumer and environmental regulation was introduced that went explicitly against the concentrated power of industry interests (Williams 1976; Wilson 1989). Capture-based accounts also have difficulties in accounting for regulatory change, especially in terms of liberalization. Why would vested interest consent to losing its privileged market position? At best, interest-based accounts can point to factors that have made the privileged position less attractive. For example, technological change may have reduced the profitability of particular regulatory regimes (for example, in telecommunications), or less regulated substitutes have emerged that threaten the position of a particular regulated industry (for example, insurance companies offering financial products that resemble those of banks which are, however, differently regulated) (see Hammond and Knott 1988; Moran 1986).

Furthermore, the likelihood that interest group politics will always lead to a capture-type outcome varies across domains. Capture accounts assume, as noted, that the benefits are concentrated on a select few, whereas the costs are widely dispersed. However, there are evidently areas where concentrated interests occur both on the 'benefit' and the 'cost' side (industries that are affected by high transport or energy prices), leading to, what James Q. Wilson calls 'interest group politics'

[handwritten margin note: Not always "captured" e.g. "soft" + "health" / social regulation]

between two broadly equal sets of interests (1980). Furthermore, there are domains where there are no concentrated interests on either side. Finally, Wilson noted that there are also fields where regulation occurs despite these interventions incurring high costs to concentrated interests, whilst benefits would apply to the 'dispersed many'. He argued that many of such initiatives were in the area of social or health regulation (consumer rights), and were the result of political entrepreneurs forging coalitions against sustained industry pressure. Capture therefore is hardly universal and applies only to select areas (and has been accused of having a very simplified picture of political life).

Elsewhere, interest group politics-based explanations have also been used to account for the tightening of smoking and of environmental regulation (Doron 1979; Vogel 1995). In both these cases, the seemingly paradoxical outcome of regulation being adopted that seems to go against the preferences of industry is explained by the existence of coalitions between regulation advocates and regulated industry (so-called 'baptist-bootlegger' coalitions, Yandle 2011). The regulated industry benefits from 'tighter' regulation (the cigarette industry from the reduced threat of emerging competition, the automobile industry from harmonized standards), while the regulatory advocates are pleased with their achievement. Tighter regulatory standards that drive-up production costs might offer particular benefits to some select producer interests. This is because the cost of complying with tight standards will fall asymmetrically on particular firms, creating competitive advantages for those facing limited transitional compliance costs.

Interest-group politics accounts have been widely used to explain the failings of financial regulation during the financial crisis, as noted. Capture accounts would suggest that the financial industry was influential in shaping the politics of regulation and in shaping the climate that made regulators seek accommodation and 'light-touch' rather than 'intrusive' regulation. It also meant that politicians were unlikely to stand up to financial interests. In addition, developer interests (i.e. housing construction) seem a likely source for identifying capture across political systems.

Furthermore, the widespread practice of 'revolving doors' between industry and regulators (the practice of career paths mixing experience in regulator and industry) is said to have further facilitated the 'closeness' between industry and regulators. Capture theory, in particular Bernstein's life cycle account, would also suggest that the future development of the regulatory regime is one where the post-crisis politics of regulation will again be dominated by the financial industry. When the attention of politicians and the public has moved from financial institutions to other issues, the adoption and enforcement of 'tough' or 'intrusive' regulatory standards will become increasingly difficult. The difficulties in adopting and implementing policies to impose structural changes on financial institutions that pose 'systemic risks', for example by separating investment from retail branch functions, or to find means to regulate private rating agencies offers potential evidence of the continuing persuasive power of interest group politics-oriented accounts.

So, what should be done about regulation, considering the prescriptions stemming from interest group accounts? One solution would be to 'deregulate' and rely solely on competition and other general consumer law (after all, it was those financial institutions that took on the most trading risks that got punished the most). This would reduce the availability of 'rents' that could be captured by the financial industry and would also reduce the distortions caused by regulatory interventions. Another option would be to create 'teflon'-type institutions (see below) that would seek to address the power asymmetry of concentrated interests vis-à-vis more widely dispersed ones. A further remedy might be to install counter-interests that act as a balance to the concentrated interests of the financial industry. Another measure would be to fragment industry interests (for example, by separating industries or firms, i.e. investment and retail banking), or to encourage market entry to reduce 'concentration' (the latter approach would build on Gary Becker's view (1983) that in a transaction-cost free environment, monopoly rents will be competed away).

Position 2: Regulation as a product of unintended consequences and inevitable 'wear-out'

As seen above, a separate argument points to the inherent unintended consequences of any intentional activity. Individual and organizations are inherently limited in their capacity to process all information given time and other constraints (Hood and Peters 2004). Regulatory instruments that may have worked in one place, may not work in another (Merton 1936; Grabosky 2005a).

Much of the contemporary fascination with behavioural economics has been about the 'discovery' of the conditions of bounded rationality (Simon 1947; Kahnemann 2003) that lead to particular decision-making biases and so-called 'satisficing' (decision making by limited choices and rules of thumb). For example, Thaler and Sunstein (2008) argue that a range of 'heuristics' lead individuals to make problematic decisions (such as the status quo bias or loss aversion). These heuristics are said to dominate decision making when we rely on intuition (our 'automatic system') rather than on 'reflection' (or 'reflective system') (see Thaler and Sunstein 2008: 21–4). Financial markets, therefore, could be seen not as an expression of the well-considered calculations of different financial institutions, but as the result of herd behaviour among traders and others that facilitates bubbles. To address such behaviour patterns, Thaler and

[handwritten margin notes:]
Bounded rationality — de-m ways e. rationality of individuals is limited by the information & the cognitive limitation of their mind

Heuristics — experienced techniques for problem solving that find a solution which is not guaranteed to be optimal.

bubbles — where asset prices appear to be based on implausible or inconsistent views of the future.

herd — acting collectively w/o centralised direction.

loss aversion — people's tendency to strongly prefer avoiding losses to acquiring gains.

Sunstein advocate 'nudges' and other 'architectural' devices to trick individuals into making the 'right' choices (see Chapter 6).

Such insights have also led to a renewed interest in the different types of observed responses to interventions. Individuals and organizations respond in different ways – and often in unanticipated ways – to regulatory interventions. Building on Merton (1936), Sam Sieber (1981; see also Hood 1974) has offered a list of seven unintended effects that any intentional strategy might trigger, all of them also applying to the field of regulation: functional disruption (change frustrates the functioning of the regulatory regime); exploitation (regulatory instruments are used by opponents to their own advantage, thereby reversing regulatory intent); goal displacement (where a focus on complying with regulatory procedures drives out a focus on regulatory objectives); provocation (where attempts at regulating leads to antagonism); classification (where regulation causes labelling effects, such as stigmatization); over-commitment (where misplaced attention to unobtainable regulatory objectives crowds out attention to obtainable goals); and placation (where the illusion of compliance and achievement filters out warning signs).

A related argument (although coming from a somewhat different standpoint) notes how interaction effects between different institutions lead to unintended and unpredictable consequences. Regulatory regimes are situated within sets of institutional relationships and regulatory authority (power) is distributed between actors. A simple change in the powers of a regulatory agency might (or might not) affect the overall distribution of regulatory power across different actors in the 'regulatory space' (others call such accounts 'decentred regulation': Hancher and Moran 1989; Scott 2001; Black 2002b).

These regulatory spaces emerge in the context of legal and historical understandings and are therefore not a result of intentional design at a particular time. Such accounts also suggest that regulation is not just about 'regulatory agencies', but is something that is spread across market participants and public bodies, thereby expanding the focus of regulatory analysis to include self-regulatory and transnational settings of regulation that may be shaped by non-state actors. Furthermore, regulation is not a simple 'one-directional' concept in which willing regulatees accept what is being 'thrown' at them. Rather, regulation is a dynamic interaction in which actors respond strategically to others' actions (e.g. counter-learning).

Related to this is the idea of *layering* as a form of institutional change which has been used to point to the side effects when multiple regulatory regimes based on different assumptions and objectives operate alongside each other and are interdependent. Pressure for reform does not lead to a 'complete' replacement of the old, but some form of filtering: demands for reform will be partly accommodated, partly rejected, leading to uncertain overall effects on the way in which the overall regulatory regime operates in future. Put differently, regulatory regimes have to be seen as historical events in which modifications and additions are added to existing regimes – often reflecting very different kinds of motives and assumptions. Over time, such competing rationales turn into conflict and lead to tension and pressures for change. Layering contrasts with *drift*, in which environmental change alters the effects of particular regulatory interventions, making them increasingly meaningless (not adjusting pensions to inflation or regulatory instruments to changing financial markets would be examples of drift). Other institutional mechanisms of change include *conversion* (in which regulatory regimes established for one purpose are used for another), *displacement* (the removal of old rules and their replacement with new ones) and *exhaustion* (breakdown and failure) (see Mahoney and Thelen 2010). Similarly, accounts based on cultural theory (see below), place a strong emphasis on social processes in which opponents of dominant institutional structures mobilize and seek to undermine and manipulate in order to mould regulatory structures according to their own preferences.

Finally, unintended effects and 'closure' to reform attempts also play a central role in theories of *self-referentiality* and *autopoiesis* (for different variants, see Teubner 1986, 1993; Clune 1992; Willke 1995; Luhmann 2004). The dominant idea – one that might explain the ineffectual nature of financial regulation – is that society is continuously differentiating into ever more distinct subsystems, each of them defined by a distinct 'language' or 'code'. These systems operate according to their own logic, but nevertheless interact with their environment in a process of self-generation and reproduction. Communication between different systems is however highly problematic and characterized by distortions. The instruments of law (regulation) do not directly translate into the language of the economy. Instead, the translation requires time and leads to potential changes in meaning. The overall effect, according to Teubner, is a 'regulatory trilemma': law may either prove irrelevant and be ignored, may irritate the viability of the functioning of the system, or it may destroy the viability of the system altogether. At best, regulation, according to this approach, is about causing 'irritation' effects (Teubner 1998). To escape this trilemma, the literature advises either a reliance on proceduralization or a process of facilitating self-learning. Proceduralization is defined by measures that without direct intervention seek to steer systems towards desired outcomes (Black 2000, 2001), whereas self-learning is said to be encouraged by means of incentives.

Regulation therefore 'fails' according to these theoretical accounts because any intervention and oversight activity cannot account for the complexity of market or other interactions that are meant to be controlled. Failure also emerges because of an over-confidence in the ability of regulatory instruments and the discounting of the kind of unpredicted side-effects noted by Sieber (as suggested above).

Furthermore, these accounts also offer limited hope for future regulatory activities: the effects are likely to be limited if they are not accommodated within the financial market itself, they point to the inevitable and unpredictable nature of side-effects and tensions that build up within any regulatory system, and also point to the inevitable loss of control. In the case of Amnesia's financial market meltdown one can therefore point to the inherent complexity of financial markets and the decentred nature of regulatory activities that made central oversight infeasible.

Considering advice, arguments would emphasize the importance of maintaining a natural caution regarding the possibility of maintaining control and in predicting the likely consequences of regulatory interventions. It stresses the importance of utilizing 'decentred' sources of regulation, that is, other interested parties, to address the inherent limitations of regulatory oversight. Nudging devices might be useful in incentivizing individuals not to fall into excessive debt, while further regulatory instruments would be required to deal with other decision-making biases that lead to 'herding' and convergent 'risk profiles' and might appear as individual 'insurance' against vulnerabilities, but cause systemic vulnerability.

Finally, the literature on historically grown systems of regulatory spaces also suggests that 'one size fits all' regulatory instruments (or fashions) are unlikely to generate similar effects. Indeed, the literature on 'varieties of capitalism' has made very similar arguments by stressing the inherent relational characteristics within the economy and between the state and the economy (Hall and Soskice 2001). Contemporary economies are shaped by different dynamics, therefore making any search for 'one' regulatory standard for predictable intervention even more unrealistic.

Position 3: Regulation as a product of dominant ideas and worldviews

As already noted, one of the key criticism has been directed at the overall intellectual mood that facilitated the rise of financial institutions and their light-touch oversight. In other words, regulation is seen, according to this explanation, as a result of the wider ideational climate that shapes politics and therefore also regulation.

Reference to dominant ideas has been a recurring theme in the regulation literature. 'Ideas' have been used to attack other theories of regulation, in particular 'interest group politics' accounts. According to ideational accounts, actors do not act 'strategically'. At least, they require a frame of reference that guides their efforts, and these frames are provided by dominant ideas.

It is further argued that ideas matter in terms of the way regulatory tools are selected. Ideas also shape how politicians position themselves towards specific regulatory issues. In the context of the financial crisis, 'light-touch' and 'risk-based' regulation were regarded as appropriate regulatory approaches since regulation was supposed to acknowledge the supremacy of the market in allocating risks and making decisions. More broadly, the rise of the regulatory state and the dominance of ideas regarding financial regulation have been part of an economic policy 'paradigm' that has shaped wider ideas on the relationship between states and markets and the type of regulatory instruments that fit within this relationships (Hall 1993). Regulation was also about protecting the market from erratic intervention of politics (Roberts 2010). The dominance of such ideas cannot only be explained by the power of industry, with politicians and regulators being captured by industry. Rather, a combination of wider ideological and societal trends and the dominance of such views in professional and academic discourse have provided the background for the support for such a regulatory model.

In the wider setting, ideas have been used to explain earlier periods of regulatory change, especially the period of 'deregulation'. For Derthick and Quirk (1985), the intellectual climate mattered in generating hostility towards and thereby shaping reforms of regulatory regimes in the late 1970s and early 1980s (ideas that emerged from the literature on interest group politics, especially capture). Reform in the United States, they argue, was not driven by interests of strategically calculating actors, but by insights from the study of regulation that learnt from earlier experiences and adopted, for example, automatic enforcement rules and cross-domain regulatory agencies (see Hood 1994: 28).

A different account stresses the dominance of worldviews and implicit theories that characterize a particular domain (Douglas 1986, Ellis *et al.* 1991, Hood 1998, Lodge *et al.* 2010). At the heart of any regulatory regime is a set of core ideas that are advocated by those sharing these ideas, and are opposed by those who have other views regarding cause-effect relationships. Grid-group cultural theory points to four rival worldviews, or implicit theories, that are inherent in particular regulatory approaches. These four worldviews, hierarchy, individualism, egalitarianism, fatalism, emerge from two dimensions: grid (the extent to which individual behaviour is bound by rules) and group (the extent to which individuals regard themselves as part of a wider collective). Table 2.1 points to the different worldviews and their underlying views about how 'best' to regulate (drawn from Hood 1998: ch. 3).

Failure, according to cultural theory, would be explained by an over-emphasis on one particular worldview (namely 'individualism'), caused by the inherent striving towards 'pure' solutions in line with dominant worldviews. This over-emphasis triggered side-effects, namely over-competitiveness in the market (with different regulatory centres competing), with light-touch regulation failing to oversee the systemic nature of

TABLE 2.1   *Contrasting regulatory worldviews in cultural theory*

| | | Group | |
		Low	High
Grid	High	**Fatalism** Control through unpredictable processes/inherent fallibility	**Hierarchy** Anticipative solutions, forecasting, and management, response to enhanced authority and hierarchical ordering
	Low	**Individualism** Control through rivalry and choice, incentives to underpin market and individual choices	**Egalitarianism** Control through group processes, network style, participation

Source: Adapted from Hood (1998: ch. 3).

TABLE 2.2   *Contrasting views on the financial crisis*

	Fatalism	*Hierarchy*	*Individualism*	*Egalitarianism*
Problem	Life and market economy are continuous and unpredictable boom-and-bust	Financial crisis a symptom of lack of order	Financial crisis a product of poor incentives and moral hazard generated by governments	Financial crisis a symptom of excessive individualism and failure of authority
Solution	Impossible to anticipate future crisis, therefore any response futile or perverse; rely on process of unpredictability	Create stronger rules and regulatory bodies	Reduce regulatory intervention to minimize 'government failure'	Increase transparency, higher professionalism and limits on authority and markets

Source: Adapted from Lodge and Wegrich (2011a: 727).

financial markets and placing too much faith in the self-regulating capacity of private market participants. Furthermore, cultural theory also highlights how different perspectives would interpret the financial crisis and what kind of responses it would favour. Table 2.2 offers an indication of how cultural theory-inspired accounts would seek to classify different arguments regarding the financial crisis (see Hindmoor 2010; Lodge and Wegrich 2011a).

A third 'ideas-based' strain suggests that regulation is inherently a communicative process. Deliberative processes are supposed to bring different perspectives together and advance shared understandings regarding regulatory issues and processes (Majone 1989; Fischer 2003). Julia Black (2002c), for example, has suggested that a better understanding of communication is central to advancing the quality of the regulatory process. In other words, regulatory failures can be mitigated, if 'conversations' between different actors are encouraged so that a shared understanding regarding the interpretation of rules and their enforcement emerges. Shared understandings further facilitate coordination and encourage distinct patterns of knowledge generation and dissemination.

In short, 'ideas'-based accounts stress the underlying ideas that shape the design and interpretation of regulatory regimes. Of course, it can be argued that ideas cannot exist separately from interests, but equally, self-interest cannot exist without underlying ideas and preferences (Wildavsky 1987). Ideational arguments point to sources of failures by highlighting the emergence and sustained dominance of particular ideas whose dominance may 'blind' participants to particular vulnerabilities and events that 'should not happen'. In response, ideas-based approaches would argue that the one way to avoid future crises is to construct settings that encourage deliberative conversations (Black 2002b) and encourage the putting together of rival worldviews in order to challenge dominant views. In other words, hybrids containing different 'cause-effect' relationships are said to offer more stability.

Position 4: Regulation as a product of institutional design

This position suggests that the failure of regulation in Amnesia had to do with the design of regulatory institutions. Most of all, it relates to the discussion about delegation and the choice of institutional forms to overcome particular analytical problems. This particular literature therefore seeks to explore why and how politicians delegate regulatory authority and how to govern the relationship between politicians and agencies as well as between agencies and regulated industry. They address these issues from the perspective of transaction cost approaches.

In terms of designing institutional structures, the key challenges shaping design choices are questions of information asymmetries, credible commitment and blame avoidance and reputation. Turning first to information asymmetry, it is inherent in any relationship that those performing a particular activity know more about the activity than those who ask them to carry out this task (such information asymmetry problems range from having one's car repaired to having nurses care for the elderly in nursing homes). Reducing information asymmetry costs to zero would mean that one would have to conduct the activity oneself or be permanently present and expert in being able to understand what the other party is doing (thereby incurring high opportunity costs). In the context of regulation, two key sources of information asymmetry exist. First, politicians (and the general public) do not fully know what a regulatory agency (or government department or whoever else is involved in regulating a particular activity) is up to. Second, regulators are also not fully informed about the activities of the regulated industry.

A further, related problem is the time inconsistency problem. This means that participants within a regulatory regime cannot know whether particular parties will accept the rules of behaviour at a future moment. If it is very costly or embarrassing to change the rules, it is likely that politicians, regulators and industry will maintain their conduct. If, however, politicians have little to fear from changing their views over time (or where an incoming government might decide that it wishes to reverse the regulatory settlements established by its predecessors), the likelihood of the time consistency problem occurring is high. This is what the literature calls the commitment problem. We return to this particular problem in more depth in Chapter 8 on infrastructure regulation. Suffice it to say that the regulation of activities therefore deals with two problems in particular: the problem of oversight (the 'agency' problem) and the problem of commitment or time consistency.

So what can be done to deal with the problems of *information asymmetry*? Three particular devices have been developed in the literature (see McCubbins *et al.* 1987). These are so-called 'police-patrols', 'fire-alarms' and 'deck-stacking' devices. 'Police-patrols' are specific units such as special watchdogs, audit offices or parliamentary committees that undertake focused oversight activities. They reduce the information asymmetry cost problem by continuous monitoring, although such constant activity is, of course, costly and might also fail to detect particular wrong-doing. It is also questionable whether wrong-doing would actually be acted upon (because of, for example, capture). 'Fire-alarms' rely on affected constituencies voicing their concerns should they regard regulatory or firm action to be 'out of line'. Politicians or regulators rely on third parties or regulated industries to complain before acting. Therefore this device is less costly than 'police-patrols'. It however requires that all affected interests have equal opportunities to mobilize and exercise the 'fire alarm'. It also requires politicians and regulators to 'listen' to all parties that raise a 'fire-alarm' (which may also be directed towards courts). Finally, 'deck-stacking' devices link to procedural and structural choices (Macey 1992). Measures used to 'stack the deck' include consultation procedures, and the need to pay attention to particular objectives. Structural choices include issues regarding appointments, funding arrangements and governance structures. These 'deck-stacking' devices place regulators on 'auto-pilots' by arranging the 'cards' that they are able to play in the regulatory games. 'Deck-stacking' forces regulators to follow particular procedural choices, therefore biasing their behaviour towards a particular set of outcomes.

The way in which controls, such as those noted above, are deployed, and the extent to which legislative provisions are designed to signal a degree of autonomy to regulatory agencies depends largely on the way the commitment problem is addressed. It might be argued, for example, that delegating decision-making power on regulatory matters to agencies is one way to address the 'commitment problem' (Levy and Spiller 1994): if politicians are taken out of decision making (at least formally) in the immediate political (elected) domain, there is a chance of more consistent decision making over time. However, the extent to which agencies offer a commitment device depends on the way in which their statutory basis provides for credible commitment. If, however, legislative reversal is relatively easy (i.e. political power is unchecked and judicial and other constraints on administrative and political discretionary behaviour do not exist), other means than using agencies might be required – such as the use of licences (see also Chapter 9).

Thus, there is no 'one-size-fits-all' solution: the way regulatory agencies are set up and what kind of control mechanisms are used varies, depending on the way in which activities are 'observable' and the way in which the relevant political system poses a distinct commitment problem. Putting these different accounts together, Murray Horn (1995) has suggested that any regulatory design therefore depends on a set of factors: namely, commitment costs; the likelihood of future reversals of initial choices; and agency costs, the (opportunity) costs of controlling an agency.

He also adds 'decision-making costs', defined as the opportunity cost arising to politicians from having to engage in a particular policy domain. Politicians are unlikely to be willing to become involved in the most complex areas of, for example, environmental regulation, preferring to delegate these functions. More broadly, it might be argued that any politician will seek to delegate (and therefore minimize decision-making costs), because of blame-avoidance motives. As noted by Fiorina (1982), decision makers may wish to seek credit where they can be seen to make electorally popular decisions, but they will seek to shift blame where decisions are likely to be unpopular (such as increased water charges). They can do so by issuing contracts that are enforceable in courts, or they can do so by tasking regulatory agencies with discretionary oversight over particular activities. Hood (2011: 67–89) has similarly noted various organizational delegation strategies, driven by the political motive to avoid the flak of public opinion should things go wrong.

However attractive such delegation strategies may appear, they also carry their own unpredictable political risk: popular opinion may still blame politicians for regulatory decisions, politicians may wish to be seen to be 'sorting things out' (therefore being against delegation), and those agencies that are supposed to play the blame-magnet role may actively engage in shuffling blame back to the political sphere. Other accounts of organizational behaviour have focused less on blame avoidance and more on reputation more generally. The argument here is that organizations will pursue strategies that enhance their reputation as this will guarantee further autonomy (Carpenter 2010; Maor 2007, 2010).

Finally, Horn also noted 'uncertainty costs', namely the inherent uncertainty about the future distribution of costs and benefits within a regulatory domain. For example, issuing a particular licence to provide telecommunications services may not offer much prospect of future returns, given the likely challenge from new technologies that undermine the profitability of particular services. The destruction of profitable regulatory arrangements is less likely to occur in technologically more stable industries (such as water).

Overall, therefore, institutional design is shaped by different factors and the outcome of Horn's framework is that different regulatory arrangements appear as 'rational' depending on the particulars of a regulatory domain, its setting within a political framework and the perceptions of those who construct the regulatory framework.

Such institutional design perspectives offer 'hope' that we can establish institutional arrangements that avoid the risks of 'capture', of politicians intervening in regulatory arrangements to please particular constituencies, or of regulatory bureaucracies pursuing their own favourite activities rather than those intended by their statutory basis.

So what can we learn from this perspective to explain why financial regulation 'failed'? One explanation would be that the institutional framework was simply not appropriate, that it was driven by blame-avoidance considerations or that it had underestimated agency, commitment and/or uncertainty costs. Institutional design perspectives are arguably on stronger ground in pointing to the implications of particular design choices, and therefore any reform suggestions based on this perspective would highlight the importance of 'deck-stacking' and 'fire-alarm' devices (rather than 'police-patrols' that might be seen as too costly). It would also consider how a regulatory arrangement that relied on the coordination (in times of crisis) between central banks, financial regulators and finance ministers can be made functional, given the potential presence of blame-avoidance motivations.

In sum, the four positions were not meant to offer a fully exhaustive or mutually exclusive account of different theoretical positions regarding regulation. Institutional design devices are advocated to deal with the inherent limitations predicted by 'unintended consequence' type arguments. Accordingly, 'deck-stacking' devices are used as devices to require organizations to collect more information in order to be able to make more informed (or 'rational') decisions. Similarly, institutional design perspective shares with capture approaches the view that information

TABLE 2.3 Overview of theories and positions on the financial crisis

Position	Theoretical claim	Causal mechanism	Why did financial regulation fail?	What remedies should be sought?
Capture	Life-cycle	Waning political and public interest makes regulator vulnerable to continued pressure from industry	Regulator became too close to financial industry as politics endorsed light-touch approach to financial sector	Institutionalize attention on regulator to balance industry demands
	Capture at point of 'origin'	Collective action problem leads to dominance of particular interest in regulatory process	Only financial interests involved in regulation, career patterns made regulators keen to appear 'light touch' rather than adversarial	Not regulate at all; introduce more interests into regulatory process (via 'deck-stacking')
Unintended consequences	Bounded rationality	Complexity of markets beyond 'rational' comprehension of any regulatory agency, need for 'satisficing'	Complex product and product interdependencies not possible to assess by regulators, firms and consumers, leading to herding and 'bubbles'	Reduce complexity of financial products, restructure financial markets, use transparency tools to enhance information availability and 'digestibility'
	Reverse effects	Side-effects of multiple regulatory regimes with different understandings and objectives operating side-by-side and overlapping; strategic responses by regulatees	Interaction of different regulations and strategic actors led to failure of regulatory instruments (and illusion of control)	Less confidence in regulatory instruments, use of hybrid instruments and elements of surprise

(Continued overleaf)

TABLE 2.3 *continued*

Position	Theoretical claim	Causal mechanism	Why did financial regulation fail?	What remedies should be sought?
	Regulatory space	Unpredictable effects of similar regulatory instruments given historical and political differences	Particular jurisdictions lacked regulatory capacity and 'responsible' behaviour to control financial markets	Less confidence in 'best in world' financial regulation
	Self-referentiality	Differentiation into sub-systems speaking their own 'code' makes effects of intervention highly ambiguous	Regulation failed as it cannot translate legal into market logic, regulation generates an 'irritant' effect at best	No confidence in regulatory control, encourage 'reflexivity', among regulatees through proceduralization
Ideas	Dominance of particular paradigms	Dominant views regarding 'cause and effect' lead to adoption of particular policy programmes and instruments that reflect dominant implicit assumptions	Neoliberal views shaped 'light-touch' regulation and belief in efficient and self-governing markets	Increase contestation between regulatory ideas
	Cultural theory worldviews	Dominant ideas are contested, opposed and over time overthrown	Dominant ideas created side-effects and could not recognize/act on signals of dysfunction	Create more 'mixed' system or 'clumsy solutions' drawing on different worldviews
	Regulatory conversations	Shared interpretations advance co-ordination given need for co-ordination and understanding	Lack of interpretative community, therefore no shared understandings	Advance professional conversations within and across regulatory domains

Institutional design	Control	Information-asymmetries cause drift, that is, regulators 'evade' political control, industries 'evade' regulatory control	Failure to exercise control mechanisms appropriately ('police-patrols', 'fire-alarms' and 'deck-stacking')	Strengthen 'fire-alarms' and improve (tighten) 'deck-stacking' devices.
	Commitment	Political systems impose different 'reversal costs' on politicians and regulators to change their preferences over time	Regulatory institutions lacked commitment as politicians were able to change intent and change regulatory regimes over time, leading to time inconsistency problems	Design and hardwire regulatory institutions that make legislative reversal too costly
	Blame avoidance/ reputation	Politicians, regulators and industry seek to avoid any reputational damage by designing institutions that allocate blame elsewhere	Blame-avoiding institutional structures led to ineffective institutions that were unable to act/detect	Clarify lines of accountability to reduce scope for blame 'shuffling'

asymmetry and capture processes can be mitigated by facilitating market entry, and thereby the number of sources of information. Ideational and unintended consequence-oriented accounts share the view that seeking to reduce the dominance of any one set of ideas or instruments is likely to advance stability and reduce the probability of dysfunction.

Table 2.3 summarizes the above debate. It notes the four positions, the different theoretical perspectives that underline particular mechanisms that lead to the predicted effect and applies these to explaining Amnesia's financial meltdown as well as to potential remedies. We are not suggesting that these remedies are all of similar relevance – nor do we wish to imply that they would be equally feasible. Different theories would point to the inherent logic of particular processes and therefore even dispute the availability of particular reform options. Table 2.3 is therefore mostly of an indicative nature. The definition of 'failure' follows the remit of the Amnesian 'Truth Commission', namely, why did financial regulation not detect warning signs and/or act on them. Other definitions of failure, for example, a failure to protect the reputation of politicians, or the failure to protect the organizational survival of regulatory bodies would offer somewhat different accounts.

Based on this overview, the Truth Commission remains divided about what advice it should give to the Amnesian government. What would you advise?

Conclusion

Theories offer particular lenses on social reality. They suggest particular cause–effect relationships. We can choose which theory offers a more persuasive account in accounting for particular events or observations. As Table 2.3 suggests, different theories of regulation point to different causes that led to the financial crisis. The various theories noted here point to a mixture of causes. These causes range from strategic actors seeking to undermine or circumvent a particular regime, the absence of sufficient resources to monitor complex environments and activities, the problem of linking different and fragmented regulatory institutions, as well as epistemological limitations, in that particular events are simply not 'understood' as a 'warning sign' (LaPorte 2007).

The intention of this chapter was not to suggest that all regulatory activity is inherently about failure. However, it is important to have theoretical insights about why regulatory regimes emerge and how they are implemented and practised. Varying worldviews will therefore also arrive at different predictions about the viability of particular regulatory strategies. The underlying assumptions of the different theories noted in this chapter also influence the more specific considerations that feature in coming chapters.

Chapter 3

Standard-Setting

A series of dog attacks on humans, including fatal incidents involving the death of two children, has caught the attention of the Amnesian public. After particularly graphic pictures appeared on the evening television news, the minister has come under considerable pressure to 'do something'. The Minister has therefore demanded an immediate 'tough and comprehensive' regulatory response.

At the same time, as a result of these public concerns there has been a rise in the number of abandoned dogs, leading to overcrowding in animal shelters. Wider attention has shifted to the shortcomings in the treatment and living conditions of dogs in these establishments. Another task force is instituted to develop standards for these shelters.

As advisors to the Amnesian government, you are asked to respond to three demands: What is a good standard for the control of dogs that are considered dangerous to the wider public? And what kind of approach should be taken towards the regulation of animal shelters?

Standard-setting: searching for good regulation

How can we develop standards that are 'tough and comprehensive'? How can we make sure that we don't present our minister with a political dog's breakfast? And, how can we develop an approach that is 'precise' in terms of easy-to-understand language, that targets those dogs that are particularly seen as accidents waiting to happen, that is easily enforceable, and that appears to address the problems of dog-related incidents?

Standards are supposed to tell us what we want to achieve, what kind of behaviours are desired, and what to do if we diagnose a difference between desired and observed states of behaviour. The development of a standard is therefore one key aspect of any regulatory regime (as illustrated in Chapter 1). At the same time, just having a standard is unlikely to achieve anything – standard-setting has direct implications on enforcement (behaviour-modification) and information-gathering. In turn, enforcement and information-gathering requirements have direct implications for the achievability of any desired standard.

At first sight, setting a standard might appear unproblematic. Standards are commands stating what is prohibited and what is

[handwritten margin note: What is signed as clarity diffes to different people]

expected: 'drive on the right', 'wash your hands', 'no vehicles in the park'. The basic characteristics of standards seem similarly uncontroversial (see Hood 1986: 19–46): they are explicit statements, intended to change behaviour, and are required to have a degree of generality to allow for broad application. The underlying desire of 'precise' and 'good' standards is the idea of 'automaticity' – the idea that those who govern can do so without having to resort to discretion and interpretation. The idea of government 'by rules not men' has been a key component in liberal political and administrative thought as it offers the promise to reduce the potential abuse of power by those in authority. At the same time, 'automaticity' through well-designed standards seemingly promises a reduction in the cost of administering rules, such as in terms of their application and in dealing with potential challenges.

However, what is a 'good' standard that would please our minister and would not appear as barking mad in the light of governmental guidelines that are supposed to ensure 'better regulation'? Following the language of the US Executive Order 13563 (of 18 January 2011), standards should be accessible and easy to understand. They should, among other priorities, reflect 'best available science', allow for 'public participation', 'predictability' that reduces uncertainty, be 'least burdensome', and take account of 'cost and benefits'.

Such lists of seemingly uncontroversial priorities hide considerable challenges. Standards allocate benefits and costs across affected actors, such as business, consumers, dog owners and street-level bureaucracies, such as dog patrols and police officers. Therefore, one key aspect of any standard is the kind of demands it places on those having to enforce rules. In addition, any standard will also be influenced by the target of the regulatory activity; it matters whether we are dealing with a highly compliant and well-informed population or with an ill-disposed and resistant population. Resisting populations are likely to require far more coercive and prescriptive standards than compliant targets. Furthermore, potential technological changes extend the feasibility of particular regulatory strategies (for example, large-scale online databases enhance information handling in surveillance strategies). In other words, standards are only at first sight the equivalent of thermostat settings that allow for the automatic and uncontroversial adjustment of behaviours. Instead, standards are political decisions about what is valued or not valued.

So how can we develop good standards, in general and for our particular example involving dangerous dogs? One way to consider a good standard would be to focus on *precision*. The idea of precision suggests that we know what is appropriate, that we can clearly distinguish between appropriate and inappropriate behaviours and that we have the means to clearly diagnose what is rightful and wrongful conduct. Precise wording might arguably reduce the possibility of ill-informed or *agreement*

misplaced discretionary action which would then encourage subsequent challenge. Precision therefore offers the prospect of reduced contestation or haggling over interpretation.

For Colin Diver (1983), the idea of 'precision' can be linked to three particular aspects: (i) the idea of transparency in the sense of the standard being easy to understand or 'idiot-proof', (ii) the idea of accessibility in the sense of the standard being applicable without requiring any major effort, and (iii) the idea of congruence in the sense of the standard representing a widely-accepted cause-effect relationship. More extensively, Christopher Hood (1986: 21–2) has noted a number of key preconditions for standards to have an effect. Standards, accordingly should display the following prerequisites. They should:

- be knowable and stable
- acceptable and visible
- consistent
- verifiable
- provide robust categories

Clarity, or the ability to know and predict what the standards are, is seen as a crucial component in encouraging compliance by those willing to comply. If people do not know what the rules are and when they apply, they are unable to comply voluntarily, and rule application will be open to challenge on the basis of obscurity. Indeed, the common law tradition has a *mens rea* ('guilty mind') convention that suggests that individuals should not be accused of wrong-doing if they were not aware that they were doing so. A rule that states 'retire on your 65th birthday' is highly transparent as it allows for little discussion as it is easy to understand, limits discretion and interpretation, and is, if birth certificates exist, easy to apply. The requirement to stop at a red light is an equally transparent rule – as is the requirement to drive on one side of the road. If we didn't know on which side we were supposed to drive or if rules were to change on a random basis, we would not know which side of the road to drive on, and we would regularly end up in gridlock, arguments or pile-ups. Clarity in rule-change is similarly problematic. A decision to switch, for example, the direction of traffic is therefore far from simple. When the Samoans decided to move to the left side of the road in September 2009 (justifying this measure in terms of harmonization with other Pacific islands and reduced dependency on left-hand car imports from North America), this switch required a two-day holiday and a three-day ban on the sale of alcohol to reduce the risk of accidents. Consequently, public buses opened their doors into the middle of the road (*BBC*, 8 September 2009).

Even when ignoring the wider contexts in which rules are set, what clarity means is contested. On the one hand, there are those that associate clarity with simplicity. On the other hand, there are those who interpret 'clarity' as extensive bullet-proof definitions of liability. Standard-setting is often driven towards becoming increasingly complex as various parties (business, consumers, NGOs) seek clarification. Different interests demand guidance on how to behave in particular circumstances; and different regulations will seek to accommodate different values (for example, regulatory objectives requiring decisions to be based on fairness and efficiency) and exemptions. Even a seemingly simple rule such as 'wash your hands' may lead to conflict over what 'hand-washing' involves and how such a rule can be validated. Similarly a rule banning animals from apartment blocks is limited by exemptions for Guide Dogs and those animals unlikely to cause disorder or injury, such as goldfish or hamsters. Indeed, such prohibitions could become increasingly challenged by competing priorities, as dogs (and monkeys) provide 'cheap' alternative health care (such as in the alleviation of depression, the detection of imminent stroke-risks, or in the sniffing of potentially gluten-containing foodstuffs) (*Newsweek*, 13 February 2011).

Furthermore, precise, written-down, and stable rules will not be desirable in all situations as 'automaticity' may not be appropriate in all situations. Some scope for informal understandings introduces essential flexibility and reduces the likelihood of creative compliance (see below) (McBarnet and Whelan 1991). We may wish to allow for some informal discretion as to rule-interpretation, thereby reducing the desirability for 'automaticity' in rule-application (do we want all drivers who are slightly above the speed limit to face an immediate penalty or might a warning suffice in at least some cases?).

Similarly, precise and tightly specified standards also have difficulties in accommodating technological change. Nanotechnology is a good case in point as it provides for potential innovations and applications that no rule can foresee. In areas with somewhat less uncertainty, similar problems exist. For example, should new food products be classified as 'food' or 'medicine', given that different kinds of licensing regimes will apply? The emergence of motorized scooters has raised similar controversy. Most of all, it has raised the question whether these motorized scooters could be defined as 'vehicles' bound by traffic codes and/or whether they should be allowed to drive on pavements. New technologies may also challenge seemingly 'clear' rules, such as the prohibition banning unauthorized vehicles from public parks (would, for example, dog-walking robots be classified as vehicles if they moved on wheels?) (Hood 1986: 46–7).

Precision in terms of transparency also leads to problems in the face of opportunistic behaviour. Any attempt to write down rules will encounter the concerted activities of those opportunist actors (and industries) that seek to exploit loopholes or linguistic ambiguities. In these cases, it might be better to rely on unpredictable standards – if the targets of regulation

Sometimes it is better to use discretion – E1 – explains why

seek to exploit standards in opportunistic ways they are less likely to be able to do so if they do not know when and how they will be monitored. In other words, the desire for knowable and stable standards largely assumes the existence of a population that is willing to comply. It also assumes the absence of other trade-offs, which will be noted below.

Similar problems emerge when considering the second pre-requisite, namely that standards should be *visible* and *acceptable* in the sense of their rationale and underlying assumptions being regarded as appropriate. We would have difficulty accepting rules that seem to fly in the face of common sense. We need to understand why rules exist and generally require rules to be based on reasonable cause–effect assumptions. However, whether acceptability in terms of rationale of the standard and its underlying causal assumptions about the world are that straightforward is questionable: many rules were once adopted for a rationale that has been long forgotten (indeed, sceptics of regulatory activity might suggest that official rationales hide the 'non-official' ones, such as capture). To use our dog example, whether dog attacks are caused by inherently dangerous dog types and breeds, by particularly 'bad' individual dogs, or by 'bad' owners is a matter of dispute, and will shape the way we design regulatory standards. Equally, any choice in terms of prescribing behaviours and devising sanctions for wrongful behaviour will need to account for different kinds of motivation (therefore allowing for flexibility about what explains particular behavioural patterns).

People have varying views about the rationale + causal assumptions of the world – E1

Consistency, the third prerequisite usually associated with 'good regulation', suggests that standards should not contradict other rules. Such contradictions occur when different institutions demand opposing kinds of responses (asking for A so that B can be granted, but A requires the proof of B and A violates the equally desirable C). Standards may demand conflicting types of behaviour, such as the need in planning to come to a decision quickly and efficiently, while also having to consult widely. Are we supposed to err on the side of speed or to consult first (in order to be able to draw on 'latest research')? And how are we to deal with particular demands – such as the need to have 'transparent rules' but also to allow for discretion? How should a new technology be classified and thus incorporated into particular legal approaches (for early railways, see Lodge 2002b: 7)? If regulators have a large number of objectives to consider at the same time, they are left with considerable discretion. As Mashaw (1983) has shown, the application of welfare regulations can lead to considerable (and necessary) diversity of behaviour in the face of discretionary provisions regarding welfare recipients. Individuals are required to make their own decisions as to how to classify any particular event, and most decisions in regulation require a degree of interpretation as to how to understand any particular event and how it has come about.

The final prerequisites of good regulation, that standards should be open for *validation* and represent robust categories, appear similarly straightforward at first sight. Standards can only be enforced or complied with if it is possible to know whether the law is being broken or not. Therefore we have speed cameras and other kinds of detection devices. This raises questions as to whether we wish to produce standards that completely prohibit a particular activity (i.e. the owning of dogs), whether particular wrong-doing should be sanctioned even if no harm has been caused (i.e. the sanctioning of dogs or owners that are falling foul of particular provisions) or if sanctions should be applied only at a certain level of harm (i.e. once a dog has caused damage). We may desire to close down restaurants that make no provisions for kitchen staff to wash their hands without requiring evidence of contaminated food (or of sick customers). Similarly, we may feel inclined to sanction nuclear energy facilities on the basis of certain deviations from the norm (for example, because of cracks in concrete walls), although no actual contamination has taken place.

However, in other cases, we may want to sanction actual harm caused rather than focusing on particular behaviours (thus allowing flexible and innovative behaviours in achieving desired outcomes). In other words, the design of the standard needs to take into consideration the nature of (potential) harm and its reversibility. Furthermore, the choice of 'target' will also be influenced by the ease with which particular aspects can be monitored: if we can't measure the level of harm caused, or have difficulty assessing 'dangerous' behaviour, we may wish to opt for ways that make particular activities 'impossible'. For example, we may wish to opt for a street-design that prohibits speeding in front of kindergartens (such as through the use of architectural traffic-calming measures, for example, flower pots or speed bumps), instead of relying on speed cameras or the imposition of punitive penalties should a child be hit by a speeding car (and then relying on evidence that proves reckless driving).

Classification is also rarely straightforward. There are always borderline cases and every boundary choice as to what is acceptable or not is a result of social choice. How behaviour is distributed around boundary-lines and the extent to which opportunistic behaviour allows for the exploitation of these boundary-lines points to the limitations of being able to specify clear categories. It might be easy to measure traffic in front of a kindergarten with speed cameras, but even here, there might be scope for measurement error. Similarly, it might be relatively straightforward to assess the level of salmonella contamination in a batch of eggs. If, however, we seek to specify the physical features of a 'dangerous dog', we are likely to witness the emergence of even more dangerous animals that fall outside our specifications – and therefore are within the letter of the law. Most standards therefore go beyond the simplicity of measuring that someone has driven at a particular speed or that a particular egg is contaminated by life-threatening levels of salmonella.

Agreeing on what is within acceptable limits and what is the appropriate measurement requires a general level of mutual agreement that is usually absent in the field of regulation. Such problems become even more pertinent in areas of technical uncertainty, such as genetically modified foodstuff or nanotechnology. Where views are contested such as in terms of compliance cost, tolerable levels of pollution or potential future consequences, then demands for and conflicts about measurement and, more fundamentally, definitions as to what is 'good' or 'bad' will increase.

In other words, precision in standard-setting might sound desirable at first sight, but the closer we look the more problematic the idea of a simple and precise standard becomes. What appeared as a seemingly uncontroversial list of five key characteristics of standards has been shown to be inherently a matter of deep controversy.

Such controversy surrounding precision is however not limited to key characteristics. It further extends to problems of *over- and under-inclusion* which emerge when deciding on the targets of particular standards (see also Hood *et al.* 2001). If we set 'clear' standards, such as the 'retire on your 65th birthday' rule, we achieve transparency in terms of administrative ease, but we are incurring both over- and under-inclusion, in that unfit but young workers continue to operate potentially sensitive machinery (such as planes or nuclear reactors), whereas older, but fit and highly competent workers are forced to retire. Regulatory regimes therefore usually are over-inclusive (false positive or type-I error) and impose unnecessary costs on companies, or they are under-inclusive and do not regulate companies or activities that do pose risks to health and safety (false negative or type-II error). How to weigh type-I or type-II errors has received considerable attention in the study of safety regulation, in particular regarding the precautionary principle, as it raises the issue as to whether one should assume that activities or objects should be 'innocent until proven guilty' or 'presumed guilty unless proven innocent' (Schrader-Frechette 1991). Apart from representing a fundamental value-based choice, there are also further side effects from opting for either type-I or type-II error. For example, in the area of 'homeland security', the debate as to whether to err on the side of 'false positives' or 'false negatives' has considerable implications for waiting times and intimidating screening procedures at airport terminals in particular, but also for civil liberties more generally (see Frederickson and LaPorte 2002). But erring on the side of caution, inconvenience and surveillance may be an acceptable price to pay for reducing the possibility of further terrorist attacks. Returning to our goal of designing 'good' standards regarding dogs deemed to be particularly dangerous, this raises the issue as to how to deal with 'over-regulation' (thereby including largely peaceful dogs) and 'under-regulation' (the exclusion of potentially highly dangerous dogs).

Given the above debate, how should we decide on standards to be applied to the design of regulatory standards? One guide could be the use of so-called 'principles of good regulation' that draw on many of the aspects noted above. The US Executive Order 13563, for example, directs agencies to follow these requirements: that benefits needed to justify the costs, that the cumulative effect of the regulation on its own and in conjunction with other provisions was least burdensome on society, and that chosen approaches maximize net benefits, rely on performance standards (see below) and prefer alternatives to direct 'command and control' regulation.

Related, the UK government has led international developments in this area of 'better regulation' by formulating five principles of good regulation that should guide the design and review of regulations in generally any domain (Better Regulation Task Force 2005: 26–7). The 'better regulation principles' suggest that regulatory standards should be:

- *Proportionate*: Regulators should only intervene when necessary, and the regulatory responses should reflect the potential risk and harm posed, while costs of regulatory intervention are identified and kept to a minimum.
- *Accountable*: Regulators should be able to justify their decisions, and the decision making should be subject to external scrutiny.
- *Consistent*: Government rules and standards should not contradict each other, and they should reflect wider legal and regulatory approaches.
- *Transparent*: regulatory standards should be 'simple' and 'user-friendly' (i.e. easy to understand).
- *Targeted*: regulatory intervention should be focused on the problem, and minimize side effects.

These principles are meant to provide useful guidance rather than hard decision-rules (cf. Baldwin 2010). They build on and reflect the basic prerequisites discussed earlier, with all their unacknowledged problems. On their own, they are largely uncontroversial and represent little else than a wish list stating the obvious. However, there is nothing in this set of 'better regulation principles' that tells the regulatory standard-setter how to weigh different criteria and how to handle trade-offs – the more targeted the intervention, the less easy to understand and more complex the standard is going to be.

Returning to the 'retire on your 65th birthday' rule and applying this rule to pilots illustrates these conflicts (see Diver 1983). This approach has clear advantages in terms of transparency, but it scores poorly in terms of ensuring that only fit and healthy captains are flying commercial airlines. Not only might the second approach fail to detect unfit pilots below retirement age, but also healthy and very experienced

[margin annotation: UK's 5 principles of good regulation]

pilots that are perfectly fit to fly commercial airplanes will be forced into retirement. A different approach would require a mandatory and regular health and fitness test for all pilots. This approach would score well in terms of targeting, but it would score less well in terms of transparency. It would require clarification as to the validity and robustness of the results from health checks and would introduce discretionary judgment. In short, the more targeted approach might be less transparent and issues of accountability are less straightforward than in the case of the age-based approach. Indeed, actual retirement regimes in many countries combine regular and compulsory health tests with a maximum age.

Finally, whether or not a regulatory standard complies with these principles hardly matters in terms of the eventual public perception of this piece of regulation. For example, the 1991 British Dangerous Dog Act has been widely accused of being the worst kind of 'knee jerk' legislation, although it fully complied with all the five 'principles of better regulation' and although no further deaths by dogs in public places occurred for a considerable time after the passing of the Act, deaths continued to occur in private places, such as family homes.

Alternative regulatory dogs' dinners?

Having considered the various choices – what are the different approaches available to deal with 'dangerous dogs'?

- a 'neutering' of all male non-breeding dogs approach; this proposal follows the advice that non-neutered male dogs cause particularly violent incidents. In addition, this measure, if adopted, would reduce the occurrence of 'non-official' or illegal breeding, and reduce the stray-dog population.
- A 'breed-based approach'; particular breeds and types (non-represented in the dog-interest universe) would be targeted that are proven to be particularly aggressive.
- A 'weight and size' approach; dogs would only be targeted that are likely to cause severe damage because of their strength and/or weight.
- An 'individual behaviour test' approach; a dog would have to fail a specific behavioural test before any measures were applied to any particular dog.
- An 'ownership test' that would require dog owners to apply for a particular licence after a training course and to provide evidence that their dog(s) would be looked after in appropriate accommodation.
- An 'insurance obligation' that would require all dog owners to purchase tailored insurance to compensate for potential injuries caused by their dog.

- A 'dogbo' approach where dog owners are responsible and liable for the conduct of their dog in public places and could be banned from particular areas in cases of repeated misconduct (*BBC*, 4 March 2011). Such a measure could also be used to deal with owners' unwillingness to clean-up after their dog; for example, Berlin's dog population daily generates over 55 tonnes of excrement.

This list is by no means exhaustive. The ownership test and 'dogbo' approaches differ from the other approaches in that they suggest that the key problem with 'dangerous dogs' is nurture and not nature. The first four approaches point to the 'dog' as the regulatory target. Targeting dog ownership may reduce the probability that 'peaceful' dogs encounter the strong arm of the law. However, it raises all sorts of administrative issues regarding enforcement, for example, when dog walkers suggest that they are not the rightful owners, or how often and by what methods enforcement officers should inspect the dog-owners' homes. The compulsory insurance option relies on price-signals to incentivize owners to switch from 'expensive' (and potentially more dangerous) to less expensive breeds and types – but it requires a licensing system and a way of enforcing dog insurance.

The other approaches also involve considerable trade-offs. Breed-based approaches encounter the challenge that dogs are 'evolving technologies', in other words, any definition of a dog breed is inherently based on constructed criteria (see Downer 2007 for jet-engine design). The more focused the criteria are, the more likely it is that breeders (especially those with connections to the criminal world) will counter-learn by breeding dogs to be within the letter but not within the spirit of the law (*Dominion Post*, 23 January 2012). In other words, breeding will concentrate on producing even more aggressive and powerful dogs. This is particularly problematic in the case of dog 'types' (such as American pit bull terriers) where no codified 'breed'-based standards by kennel associations exist. Breed-based approaches are also problematic in that they are over-inclusive (there may be many peaceful American pit bulls), and under-inclusive (as such a breed-based approach may not include the German Shepherd/Alsatian which might be seen as problematic to include given the size of the dog population and that breed's widespread middle-class ownership). Furthermore, breed-based approaches have boundary issues: how do you justify that some dogs are regarded as particularly dangerous in contrast to others in the face of rather limited information regarding what kind of dogs are present within Amnesia or elsewhere. Dog licensing is generally not associated with high compliance rates and therefore records do not provide a good indicator as to the overall dog population; and those licence-paying dog owners are not usually those interested in owning a 'dangerous' dog. Which dogs cause severe injuries is also not particularly well-known (if you are attacked by a dog and end up in hospital you are unlikely to remember to enquire as to the dog's genetic stock)? In other words, breed-based approaches are faced with issues of over- and under-regulation at the same time.

Relying on an individual test reduces the problem of 'over-inclusion', as it gives each dog a chance to prove its innocence (or lack of vicious tendencies). However, this requires a behavioural test that produces relatively error-free messages (any test has over- and under-inclusion outcomes) and it places also great trust in the measurement by and the discretion of the official conducting the test. Tests also impose administrative costs and their implementation will take time (time that a minister in media-heat does not have). Nor does it deal with the 'illegal' dog population whose owners are already largely outside the law and are therefore unlikely to follow requirements to take their dog to behavioural assessment centres. In contrast, relying on weight and size measures to qualify any particular dog for special measures (such as having to wear a muzzle and a leash in public or for dog behaviour tests) would somewhat reduce the amount of over-inclusion, but would potentially lead to conflicts over enforcement (should a dog who happens to weigh-in 100g above the required weight limit on one particular day be penalized for not having been put on dieting pills?). It also means that smaller dogs may be trained to be dangerous, by, for example, advancing their ability to jump and by strengthening their jaw muscles. There might also be a straight switch towards other animals – as is said to have happened in France (where the fashion moved to small apes as weapons of intimidation) (Hood and Lodge 2005).

An insurance-based approach faces the problem of over- and under-inclusion as it imposes additional costs on those dog-owners that are likely to be law-abiding in the first place, whereas the damages caused by the uninsured dogs (those more likely to cause injury) will remain uncovered. In other words, the price mechanism via an insurance premium is unlikely to deal with the problem of dogs perceived to be particularly dangerous. Similarly, an approach that makes dog owners liable for the conduct of their dog faces issues regarding enforcement and problems of traceability should a dog cause injury and ownership be difficult to establish.

Finally, all those approaches require enforcement (see Chapter 4). Enforcement could be enhanced by the use of micro-chips and/or visible badges for 'good' dogs. Neutering all male dogs that are not exempted for breeding purposes would reduce a range of dog-related problems, especially those arising from stray dogs. However, this proposal could be unacceptable to those professional enforcers who may not wish to be associated with investigating particular parts of dogs' anatomies.

In short, we are dealing with counter-learners, a population that cannot be assumed to be voluntarily complying and also reluctant enforcers. There is also the difficulty of a potentially rapidly evolving technology in terms of 'dogs of choice'. Table 3.1 highlights the different

TABLE 3.1 Overview of different approaches towards dog regulation

Approach	Transparency	Acceptability	Verifiable	Administrative cost/discretion	Over/under-inclusion
Neutering	High	Limited, as dog owners may contest the need to neuter their dog	Easy	Costs of neutering, professional resistance to enforce compliance	High degree of over-inclusion if all male dogs involved
Breed-based	High, although contestation about boundary cases	Potentially high if tightly drawn, potentially low if extensive list chosen	Difficult	High, requires knowledge regarding breeds and types	Both high
Size/weight	High, although contestation about boundary cases	Relatively high, as strength associated with likely injury caused	Relatively easy, but conflict over interpretation of boundary cases	Relatively high, as requires means of assessing dogs	Both medium, many big dogs might be peaceful, many smaller dogs might be aggressive
Behaviour-tests	Low – requires test and involves discretion	High – suggests that individual dogs are 'bad' not whole breeds/types	Medium – requires robust and valid test without high Type I or II errors	High, requires trust in professional knowledge and capacity to conduct tests	Potentially both low

Ownership criteria	Potentially high, but complex rules likely (to define appropriate standards)	If nurture argument accepted relatively high	Very difficult	High, as it requires registration and ongoing inspection	Largely under-inclusion as dog owners will not comply/not register
Obligatory dog insurance	High – although requires choices regarding dog types/breeds	Medium – as law-abiding dog owners may dislike additional charges caused by 'illegal' dogs	Medium – if visible signs are provided for	Medium – relies on registration system	Both high over- and under-inclusion; Lack of register of injuries sustained in dog incidents
'Dogbos' – social control orders on dog owners	Low – requires understanding of required behaviours	Medium – largely problems with those resistant to prescribed behaviours.	Low – requires discretionary understanding of 'dog officials'	High, requires policing of public places	Potentially low, as interference only on basis of incidents and displayed behaviours

choices, reflecting also how different jurisdictions have sought to address demands to regulate dogs deemed particularly aggressive. How would you decide – or what mix of approaches would you choose?

In sum, designing clear, precise and transparent standards is less straightforward than initially suggested. Rather, setting standards requires dealing with trade-offs inherent in almost any case of regulatory design. A call for 'precise' standards that will somehow emerge from a straightforward balancing of benefits and costs of intervention inevitably leads to difficult trade-offs.

Rules versus principles

Apart from the immediate concern regarding the lack of capacity in Amnesia's animal shelters to deal with abandoned dogs, there have been more long-standing issues regarding the quality of care inside these establishments. At the same time, members of staff have complained about the 'red tape' that impedes their ability to do their work and about regulatory inspectors' inconsistent and aggressive behaviour. Again, therefore, we are faced with a difficult choice: What kinds of standards are likely to encourage an improvement in the quality of care in these animal shelters?

One initial distinction can be made between those that ask for 'clear rules', whereas others advocate a reliance on 'principles' (Baldwin 1990; Black 1997; Braithwaite 2002). Rules in this context are defined as specific prescriptions, whereas principles are defined as standards that offer broad guidance. An example of a rule would be a speed-limit, whereas a principle would ask for drivers to choose their speed 'appropriately' or 'with due consideration of the specific context'. The latter approach might be regarded as too vague – there might be too much scope for disagreement over appropriate speed or other forms of careless driving. Indeed, encouraging people to responsibly interpret particular regulatory objectives might mean that they will either ignore these objectives or interpret them in their own favour. As a result, we may wish to specify clear rules to guide animal shelters.

Although there are considerable rhetorical attractions to the idea of 'rules-based' standards, these standards are vulnerable to the kind of problems we discussed in the previous section. Indeed, Robert Baldwin (1990) has noted that 'rules don't work'. John Braithwaite (2002) has suggested that rules are only superior under conditions of stable and relatively simple environments (such as telling people not to dive off cliffs or motorway speed restrictions). Under conditions of higher complexity and more rapidly changing environments, rules are arguably highly limited in their benefits and even potentially counter-productive. The applicability of rules is limited in the face of complex environments characterized by the presence of (highly complex) corporations, transitional technologies and strategic behaviours (for example, involving taxation). Furthermore, rules, as noted already, are likely to interact with other rules, and attempts to clarify complex laws by ever more complexity also has a redistributive impact (see Braithwaite 2002: 57): only the well-resourced are likely to be able to cope with the costs of playing the regulatory game.

In his studies of nursing home regulation, Braithwaite (2002: 60–5) observed that the rules-based approach in US care homes encouraged a box-ticking type compliance approach that hardly represented regulatory intent. The consequence of this compliance style was that patients received a lower level of care that hardly took into account specific or individual circumstances. It also meant that regulatees and regulators were hardly motivated in their job as they merely focused on completing checklists. A further problem was that a concentration on completing checklists also bred complacency which is often seen as a key source of failing to identify deeper or underlying problems (see Power 1997). Furthermore, as the US approach was characterized by growing complexity, with the discovery of loopholes being followed by additional rules, there was also a growing problem of ensuring consistency in assessment.

In contrast, the Australian regime of nursing home supervision was based on 'principles' and outcome-based standards. For example, nursing homes were to offer a 'homelike environment', without specifying what this environment should look like. Although widely condemned as being merely aspirational and unenforceable, John Braithwaite (2002) argues that nursing home managers and inspectors were encouraged to engage in professional conversations regarding the provision of a 'home-like environment', and had few problems in agreeing if this objective was achieved or not. Rather than following a rule-book and ticking boxes in a checklist, managers developed bespoke responses to general principles. In other words, they did not turn into 'rule-following automatons' (Braithwaite 2002: 66). This meant that nursing home staff sought to respond to the substantive needs of their patients rather than the demands stated in regulatory provisions. Indeed, he argues that nursing home regulation in Australia provided for more consistency than in the United States. Inspectors in the United States were required to address an overwhelming number of standards (over a thousand) and therefore enforced those unevenly. Their Australian equivalents displayed more consistent enforcement activities, having to cope with 31 standards.

Similar patterns were also evident in other policy fields, such as taxation. Valerie Braithwaite (2007) suggests that resource rich companies and individuals, who could draw on specialized lawyers and advisors to find loopholes, could exploit such inconsistencies to their advantage, making the enforcement of the tax code extremely difficult. In contrast, she argues that a principles-based approach was less likely to be vulnerable to such gaming.

Relying on principles is more demanding on regulatory subjects, requiring them to decide for themselves how to translate broad principles into action (this is arguably reflected in Bob Dylan's famous line 'to live outside the law, you must be honest'). A principles-based approach views organizations as self-regulating entities that can be encouraged to behave responsibly. But, such self-observing requires oversight where regulators concentrate on firms' activities in managing particular risks or activities. A principles-based approach is, however, also more demanding on those who inspect regulated activities. Inspectors are required to interpret and evaluate an entity's regulatory responses rather than merely tick boxes. It also requires considerable regulatory capacity in ensuring consistency of interpretation across different inspectors – it is easy to have consistency between inspectors if the sole requirement is to tick a box that a particular piece of equipment has been installed. Consistency is more problematic if inspectors have to judge on broader categories such as 'home-like environment'.

In general, therefore, a principles-based approach places demanding challenges on regulatees and regulators alike. Both sides will be tempted to demand a move towards more rules in order to reduce the scope for discretionary decisions (firms will demand to know what to do in order to reduce compliance costs, inspectors will not want to risk their reputation by allowing for individual interpretation, rather, due to risk aversion, they will want to hide behind verifiable rules). Thus, principle-based standards require a good understanding by regulators of the activities of the regulated parties, namely whether the observed activities are really a good indicator of the wider 'health' of the regulate entity. Furthermore, it requires an ability to understand whether observed misconduct is due to a lack of capacity, a lack of disposition, or both.

Returning to our animal shelter example, we may therefore tend to agree that a reliance on principles offers a superior solution to rules. However, we also need to acknowledge the potential limitations of such a strategy. Most of all, principles-based regulation also requires interpretation from both regulators and regulatees. For Julia Black (2002b), the emphasis therefore has to be on encouraging 'regulatory conversations'. These conversations, based on shared rules of conduct and the existence of shared views of the world, allow regulatory communities to have conversations about intended effects of principles and how to apply them. Such conversations establish certainty as they establish informal institutions, whereas gaming and 'rule-cheating' can be seen as an explicit refusal to share the kind of tacit understandings that support regulatory activities.

Technology-, performance- and management-based standards

On the basis of the preceding discussion, Amnesian animal shelters might arguably be best regulated via principle-based standards. This would reflect a general preference of principles over rules, and a more general preference for relying on the regulatee to flexibly interpret the requirements of regulatory standards. Delegating responsibility to the regulated entities reflects wider themes that feature throughout this volume, namely the information asymmetry between regulator and regulatee, where the latter is better informed about its own activities and the idea that the regulatee has a higher degree of expertise to deal with the problem. Such concerns might be less critical if all areas of regulation were characterized by the certainty that specific regulatory interventions will rectify particular problems. However, most areas of regulation deal with degrees of uncertainty regarding the origins of particular problems and the effectiveness of regulatory strategies. As a consequence, increased attention has been placed on decentralized approaches, that is, those that impose the obligation on organizations to self-observe and to find flexible solutions to broad regulatory requirements.

Such preferences are also evident in 'better regulation' requirements, such as in the US Executive Order 13563, noted earlier, that states a preference for specified 'performance objectives', instead of attempts that would place an emphasis on 'the behaviour or manner of compliance'. In addition, delegating responsibility for enacting regulatory objectives to regulated entities also promises a less intrusive and coercive regulatory approach, allowing regulators to focus their (depletable) resources on the more problematic cases. As noted, however, broad principles are highly demanding, require a willingness and capacity among regulated entities to comply, and a preference for 'performance standards' assumes that the measurement of outputs and outcomes is feasible.

In response to a growing awareness of the distinct advantages and limitations of diverse regulatory standard-setting strategies, an extensive discussion has emerged about different kinds of regulatory standard-setting strategies (Gilad 2010). Industries are heterogenous in type, capacity and motivation. As regulators need to account for different contexts, it is important to explore differences in terms of observability of regulatory activities, outputs and outcomes. Accordingly, we can distinguish, as illustrated in Table 3.2, between three different regulatory strategies: technology-based, performance-based, and management-based standards (Parker 2002; May 2003; Coglianese and Lazer 2003; Gunningham and Sinclair 2009; Gilad 2010).

Technology-based standards are often regarded as 'traditional' and 'rules-type' approaches (Coglianese and Lazer 2003). Problems include those associated with the imposition of particular technologies that

TABLE 3.2   *Overview of standard-setting approaches*

	Technology-oriented	Performance-oriented	Management-based
Focus	Prescriptions of technology	Outcomes	Specification of managerial systems
Nature of standards	Specifications of technology or procedures	Specifications of outputs or outcomes	Design system specifications (such as emphasis on critical control points), 'enforced self-regulation'
Rationale	Homogeneous organizations, regulators have good understanding of association between intervention and desired regulatory objectives	Heterogeneous organizations can be controlled by monitoring outputs and outcomes	Heterogeneous organizations are themselves best placed, and are motivated and capable of developing and monitoring practices and improving performance, especially as outputs/outcomes are difficult to monitor
Examples	Prescriptions of particular technologies to reduce pollution, prescription of building standards (best available technology), prescription of school curriculum material (i.e. specification of specific authors, textbooks etc)	Measurement of air quality, building standards (New Zealand), school quality assessment on exam results	Safety systems in food production (HACCP), nuclear reactors.

Sources: May (2003); Gilad (2010).

thereby hinder the discovery of innovative alternative kinds of technologies. For observers, therefore, technology-based standards are associated with considerable opportunity costs (i.e. the costs of opportunities forgone: Coglianese and Lazer 2003: 700; Wildavsky 1988). More flexible variants, such as the 'best available technology' approach seek to address this problem of inflexibility by institutionalizing continuous updating of technology-based standards (however, critics point to the inherent inertia of such processes, see Sunstein 1990). In general, technology-based standards are said, at best, to be an appropriate response when there is an overall certainty (or agreement) about the expected benefits from a particular technological choice. A further pre-condition for technology-based standards is a certain degree of homogeneity among the industries affected. When faced with a heterogeneous set of actors and concerns, imposing uniform technological demands is likely to be costly and ill-judged; for example, small firms would be forced to adopt the same costly technology as large corporations, and all schools in ethnically-diverse populations would be required to adopt the same curriculum. Such choices are inherently political. In a regulatory context, diverse contexts require flexible responses to achieve desirable outcomes, in terms of encouraging regulatee cooperation, innovative discovery of potential solutions and 'heedful' compliance rather than box-ticking (Weick and Roberts 1993), as noted above (let alone the potential market distortions that emerge from the imposition of uniform standards that may benefit one particular set of industry interests).

Performance-based standards have been a well-established feature in regulation for some time, especially in environmental regulation. Setting performance objectives rather than specifying technologies or behaviours has been regarded as preferable approach in the United States in general (as specified in Executive Order 13563), and elsewhere too. Performance-based standards have become particularly prominent in building regulation, health care (such as hospital waiting times), and education (exam results). The advantages of performance-based approaches are said to lie in allowing regulated entities to decide their own responses to effectively meet a particular objective. At the same time, performance-based standards assume that outputs and outcomes can be measured (such as air control or building quality), it also assumes that regulators have sufficient capacity to understand the kind of responses that firms have chosen. The latter pre-condition is particularly problematic. For example, in New Zealand the move from a technology- to a performance-based standard is said to have encouraged a 'race to the bottom' in terms of building materials. In particular, the use of unsuitable building materials (untreated timber and monolithic claddings) and a preference for 'Mediterranean'-style architecture contributed to a rapid deterioration (peaking in the early 2000) of a large number of newly constructed homes built in the 1990s. The inevitable result was that building started to 'leak' and houses deteriorated rapidly. The New Zealand government estimated that the cost of 'leaky buildings' amounted to NZ$11bn (approx. €5.9bn), although other experts suggested that the real cost was double that of government estimates (*Dominion Post*, 5 April 2011). According to Peter May (2003), one key problem was that the overall preference for 'light-touch' regulation went hand-in-hand with a regulatory inability to monitor and understand the industry's adoption of new (and inappropriate) building materials. In addition, performance-based standards require a motivation and capacity by industry to comply (rather than, for example, just shifting from one mode of pollution to another). It also raises an issue of inequity as different regulated entities are likely to face different compliance costs (e.g. firms in certain locations will find it less difficult to comply with pollution targets). A further issue is also the choice of performance 'target', for example, setting a non-ambitious objective hardly encourages regulated entities to improve beyond that particular objective (such as the achievement of a particular air quality standard).

Management-based standards focus on operational practices within regulated entities (Gilad 2010). Organizations are required to identify core issues that affect their production process and to develop measures to address these potential problems. Such approaches have been particularly prominent in the areas of food safety ('HACCP', discussed in the following chapters, see also Demortain 2010), in health and safety in the workplace and, in the United Kingdom at least, in university teaching quality. Management-based regulation assumes that organizations are capable of self-diagnosing vulnerabilities (in the light of set priorities) and of developing effective remedies to tackle these potential risks and hazards. The role of the regulator is primarily concentrated on ensuring that these management plans are not just a work of fiction, but that they offer robust frameworks. Coglianese and Lazer (2003: 695) argue that management-based regulation has a number of potential advantages compared to the other two types of standards. By delegating responsibility to regulated entities, management-based standards grant a certain degree of flexibility in that firms are in a position to develop potentially 'innovative' ways to achieve regulatory objectives, especially as they are in an advantageous position to exploit their superior expertise and information (Gilad 2010). In line with risk-based approaches, these approaches allow for industry and regulators to concentrate their resources on auditing production processes. In contrast to performance-based standards, management-based approaches do not require measurable outputs or outcomes. Furthermore, in contrast to technology-based standards, management-based standards are able to accommodate industry diversity, which would otherwise make the imposition of a uniform technology costly. Moreover, management-based standards are said to provide incentives (or at least do not cause disincentives) to excel beyond some level of performance (as the required level of performance is not set).

Management-based standards therefore seem to be a particularly attractive option for standard-setting. They place responsibility on regulated organizations to develop and reflect on their practices. The regulatory activity is concentrated on monitoring and enforcing organizational self-regulation. However, this activity is hardly problem-free. Private organizations are widely said to err on the side of under-investment when faced with concerns regarding health and safety (for diverse reasons, such as optimism bias or profit-maximizing). It is therefore critical for regulators to be able to understand the regulated entities' response (or 'plan') in terms of understanding the information provided, understanding whether the information provided represents a truthful and faithful representation of the entity's activities and whether the regulated entity in general is not just capable but also motivated to comply with the intentions of management-based standards.

The meltdown of banks during the financial crisis in the late Noughties revealed that banks were hardly interested in or capable of developing effective self-regulatory risk management systems. The financial crisis also revealed the difficulties of containing systemic risks when management-based standards operate solely at the level of the firm. Indeed, wider criticisms of the management-based approach focus on problems of achieving compliance within companies. For example, Gunningham and Sinclair (2009) note how management-based standards face compliance issues given organizational subcultures and tensions between corporate headquarters and specific sites. Management-based standards therefore are highly demanding of both regulators and regulatees, they demand a careful and arguably highly fragile balance between encouraging 'mindfulness' (Weick and Roberts 1993, Reason 2008) and surveillance. How supportive communication and trust within organizations can be fostered is therefore one key challenge for management-based approaches.

In terms of surveillance, management-based standards require choices as to what is being 'surveyed' and approved: this could include advanced approval of particular operational plans, a 'completion check' (before production can begin) and ongoing inspections. In other words, management-based standards are hardly a 'regulation-free' zone and they may be seen as particularly problematic in the case of irreversible risks that are hard to detect.

Despite the widely presented advantages of management-based standards, the literature has therefore come to less enthusiastic findings, given the extent to which management-based standards rely on highly demanding pre-conditions (Coglianese and Lazer 2003: 724). Indeed, management-based standards are faced with the kind of vulnerabilities associated with principles-based approaches towards regulation noted earlier. That is, both regulator as well as regulatee will demand specifications of managerial practices which then can easily turn into a more rules-based or 'technology-based' approach. In defence, Christine Parker (2002) has noted that despite evidence of non-compliance, studies of management-based standards have diagnosed an improvement in working practices and a reduced number of complaints regarding enforcement.

A dog's life

In terms of standards for animal shelters in Amnesia, the choice therefore is between these three broad approaches.

- Technology-based standards: These would rely on specifying the conditions of care, such as the size of kennels, the amount of food, behavioural and other training and such like.
- Performance-based standards: These would rely on indicators such as successful 'retraining' and 'resettlement'.
- Management-based standards: These would rely on providers of animal shelters to develop verifiable plans as to how to treat homeless dogs in order to 'rehabilitate' and 'rehouse' them.

Table 3.3 notes the advantages and disadvantages of these three approaches as applied to Amnesian animal shelters. Which approach, or combination of approaches, would you choose?

As in the previous discussion regarding the standards for dangerous dogs, the choice of standards for animal shelters is far from simple. We cannot simply assume that people will comply with standards, and we

TABLE 3.3   *Overview of regulatory approaches towards standards for animal shelters*

Approach	Design	Potential benefits	Potential limitations
Technology-based	Specification of size of kennels and accommodation standards, detailed provisions regarding training and support	Potentially easy to enforce as simple assessment of presence of particular provisions/ standards being monitored	Encourages tick-box approach and lack of bespoke approach
Performance-based	Diagnosed well-being of animals and their rehabilitation/ rehousing	Encourages shelters to develop their own responses	Outcome/output specification will encourage gaming response (concentration on some aspects of care rather than others)
Management-based	Shelters to develop their own programmes to provide for care for animals	Encourages shelters to develop their own responses	Requires regulatory understanding of the capacity and motivation of shelter

need to consider the implications of any regulatory strategies on those that are required to enforce standards.

Of course, we have adopted a somewhat over-instrumental view of standards here and one central objection could be that ultimately standards hardly matter. Standards only matter if there is a political and legal system that requires actors to follow rules, at least to some extent. What kind of standards emerge also depends on *who* sets the rules. Should we require ministerial bureaucracies (and in the end, therefore, politicians) to decide on regulatory standards? This might be regarded as democratically legitimate. Others may wish to delegate such tasks to regulatory agencies that are outside the electoral cycle. As the discussion regarding alternatives to regulation shows (Chapter 5), there are considerable criticisms of regulation through bureaucratic bodies (ministerial bureaucracies or regulatory agencies). We may therefore wish to place an emphasis on rule-making by professional bodies. However, professional rule-setting may be argued to limit, if not exclude external scrutiny (thereby raising concerns regarding accountability), leading to over-lenient standards. Professional bodies may not be interested in or have the capacity to regulate particular technologies. For example, kennel clubs (i.e. dog associations) are usually organized on 'pure breed' lines, and are therefore unlikely to welcome responsibility for dealing with non-recognized dog types or 'mixed breeds', exactly the kind of dogs that are widely associated with heightened levels of aggressiveness.

Our examples suggest that standards *do* matter, although they might arguably matter less in terms of leading to a particular intended outcome or output. Rather, standards do shape the rules of the game, they allocate benefits and costs and they become a source of conflict. They allocate responsibilities across regulators and regulatees. In other words, any regulatory regime requires standards as their 'director', however, at the same time we need to be fully aware that merely prescribing a standard and hoping for intended change is highly unlikely to lead to desired results.

Conclusion

This chapter has highlighted debates and controversies surrounding the setting of regulatory standards. Starting off with the basic idea that standards are about limiting arbitrary discretion, we have noted how 'standard-setting' is inherently about choices and trade-offs. The examples of dangerous dogs and animal shelters have suggested that simple choices do not exist. It is therefore impossible to make simple statements regarding what is 'best'. Instead, every standard comes with distinct benefits and costs, advantages and weaknesses. What the distribution of these different factors is depends on the specific contexts. However, in order to make these choices, the regulatory analyst needs to explore these different aspects.

More generally, each choice reflects particular assumptions about causes and effects and the capacity and willingness of various parties to comply with the spirit of the regulation. Finding an 'ideal' standard is further limited by the inherent limitations to individual and collective decision-making. Given the lack of information, time and other resources, it is impossible to expect that decision-makers will be able to scan the environment for all possible options and provide for a critically and bespoke evaluation of each option.

The various approaches towards standards that have been explored in this chapter have distinct implications in terms of costs, discretion and regulatory monitoring and enforcement. It is impossible to establish standards that will cover every conceivable situation that may arise. Every regulatory standard therefore represents an 'incomplete contract' that relies on informal understandings to deal with differences between the formal standard and the kind of behaviour or output that can be observed. Indeed, we have noted that each of these approaches towards regulatory standards also assumes a particular type of motivation and capacity to comply; and it might be argued that a sophisticated approach towards standard-setting needs to consider both the limitations of relying on discretion (that is why we have standards in the first place) and the limitations of relying on 'fixed rules' as it encourages gaming and disagreement about the applicability of rules to particular situations. In short, regulation cannot exist without any form of direction or standard. However, how we set this kind of standard also has considerable implications for the way we can enforce and gather information.

Chapter 4

Enforcement

'Amnesia belly' has entered the international tourist vocabulary. To combat this impression of poor food safety, the Amnesian government has called for a fundamental overhaul of food safety regulation. A particular emphasis has been placed on the enforcement of safety standards. The government has asked the Amnesian Food Enforcement Agency (AFEA) to disseminate information and to inspect restaurants and other food-sellers. Training and 'capacity building' for inspectors is to take place. Tourists are particularly attracted to the food sold by Amnesian street vendors. Recent studies have shown that 40 per cent of all food sold by these vendors poses a risk to human health. At the same time, larger restaurant chains have been complaining about the rude and seemingly inconsistent and unreasonable conduct of the officials tasked with enforcing food standards.

Consider alternative strategies to deal with the enforcement of safety standards for restaurants and street vendors, their implications in terms of costs and wider effects, and recommend enforcement strategies. This requires an assessment of what the underlying problem is, why voluntary compliance might not forthcoming, and what strategies are likely to make regulated parties do what we want them to do.

What is enforcement?

Regulation is about seeking to achieve objectives that otherwise would not be obtained. Enforcement, the use of force to compel particular parties to do things they would not otherwise do, is therefore central to regulation. This seemingly obvious point, however, requires us to consider the motivations and capabilities of those whose behaviour needs changing and also the motivations and capabilities of those who are supposed to do the enforcing.

So how can we make rules 'stick'? 'Keep it simple' might be seen as the obvious answer. For example, the Amnesian street vendors are unlikely to have advanced degrees in food science. It seems therefore appropriate to rely on accessible rules that are uncomplicated and easy to understand. We can also assume that they will get most information regarding hygiene through their interaction with inspectors rather than through the study of rules or handbooks (Fairman and Yapp 2005). However, as we have seen in the previous chapter, 'precision' may require complex rather than simple technical definitions. One further key question is whether enforcement activity should be focused on prevention, the active violation of a standard or the cause of actual harm (Shavell 1993, Polinsky and Shavell 2000).

Enforceability, however, is not just about rule-design it is about the kind of strategies that are adopted to gather information on compliance and to change behaviour in the case of diagnosed wrong doing. In other words, enforcement includes 'detection' or information-gathering *and* 'effecting' or modifying behaviour. Detection deals with the information asymmetries that are inherent in any inspection of a particular activity, that is, how robust and valid are the 'snapshot' impressions of an inspection visit for an overall picture of the 'health' of a particular organization. Any enforcement strategy is not just about those things that are being investigated, but also about what is knowingly and unknowingly 'under the radar', as those 'under the radar' activities might affect the overall health of the regulated activity.

In contrast, behaviour-modification links to debates regarding sanctioning styles, and highlights the considerable motivational impact that different sanctions might have on different types of regulatees. Sanction-related discussions consider activities such as monitoring, inspecting, advising, warning, licence revocation, fining or prosecution. This range of behaviour-modification tools can be seen as an escalating continuum, but each one of these responses has distinct resource and motivational consequences for both inspectors and inspected. The challenge for any enforcement strategy is therefore to achieve a high level of compliance at reasonable cost to both sides.

Furthermore, any attempt to devise appropriate instruments has to take into account the underlying conditions that apply to particular institutional settings, for example, whether the target population is homogeneous or heterogeneous, concentrated or diffuse, and whether the overall domain is broadly static or dynamic (Baldwin and Black 2008).

In sum, enforcement-related discussions are about the limitations of hierarchical sanctioning activities and the complexity of motivations and capabilities among regulators and regulatees. We cannot safely predict the ways in which regulated companies and citizens will respond to enforcement activities, both in terms of information-gathering and behaviour-modification. Indeed, it is the complexity of this interaction that makes enforcement one of the most contested areas of regulation (Braithwaite *et al.* 1987). The rest of this chapter progresses as follows. First, it explores the underlying questions that inform any debate regarding enforcement strategy. Second, it discusses the viability of deterrence- and/or persuasion-based strategies in enforcement. Third, it considers a variety of contemporary 'mixed strategies' before finally returning to a discussion of the various options that might be put before the Amnesian government.

Core questions

As noted already, enforcement is about making people and organizations do things that otherwise they would not do. This leads to a range of questions. Can we assume that regulated parties will voluntarily comply with rules assumed to be in their self-interest? What should we do when faced with non-compliance? Who should do the inspecting – actors that share the same professional background or other, more remote observers? Should inspectors be civil servants or come from the same industry with fluid boundaries between poachers and gamekeepers? Finally, what resources should be put into enforcement, in particular how much non-compliance are we willing to tolerate? The rest of this section considers these questions.

The first question focuses on the underlying motivation that underpins individual and corporate behaviours. For George Stigler 'all prescription of behaviours for individuals requires enforcement' (1970: 526). Such a position assumes that individuals and organizations are strategically motivated and well-informed. Accordingly, compliance with standards will only be forthcoming if the costs of non-compliance are higher than the prospective benefits of rule-breaking. Such a view of individuals as 'amoral calculators' might apply in particular to economic regulation (as material calculations are likely to outweigh any interest in appearing as a 'good citizen' as this has direct implications on the balance sheet if the rise in production costs cannot be passed on). This assumes, however, that all regulated entities are capable of 'amoral calculation' whereas non-compliance often occurs because of a lack of information or resources. After all, not all street vendors are likely to be willingly contaminating food, but may do so because of a lack of education or resources to upgrade their stalls. Furthermore, voluntary compliance might be motivated by the wish to appear as a 'moral' agent who 'does the right thing'.

A second core question follows from this: what should regulators do when faced with non-compliance? Should sanctions follow rule-breaking behaviour more or less automatically or should inspectors be granted some discretion to accommodate specific circumstances at the risk of appearing inconsistent? At the same time, the imposition of fines will only reduce the resources of the regulated party to rectify its failings. Generally, when faced with non-compliance, we can respond in four ways (see Hood 1986: 51–60):

1. Amend the rule. In this case, we may be persuaded that the observed behaviour complies with the spirit rather than the letter or that the rule serves no obvious function.
2. Rely on persuasion and advice so that regulated parties understand why complying with particular standards is in their interest. This

assumes that non-compliance is largely a result of a lack of information or resources.

3. Rely on punishment, such as the imposition of fines or the revocation of licences so that regulated parties are 'afraid' to break the rules. This assumes that parties calculate the costs and benefits of complying with regulatory objectives and that therefore the 'cost' of non-compliance needs to be escalated.

4. Make it impossible to break rules, for example, through technical and other architectural means. Such measures could include technical fixes, such as a device that would require all passengers to have fastened their seat belts or to have passed a breathalyzer test before being able to start a car.

A third core question focuses on those responsible for enforcement. One solution is to rely on a public agency that is seen as less partial to the interests of the industry than a self-regulatory system. Organizational choices influence the degree to which boundaries between regulated and regulatory worlds are porous or not. One example might be the facilitation of career-structures that would allow for a 'revolving door' career pattern (Makkai and Braithwaite 1992). Such a pattern allows interchanges between industry and regulatory experience. This contrasts with career structures that create clear boundaries between regulatory and industry careers (for example, such boundaries can be created through pension systems). For some, a revolving door pattern is a recipe for industry-friendly regulation, as regulators will be keen to accommodate potential employers. However, others argue that revolving door career patterns are unlikely to lead to captured regulation as nobody would wish to employ staff that demonstrated they were open to capture (Horn 1995). Instead, regulators with a potential occupational future in the regulated industry are likely to be interested in appearing competent rather than partial. However, it also means that their time horizons are relatively short-term. Therefore, a revolving door career pattern will incentivize regulatory enforcement activity away from long-term, hardly visible tasks, whereas easy wins that would look good on regulatory staff's résumés would feature highly on regulatory enforcement agendas.

A related debate focuses on professional background. It might be argued that the most informed inspectors are those that are close to the regulated profession – others might argue that such close 'relational distance' (Black 1976) is a recipe for laxity and cosiness in enforcement. An example of close relational distance would be the deployment of former teachers to inspect schools, or of former prison directors to inspect prisons. A shared professional background is said to allow 'professional conversations'; for example, a UK report on regulation in the farming sector noted that farmers complained about the lack of farming experience displayed by inspectors (Independent Farming Regulation

Task Force 2011: 41). A shared professional background might also enhance the acceptability of enforcement activities.

More broadly, it has been argued that enforcement tends to become more formal in metropolitan (and socially heterogeneous) settings where issues such as housing might enjoy higher political salience and where overall social relations are less established and informal (Hutter 1988). A further related challenge links to the way in which enforcement activities rely on specific expertise and/or seek to combine an inspection of different activities. On the one hand, regulatees wish to reduce the cost of having to deal with individual inspections and specific (and possibly incompatible) requests. On the other hand, they do not wish to deal with 'jack of all trades' inspectors who might have expertise in one area, but not in all. As a result, any attempt to introduce 'cross-media' inspections requires regulatory capacities to assemble competent inspection teams that draw on different specialisms.

Limited resources are a further key issue affecting enforcement style. Enforcement activities are not cost-free and it is therefore important to question to what extent non-compliance will be tolerated. Perfect '100 per cent' compliance is unlikely to be achievable, and even if it were possible, it could be argued that achieving compliance among the 'final 10 per cent' would be disproportionately expensive. For example, it would be prohibitively costly to aim for a 100 per cent detection rate regarding speeding motorists in any given jurisdiction. Inspecting all Amnesian street vendors at all times might be seen as impossible.

Equally, however, resources allocated to enforcement are affected by the wider political setting, namely the extent to which the regulatory responsibility to enforce is met by a commitment to allow intensive inspection activity. For example, in 2011 a major scandal in the quality of care home provision in the United Kingdom was partly linked to problems in regulatory oversight. The responsible Care Quality Commission could rely on roughly 900 inspectors to deal with 409 National Health Service trusts, 9,000 dental providers, 18,000 care homes and thousands of home care agencies run by a highly fragmented set of providers, and, as of 2012, was to inspect 8,000 general practitioner practices – without expanding its inspection-related staff due to budget cuts. At least temporarily, this led to a sharp decline in inspection activity and a change in rating regime away from a differentiated 'star rating' to a basic confirmation of minimum standards. In addition, due to budget cutbacks and its expanding jurisdiction, the Quality Care Commission was increasingly dependent on local authorities to raise concerns – exactly at the same time that local government budgets were being cut (*Financial Times*, 31 May 2011: 3).

In short, enforcement strategies are fundamentally about key choices in the light of resource and capacity limitations. It is also about the setting in which enforcement activities can take place, in particular regarding the type of domain as well as the wider political setting in which any enforcement activity takes place.

Deterrence versus persuasion

At the heart of any enforcement-related discussion is the question why people or organizations do not voluntarily comply with rules and standards. This fundamental debate into human behaviour has been reflected in the distinction between deterrence- and persuasion-based approaches. As their labels suggests, the two approaches rest on different assumptions about why regulated companies or individuals comply, and they therefore generate conflicting advice in terms of enforcement style.

The *deterrence* approach assumes that individuals and organizations calculate the utility of rule-breaking. As 'amoral calculators' (Kagan and Scholz 1984; Scholz 1984) they weigh the costs and benefits of complying and not complying with regulatory standards. Since compliance with standards is seen as imposing costs on companies, they will only comply when non-compliance is likely to be detected and sanctioned (implying that rules have been drafted in a way that allows for their application). Therefore, compliance represents the calculus of the benefits of non-compliance and its costs – which are constituted by the probability of detection, the level of punishment, and the probability that the sanction will actually be imposed (cf. Becker 1968; Stigler 1970; Shavell 1993; Ritchey and Nicholson-Crotty 2011).

Such an understanding of 'economic calculus of compliance' leads to a simple production function of enforcement: if the likelihood of detection is low, the level of punishment needs to be increased to achieve compliance. Accordingly, tough penalties succeed in motivating firms more than any other device (Gunningham *et al.* 2005). Calling for tough sanctions in the face of non-compliance is a widespread policy response. For example, the Swiss village of Reconvilier considered whether non-payment of the annual dog tax should be punished with the mandatory destruction of the dog (*Time*, 11 January 2011). More broadly, deterrence-based approaches have enjoyed widespread currency, ranging from attempts to impose speed limits, mandatory seat-belts or restrictions on drink-driving to efforts to reduce the amount of litter produced by visitors to public parks (*Tagesspiegel*, 25 April 2011).

However, the compliance calculus also suggests that fines have no deterrent effect if the perceived probability of detection is negligible. A strategy that solely relies on high fines for food safety violations (or any other violation, such as drunken-driving or illegal waste disposal) will not lead to any adjustments in behaviour if it is not accompanied by a credible 'detection' threat. Pointing to the largely mixed evidence regarding deterrence-based approaches in road safety, Ritchey and

Nicholson-Crotty (2011) suggest that it is mostly enforcement 'presence' (i.e. the perceived rate of detection and actual sanctioning) that produces a compliance effect. Similarly, if corporations can assume that no actual sanction will be forthcoming as such attempts can be frustrated in the legal process (even if, formally, considerable material or immaterial fines could be imposed), then it is unlikely that deterrence-based approaches will provide an effective strategy to achieve compliance.

Furthermore, deterrence-based approaches have been criticized for their potential to be indiscriminately used or abused (Bardach and Kagan 1982). For example, firms might be punished although they believed that they had acted in good faith. This could then lead to a reduced interest in cooperative relationships with inspectors in the future, leading to 'creative compliance' (McBarnet and Whelan 1991; Bevan and Hood 2006). Concerns with the deterrence-based approach have also been raised regarding its differential effect. For example, large firms are said to be less affected by deterrence than smaller or medium-sized firms. Among small and medium-sized firms, the threat of persecution and personal liability is more directly 'felt' than in organizations where responsibilities and liabilities are complex and diffuse (Haines 1997). Among larger entities, persuasion and the availability of alternative 'carrots' (such as certification schemes) might offer a more palatable route towards achieving compliance (Law 2006).

Empirically, it is difficult to assess whether 'deterrence' works, as firms might be complying with regulatory standards for other reasons, such as reputation, or for normative reasons that actors do indeed wish to do 'the right thing'. However, studies suggest that deterrence still plays an important background role, even in cases where 'values' are motivating 'compliant' behaviour. Such background roles operate in at least two ways (Simpson 2002; Gunningham 2010). One is the importance of seeing other firms being sanctioned against, thereby reminding firms about potential sanctions they themselves could face. The second role is the experience of previous fines and other sanctions that might have left a reputational legacy ('never again'). Such attention-directing experiences need not have included prosecution. Nevertheless, it is argued that inspections without a 'big stick' are unlikely to alter firms' conduct (Shapiro and Rabinowitz 1997: 713). Critics, however, suggest that such immediate 'knee jerk' responses to enforcement actions are likely to fade as time passes.

The contrasting approach relies on *persuasion* and is based on the assumption that it is better to prevent harm from occurring than to punish wrong doing (Hawkins 1984). Mediation and negotiation are seen as primary strategies for achieving compliance, whereas a reliance on a legalistic process to punish wrong doing is seen as a last resort. The core assumption here is that wrong doing is not based on 'cold-blooded' cost-benefit analysis, but because of non-strategic motives, namely a lack of resources or ignorance. For example, Berlin's public transport system formerly relied on German-language only signs. Non-German speaking tourists were therefore regularly caught unaware of the rule that tickets needed to be validated before commencing a journey (there are no machines on board apart from buses). Enforcement officials were granted with some discretion to waive the automatic €40 fine to account for such 'ignorant' violations. Similarly, the Berlin transport system waived penalties payable by highly indebted individuals. As a result, only 38 per cent of all 'automatic' €40 fines were collected (*Bild*, 20 November 2008).

In our case of Amnesian food safety, the basic assumption would therefore be that food vendors and restaurants are interested in providing hygienic food, maybe even because they 'want' to behave properly. They therefore would mostly require information and, maybe, some additional resources to convert their stalls to allow improved hygienic food preparation.

According to the persuasion-based approach, information, advice and argumentation are seen as critical tools and sanctions only operate in the background. Indeed, advocates of a persuasion-led enforcement strategy would suggest that deterrence only breeds adversarial relationships and gaming. Furthermore, it is argued that one-off inspections are unlikely to uncover deep-seated problems within organizations. To 'really' understand complex operations (ranging from slaughterhouses, universities and schools to prisons) one needs to encourage open conversations, and such open conversations are, according to this perspective, only possible if enforcement activities are based on advice and persuasion. For example, Steven Kelman (1981) has suggested that the confrontational, hard-nosed approach of regulating workplace safety in the United States is less effective than the cooperative enforcement style deployed by Swedish authorities.

Persuasion-based approaches are far from problem-free. Companies are likely to require more than just persuasion that strict health and safety enforcement will provide better working conditions and higher productivity unless any additional costs can be easily passed on. It is therefore important to assess the 'motive' and the 'opportunity' for any firm to under-invest in regulatory compliance as this may directly benefit company profits. For example, this disinterest in checking on its own practices was evident in January 2011, when a large number of German pig and poultry farms had to be closed after the discovery of dioxin-contaminated animal feed. This followed the discovery that one major producer had sought to reduce production costs by (illegally) mixing dioxin-contaminated industrial fatty oils into animal feed (*BBC*, 5 January 2011).

Furthermore, persuasion-based approaches have a tendency to turn into excessively cozy regulatory arrangements that might discourage attempts at improving regulatory performance and compliance: why should 'good performers' incur costs of higher regulatory compliance if 'poor compliers' are not punished? More basic, but even more problematic is the need to prevent 'friendly' relationships from becoming over-friendly, that then turn regulated entities' responses into a form of 'negotiated non-compliance' (Gunningham 1997). Similarly, it is often argued that any inspection requires an element of deterrence, if not surprise, to maintain a basic level of mistrust between regulator and regulatee. Therefore, persuasion-based approaches face difficulties in dealing with reluctant compliers or 'amoral calculators'. Enforcement officials are thus highly exposed when facing these extremely complex questions, and it is therefore hardly surprising that empirical studies point to a fear of exercising discretion and a reluctance not to just 'go by the book' (Bardach and Kagan 1982; Pires 2011)

Both of these approaches therefore raise considerable challenges (Gunningham 2010). They offer contrasting accounts as to the causes of wrong doing, and the motivations to rectify non-compliant behaviour. Neither approach pays too much attention to the issue of whether regulatees are *capable* of responding. Deterrence-based approaches seem particularly appropriate in those cases where regulatory targets are reluctant compliers, that is, unwilling to comply. In contrast, in cases where compliance is 'well-intentioned', a deterrence-based approach might trigger perverse effects: the experience of being punished despite having acted in good faith might encourage firms to become increasingly reluctant to engage with regulators in an open manner. In other words, deterrence-based enforcement strategies may turn 'honest triers' into 'amoral calculators' and foster an overall culture of resistance.

Persuasion-based approaches are more likely to have an effect as regulated entities may wish to display some social conscience (Haines 1997). In contrast, a deterrence-based approach seems to be appropriate where regulatees are seen to be ill-informed and ill-intentioned. These 'principled objectors' are generally hostile to any interference and therefore unlikely to be willing to be persuaded. Here 'deterrence' is likely to offer more scope for compliance than persuasion. Similarly, deterrence also seems to be the preferable strategy when dealing with the well-informed and ill-intentioned. Any enforcement strategy will, however, face problems when faced with hostile and well-informed regulatees who will game any regulatory strategy. Arguably, it is exactly these 'rational maniacs' (an extreme case of amoral calculators, see Bevan and Hood 2006) who will strategically game to avoid any form of detection and who are likely to evade regularized enforcement strategies – raising issues about whether it will ever be possible to catch such 'rational maniacs', or about what kind of resources will be required to permit their detection.

In other words, enforcement strategies require an awareness of the

TABLE 4.1   *Two dimension of enforcement characteristics*

| | | Willingness to comply | |
		Low	High
	High	I **Amoral calculators** well-informed, but unwilling to comply	II **Honest triers** well-informed and willing to comply
Level of *knowledge* *about*	**Low**	III **Principled objectors** ill-informed and unwilling to comply	IV **Organizationally** **incompetent** ill-informed, but willing to comply
regulatory *requirements*			

potential diversity of motivations among regulatees along two dimensions – willingness to comply and 'information', as illustrated in Table 4.1. Persuasion-based approaches are likely to be more appropriate for types II ('honest triers') and IV ('organizationally incompetent'), whereas deterrence-based approaches might be appropriate for I ('amoral calculators') and III ('principled objectors') (see also Baldwin 1995: 185–9, 2004).

In sum, without information regarding the type of organization they are dealing with, any regulatory enforcement agency will be largely ignorant as to the usefulness of its strategy. So before we turn to our example of Amnesian food safety, we need to explore different developments in the enforcement literature that have sought to address the challenges for enforcement regimes when faced with any combination of characteristics shown in the table above.

Developing mixed strategies

In the light of the variety of motivations and capacities to comply with regulation, it is not surprising that the discussion has moved beyond deterrence- versus persuasion-based approaches and towards the consideration of mixed strategies. This section considers three contemporary approaches, those that advocate 'responsive regulation' and 'smart regulation', those that advocate 'risk-based regulation' and those that recommend 'meta-regulation' or 'enforced self-regulation'. The various 'recipes' partly overlap, in that they rely on escalating sanctions and the involvement of non-state actors in controlling regulatory activities, and partly they are also in competition with each other. For example, it is difficult to see how in all cases an approach that relies on 'risk-based' assessments can easily be combined with a 'responsive' approach (but see Black and Baldwin 2010).

Responsive regulation and 'smart regulation'

As noted, any enforcement strategy needs to deal with those who are willing to comply and those that are reluctant to do so (see Table 4.1). It seems obvious that regulatory enforcement is more likely to achieve its objectives where it responds to the 'culture' of those that are being regulated by appealing to their professional responsibility. Enforcement is resource-intensive, and a deterrence-based approach is arguably particularly resource intensive as it requires not just detection and the imposition of sanctions, but also administrative perseverance should regulated entities seek to challenge the imposition of sanctions. Thus, encouraging voluntary compliance through persuasion is arguably much 'cheaper' than reliance on deterrence-based strategies. However, as noted, relying on persuasion on its own is likely to lead to exploitation.

These conditions have generated the concept of *responsive regulation*, an idea developed initially by Ayres and Braithwaite (1992). The underlying idea of responsive regulation is that enforcement should be perceived as an iterative interaction between regulators and regulatees. Ayres and Braithwaite (1992) suggest that an 'enforcement pyramid' offers an advantageous mixture of persuasion- and deterrence-based components. Figure 4.1 illustrates the enforcement pyramid.

Accordingly, the starting point of any enforcement activity should be based on persuasion and dialogue. Any escalation should only occur where cooperation on the side of the regulated is not forthcoming. It is argued that such cooperation will be forthcoming, if the potential imposition of sanctions has a credible deterring effect. In other words, regulators need to carry a credible 'benign big gun' in their enforcement armoury.

The image of a pyramid has two central messages. One, the number of cases that can be resolved at the 'bottom' of the pyramid is high, that is, persuasion and warnings are usually sufficient and the number of cases to be considered declines the further up the pyramid we go. Therefore, informal warnings and positive encouragement motivate desired change in most cases. Two, the pyramid points to the availability of escalating sanctions ('the benign big gun'), starting with advice and warnings, to 'mild' administrative penalties, to criminal sanctions and ending with incarceration. This means that care homes, hospitals or schools could be publicly 'shamed', be refused access to funding schemes, or be simply closed down (or witness a transfer in managerial/ownership responsibility). (Whether it is feasible to simply close down a large hospital is a different matter).

According to 'responsive regulation' accounts, enforcement should be

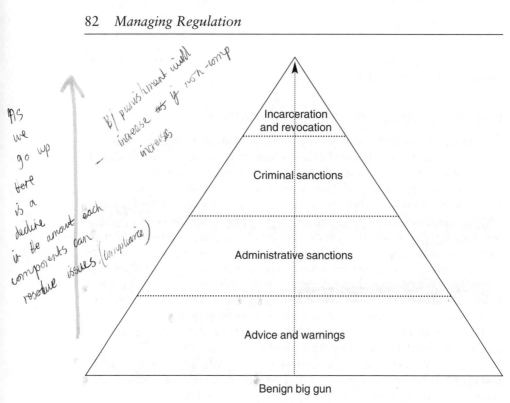

(handwritten margin notes:)

As we go up here is a decline in the amount each components can resolve issues (compliance)

b/ punishment will increase as if non-comp increases

FIGURE 4.1   *Enforcement pyramid*

Source: Ayres and Braithwaite (1992: 35) (by permission of Oxford University Press, Inc.).

responsive to the observed conduct of regulated entities. Cooperative behaviour, that is, a high level of compliance and a willingness to correct non-compliance voluntarily, is rewarded with a cooperative, non-intrusive and 'light-touch' behaviour by enforcement authorities. Ill-informed rule-breaking is to be addressed by persuasion and warning. In short, regulatory enforcement is a cooperative game of tit-for-tat. The regulator offers 'cooperation', but if this offer of cooperation is not reciprocated, there is the threat of escalating sanctions and, eventually, the 'big gun' to punish 'cheating'. However, as noted, the gun is 'benign' in that it offers 'persuasion' first.

A strategy based on 'responsive regulation' therefore offers a view of enforcement that combines persuasion and deterrence. It assumes that the intention of regulation is to make regulatees reflect on their activities. The enforcement pyramid has attracted considerable academic and practitioner attention as it offers a method that promises to reduce the considerable cost of pure deterrence-based approaches without resulting in over-friendly or 'captured' relationships. Its popularity has led to an increasing attention on the activities at 'the bottom' of the pyramid and a willingness to 'forgive' as part of regulatory tit-for-tat strategies.

However, it is far from a 'cost-light' or non-demanding enforcement strategy. It requires regulators to be able to observe regulatees' responses. It also faces the further challenge that 'responsive regulation' may be seen as inherently 'unfair', as some violations will be met by persuasion. In other words, not everyone is equal in the face of the law.

Numerous further challenges to the 'responsive' idea of the enforcement pyramid can be identified. One, it assumes an almost costless transition along the 'big gun's' escalating sanctions that hardly reflects the organizational and political processes that can be observed within regulatory agencies. Instead, it is likely that inertia and limits to information-gathering will hinder the immediate adjustment of enforcement strategies. Furthermore, seeking to build an army of enforcers who are capable of consistently interpreting 'responsive regulation' may require considerable instruction or guidance which, in turn, might place considerable strain on professional inspectors whose identity is built on individual professional judgement, not prescription and reporting requirements.

Second, the enforcement pyramid assumes that most firms are not only willing but also *capable* of following regulatory advice (Parker 1999), in particular not just in terms of responding to the immediate warning regarding a particular problem, but in terms of reflecting more generally about approaches to, for example, safety in the long term.

Third, an enforcement pyramid based on 'tit-for-tat' requires iterative interactions between the different parties. It is therefore arguably less viable in circumstances where regulators are able to conduct only occasional visits, or where regulated entities are able to move across jurisdictions. Similarly, it has little to say about what happens to the interaction between regulator and regulatees after the regulator has used the 'big gun': will regulated entities remain cooperative or will they alter their motivation towards becoming 'amoral calculators'?

Fourth, and related, not all regulated activities represent equally dangerous risks. Some activities might be so risky that we may not wish to tolerate their occurrence or their potential redress through a 'warning'. In such cases regulators have to start higher up the pyramid than with other tasks. Differentiated risks that might be present in one single regulated firm might call for a differentiated approach towards responsive regulation – allowing for 'speaking softly' for some risks and requiring an immediate 'big stick' deterrence-based approach for others. However, how regulated entities will respond to such differential treatment is also an open question – and poses further challenges for the analytical capacities of regulators and the overall interaction patterns between regulators and regulatees. Such different approaches affecting regulated entities is one of the common complaints raised by business interests. However, such inbuilt conflicts usually reflect not just different organizational approaches, but also competing legislative frameworks and objectives. They also reflect the fundamental difficulty of any enforcement activity to display consistency across activities and a high degree of informed insight at the same time. For example, it is often said that environmental enforcement should take a 'cross-media' perspective in which enforcement considers aspects across different forms of pollution. However, forcing inspectors to operate across different technologies may stretch their subject expertise.

The need to accommodate different risk profiles across and within regulated entities reinforces the highly demanding prerequisite that regulators should be able to understand the regulated entity and the kind of risks that it represents. Such decisions are inherently problematic and are likely to demand a regulator that is autonomous and well-resourced. Fifth, it requires the existence of a credible 'big stick' – and therefore reintroduces all the kind of problems associated with deterrence-based approaches noted earlier.

Furthermore, the enforcement pyramid is based on the assumption of a unified regulator that combines information-gathering and behaviour-modification. However, empirical studies suggest that these functions are usually fragmented across different regulatory parties, leading to problems of joining up different sources of information and responding with behaviour-modifying strategies (Hood *et al.* 2001). Fragmentation exists within regulators, especially when having to apply different legal regimes or having to deal with various sectors or activities, or when regulation is divided across different layers of government, such as the reliance on local authority enforcement officers. Such organizational fragmentation will pose further challenges to any attempt at smoothly applying escalating sanctions.

Such a view of enforcing rules within a fragmented 'regulatory space' have underpinned the development of the *smart regulation* perspective (Gunningham and Grabosky 1998). The smart regulation perspective highlights the importance of diverse sets of actors that might influence compliance with regulatory objectives, such as financial markets, insurance, supply chains, non-governmental organizations or international private standard-setting organizations.

The argument is that one can use such 'co-regulatory entities' as initial quasi-regulators who can rely on the backing of formal regulators should regulated entities be found to be non-compliant with the more informal quasi-regulators. In addition, cross-sanctions and other mechanisms can be used to facilitate a self-interest in compliance: such as the availability of favourable tax treatments in exchange for the certified compliance with environmental standards. Inherent in the view of smart regulation is a responsive view that suggests that enforcement should be gradually escalated in cases of non-compliance, they rely on iterative interactions and they require quasi-regulators to be sufficiently resourceful to detect non-compliance and be willing to and capable of escalating sanctions.

Therefore, while the incorporation of third parties and the use of administrative cross-sanctions might reduce the difficulties of formal (state-based) regulators in enforcing standards, such an approach is faced with numerous limitations. One limitation is the reliance on the capacity and motivation of different participants to escalate sanctions.

In their original responsive regulation framework, Ayres and Braithwaite (1992) suggested the deployment of 'public interest groups' would support regulators in their information-gathering work and therefore reduce the information asymmetry or dependency relationship between regulators and regulatees. They also suggested that such groups should be subsidized to provide them with sufficient resources. To reduce such arrangements from becoming lax and institutionalized, they also advocated regular competitions among potential public interest groups for these publicly subsidized observation functions.

In addition, a reliance on self-certification schemes as a first resort is faced with potential problem of transparency and accountability. Will so-called industry audits provide for open and transparent information regarding the type of information required? And how will the robustness of these checks be validated? In other words, a reliance on private parties as frontline regulators requires considerable trust in their active pursuit of regulatory compliance.

Both responsive regulation and its related smart regulation offer limited insights as to how to distinguish between those types of activities that are highly catastrophic and those that might be 'tolerable'. They both also face issues in terms of determining how to maintain responsive regulation in the light of limited interaction frequencies. Robert Baldwin and Julia Black (2008, Black and Baldwin 2010) have therefore developed these frameworks further into their 'really responsive' framework which emphasizes the extensive considerations that regulators are required to make 'responsive regulation' work. It also noted that far from being offering a 'resource-light' enforcement pattern, responsive regulation has placed considerable informational, analytical and material demands on all participants. It is therefore unsurprising that empirical investigations have found, at best, a mixed success pattern.

Risk-based regulation

As noted, resources are not limitless and we may wish enforcement activities to focus on those activities that 'matter' rather than those that might appear to be symbolic or merely opinion poll-enhancing. Such a view may not just be informed by a regulatory longing for friendly treatment. Rather, it is widely accepted that human decision-making is likely to be more focused on those few big risks than those that are frequent but have low impact. To redress these inherent biases, ideas have moved towards a 'risk-based' view on enforcement activities – an idea that became formal UK policy for all regulatory enforcement agencies following the pronunciation of the so-called 'Hampton Principles' (Black 2005; Hampton 2005; Hutter 2005). The OECD similarly advocated risk-based regulation to achieve superior and 'efficient' compliance (OECD 2010b).

Risk-based enforcement is defined by the prioritization of enforcement activity in line with an assessment of risks that stand in the way of achieving core regulatory objectives. The assessment of risks builds on two dimensions, (1) the probability of something going wrong, in particular the violation of standards and (2) the impact of something going wrong, that is, on consumer health or the stability of the financial market. In other words, risks have to be somewhat weighted in terms of their impact severity and their likelihood. A third key aspect in assessing the probability of violation is the compliance history of the firm, and, in particular, an assessment of the propensity of the firm to control or manage the kind of risks their business activity incurs. In terms of information-gathering, therefore, risk-based regulation requires robust and valid information regarding the type of risk at hand and regarding the compliance history and capacity of the regulatee. This contrasts to some extent with the information requirements of responsive regulation that largely rely on perceptions of the motives (and opportunities) of regulatees to comply (or not).

Regulators are required to develop decision-making frameworks – in the form of 'framework documents' and spreadsheets documenting monitoring and behaviour-modification activities – that prioritize regulatory activities and allocate resources around the assessment of regulated firms' particular risks. The supposed advantages of a risk-based strategy are that it is explicit about the inherently limited resources available to enforcement. It therefore makes the obvious point that some low-risk regulated activities might need less observation than other, more risky activities. Thus, enforcement is to focus on potentially 'systemic' risks rather than time-consuming 'low-level' risks. Sparrow (2000) has noted how a 'problem-solving' approach should advance conversations regarding compliance-inspections (in his case, policing). His argument is that such a focus on problems facilitates a more informed conversation regarding what tools or resources are required. Too often, according to Sparrow, organizations focus on their tools first before considering what tasks they are able to perform.

A risk-based enforcement strategy therefore appears highly attractive on numerous grounds. It provides a 'formula' to justify why certain areas are inspected more frequently. This formula can be legitimized in the language of scientific risk assessment and economic cost-benefit analysis (Sunstein 2002). It potentially makes value choices transparent. In addition, it signals that organizations will respond appropriately to the analysis and will manage risk sensibly. It also offers a defensive shield against the complaint that compliance and inspection cannot be perfect and require inevitable choices (Black 2005).

However, it is far from clear whether risk-based enforcement offers the panacea towards enforcement. First, it is doubtful whether the assessment of risks can be conducted in a 'politics-free' zone. Assessments are unlikely to easily identify those risks that can be regarded as 'intolerable'. Furthermore, whether the popular perceptions of 'intolerable' risks clashes with more 'economic' understandings of low probability events and whether a difference between the two can simply be dealt with through information or education is also questionable, as discussions regarding nuclear energy have illustrated (Douglas 1992; for a discussion of extreme events, see Posner 2004). Indeed, risk-based enforcement seems to have little to say about 'herding' mechanisms that appear more widespread in markets than risk calculations allow for.

Second, besides such fundamental objections, it is far from clear whether the basic definition of an 'assessment of risks to achieving regulatory objectives' is that easy to fulfil. This requires not just an understanding of objectives (and an assumption that these objectives are not contradictory). It also requires a sophisticated system of conducting risk assessments. This raises issues about how objectives are identified, how transparent the conduct of risk assessments is, and how biases in risk perception shape the development of enforcement strategies (how much attention, for example, should be paid to extreme outliers, or so-called 'black swan' events). Even if all such hurdles can be overcome, it still requires high-quality information – which often can only be provided by those entities whose activities are supposed to be monitored. For example, in the case of the UK Care Quality Commission (mentioned above), information was widely available regarding public (NHS) hospitals, whereas private hospitals refused to provide sufficient information (as illustrated in the uproar about faulty breast implants in early 2012: *Financial Times*, 7 January 2012).

Third, there are considerable issues as to how a 'risk-based' approach that focuses on the 'systemic risks' stemming from any one organization can 'join the dots' when risk-based enforcement is about specific organizations rather than a wider system. Fourth, and related to all other enforcement strategies considered so far, risk-based enforcement requires analytical capacities to understand the motivation and capacities of regulated firms to manage their risks, given that it is not likely that most firms are either willing or capable of risk managing their future. Furthermore, we are likely to encounter the regular enforcement problem that firms may not comply uniformly and they may also alter their strategies following particular interventions (i.e. does the imposition of a sanction lead to undesirable behavioural changes that encourage gaming). Indeed, it requires an analytical interest in the kind of activities that might not be seen as 'systemic risks' in the past, but might become so in the future.

Most fundamentally, the financial crisis that began in 2008 has illustrated the intellectual bankruptcy of risk-based regulation as an enforcement strategy, despite the continued campaign advocating risk-based enforcement by consultancies, special interests and governments (Gray 2009; National Audit Office 2009). The collapse of the UK bank, Northern Rock, in the wake of the 'credit crunch' pointed to considerable limitations in risk-based regulation. Prior to the collapse, the then UK regulator, the Financial Services Authority, had widely advocated the use of risk-based regulation as the key tool to avoid any systemic problems in financial regulation. The post-mortem of the banking collapse and the subsequent collapse of further banks was highly critical of the FSA's activities in general and risk-based regulation in particular (FSA 2011). At one level, risk-based financial regulation was accused of having failed to identify failing banks. The risk-based approach which thought it could neglect 'irrational' behaviour was challenged by the moral panic that emerged once the story of the banking collapse had been leaked. At another level, it was argued that risk-based regulation had indeed succeeded in identifying financial institutions in danger. However, problems then emerged about what to do with these warning signs. It was feared that raising concern publicly would encourage a self-fulfilling prophecy effect in that faith in financial institutions would vanish leading to moral panics and runs on banks. Furthermore, political masters were also said to have sought to avoid bad news, and thereby to suppress such information.

Finally, risk-based regulation may also be seen to come into conflict with responsive regulation and the idea that at least some regulatees will learn from a conversation with regulators. For example, Fairman and Yapp (2005) have noted that for small-and-medium sized enterprises the key 'learning' about regulatory standards occurred during actual inspections as they otherwise did not commit resources to keep updated on regulatory changes. In other words, for these companies, compliance was doing what they were told by inspectors and not about adherence to formal legislative texts. A risk-based approach would potentially exclude such enterprises from regular inspections (as they pose little systemic risk). As a consequence, learning effects stemming from iterative exchanges would disappear, leading to the potential build-up of considerable non-compliance (and risk) over time. As the area of food (and finance) in particular have shown, for any regulator to have a view as to which activities have systemic significance and therefore need to be regularly inspected requires considerable confidence in their own intellectual capacity.

Of course, critics of this view will suggest that risk-based regulation has not failed. Instead, risk-based regulation suffered as the events were either so extreme, or the politics so 'high', and that only risk-based regulation offers a rational way to allocate resources to enforcement activities. Nevertheless, the controversy surrounding risk-based regulation highlights the basic tension in regulatory activity, namely that a belief in 'technical fixes' often turns into over-confidence and limited ability to update strategies.

Meta-regulation and enforced self-regulation

Finally, our discussion turns to approaches that focus on enforced self-regulation (Parker 2002). We have pointed to management-based regulation in the previous chapter. As noted, much of the regulation literature has observed the inherent limitations of hierarchical oversight. Therefore, strategies to push enforcement activities into regulated entities have become a widely favoured strategy (Parker 2002). Both responsive regulation and risk-based regulation build on an understanding of enforcement being conducted first and foremost by the organization itself – with regulators assessing the importance of regulatory intervention on the basis of risk and/or compliance history. Accordingly, regulatory enforcement strategies prescribe the establishment of company- or industry-level self-regulatory systems. One prominent example of such a strategy (that also utilizes risk-based elements) is the HACCP standard, but similar ideas have been prominent in the 'safety case' accreditation regime for oil rigs, the development of hospital-hygiene programmes, or the operation of 'near miss' reporting among airlines. HACCP (Hazard Analysis Critical Control Point) focus on hazards that arise in the production of particular goods rather than concentrating on inspecting the final product. It emerged initially in the private sector as a response to NASA's request to develop food for space flights (Demortain 2010). As a result, regulatory activities concentrate on the validity and robustness of the safety systems of the regulated entities themselves. We have noted the limitations of management-based systems or 'meta-regulation' previously; therefore, it is sufficient to say that this approach towards reducing the inherent information asymmetry in regulatory enforcement faces considerable limitations as well.

Most of all, meta-regulation faces problems with organizations that are 'amoral calculators' who, at best, comply reluctantly. Enforcement capacity and emphasis is therefore required to be placed on actual managerial compliance with the goals of the regime rather than on the presence of management systems alone, as safety standards may not be an inherent part of an organization's 'DNA' (or code). Similarly, as noted in Chapter 3, even if the industry is relatively concentrated and therefore may be interested in avoiding disaster for reputational reasons, the likelihood that complex organizations are uniformly committed to reflexive safety plans might be questioned. Such problems are further

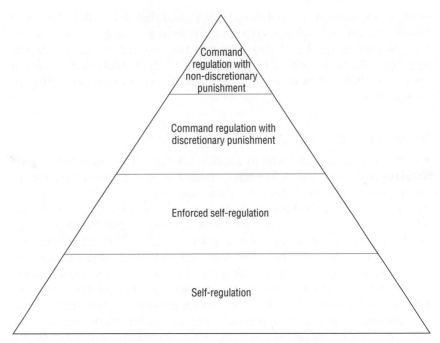

FIGURE 4.2   *Enforcement strategy pyramid*

Source: Ayres and Braithwaite (1992: 39) (by permission of Oxford University Press, Inc.).

accentuated in the case of highly fragmented industries where inspections inevitably have to choose between width or depth in terms of
assessing self-regulatory systems. In the end, it is management rather
than management-based systems that matter in enforcement.
Furthermore, it not even clear whether management-based 'enforced
self-regulation' will provide for the kind of discretionary and innovative
self-evaluative managerial learning that is foreseen by advocates of
'meta-regulation'. Such an approach requires considerable resourceful-
ness and capacity among regulatees, whereas it is more likely that for
reasons of conformity-seeking and risk aversion highly cautious
approaches will be evident (see Brandsen *et al.* 2006).

This section has presented three, partly overlapping approaches
towards regulatory enforcement. Indeed, it is often argued that meta-
regulation and responsive regulation offer a similar account regarding a
reliance on different organizational responsibilities, depending on organizational 'responsiveness' and also type of risk. These different levels
are illustrated in a further 'pyramid', namely a pyramid of enforcement
strategies, as noted in Figure 4.2. As noted above, the problem with
such a view is caused by the communication channels and the motivations and capacities of different actors across all the levels within the
pyramid.

Some accounts have sought to combine insights from 'responsive' and 'risk-based' regulation (Black and Baldwin 2010), but again such accounts have escalated the resource demands on regulators. In other words, enforcement is about accepting inherent limitations – of the potential ability to change behaviour among regulatees, and of the limited resources of regulators themselves.

Amnesian food safety

So what are the various options that might be considered for the enforcement of food hygiene standards for Amnesian chain restaurants and street vendors?

At the most basic level, deterrence-based approaches are unlikely to work for either type of regulatee. For chain restaurants, a deterrence-based approach would not address their complaint regarding 'unreasonableness' in enforcement, as inspectors would continue to punish wrong doing regardless of inherent intent. It would further aggravate tendencies within the industry to display amoral calculator behaviours. At the same time, such a strategy would only work if the threat of rule-breaking being detected and punished was sufficiently credible. For street vendors, a deterrence-based approach would potentially have most undesirable consequences as the ultimate sanction (the removal of the ability to operate) would potentially mean the elimination of individual economic livelihoods. It is also difficult to imagine that a deterrence-based approach could properly deal with the largely informal way in which street vendors ply their trade.

A persuasion-based approach would similarly be faced with considerable limits. Such an approach would be potentially most appropriate for street vendors, as here persuasion and advice are likely to lead to an increased level of information, and therefore compliance. However, persuasion requires iterative interactions which it is unlikely that the nature of street vendor work allows. Even if such repeat interactions were potentially feasible, this would require considerable resources to be allocated to Amnesia's food safety enforcers. In the case of food chain restaurants, persuasion also may offer considerable benefits, especially in terms of addressing their complaint regarding the 'unreasonable' behaviour of regulators. However, inevitably there will be worries about consistency in enforcement actions, and there will also be concerns that such an approach will not ensure that some non-compliant activities will remain undetected.

Table 4.2 points to the implications of the three 'mixed' strategies that have been discussed. There are clear trade-offs between the different strategies and there will be disagreements as to how to resolve conflicts regarding potential limits.

TABLE 4.2　*Enforcement strategies and Amnesian food safety*

Strategy	Target	Advice
Responsive regulation	Chain restaurants	Should offer an appropriate strategy. However, there are limits in terms of decisions regarding escalation of sanctions, and detection of motivation of regulatees
	Street vendors	Persuasion should offer information and advice. However, highly limited strategy as iteration in relationships highly unlikely
Risk-based regulation	Chain restaurants	Offers an appropriate strategy to focus on key risks and therefore offers redress to complaint of 'unreasonableness' through discretionary behaviour. However, strategy raises issues regarding issues that might be 'under the radar'
	Street vendors	Highly problematic, as risk analysis might suggest that street vendors do not present a systemic risk to food safety, despite the reputational risk to tourism. Unlikely to identify black sheep
Meta-regulation	Chain restaurants	Potentially appropriate strategy, but requires effective management of self-control system and regulatory capability to detect malfunctioning management-based systems
	Street vendors	Not appropriate given lack of capacity to establish a system of reflective self-control and evaluation

One of the key themes that emerge from Table 4.2 is the difficulty in enquiring into the way in which food restaurants and street vendors conduct their operations. Table 4.2 notes that the key challenges are gaming by regulatees, generated either by creative compliance with the reporting duties and other requirements, or by the closeness of a 'professional conversation'. There are at least two strategies to deal with such limitations, namely strategies using rivalry and those using contrived randomness (Hood 1998).

Strategies employing *rivalry* would seek to motivate compliance among restaurants and street vendor by appealing to their own commercial self-interest. Such strategies might include league-tabling, or the use of certification measures (such as stickers and other visible signs) that would allow restaurants and street vendors to 'compete' on quality. Such a strategy would also address restaurants' complaints regarding inspection styles. However, the downside of this strategy is that it might encourage corner cutting and potential conflicts with objectives that might not be exposed to competition (as they are not 'measurable'). It is questionable whether such rivalry mechanisms can operate in the case of mobile street vendors, although some form of certification system might be feasible. However, such an approach still requires inspection rather than mere comparative information provision to allow for consumer choice.

A different strategy to accommodate potential gaming is to rely on elements of surprise and *contrived randomness*. Such a strategy assumes that any intentional and regular activity will be faced by inevitable gaming and evasion. As a result, the only way to keep regulated entities 'honest' is through a system of 'organized' surprise, for example, by conducting unannounced inspections, or by evaluating organizations on the basis of randomly selected sets of indicators (rather than all of them). A system based on distrust is however likely to generate further distrust. It might be argued that 'surprise' (or unannounced) inspections might be helpful in gathering information on a superficial level. However, it is less helpful for engaging in any in-depth advisory type relationship as such a conversation would require trust rather than distrust. An inspection style based on contrived randomness is therefore likely to enhance food restaurants' criticism regarding arbitrary inspection practices. In terms of mobile street vendors, it is likely that contrived randomness is the default inspection style. However, it is unlikely that such an inspection style would allow for learning and persuasion.

It is therefore essential to understand the limitations of any strategy rather than focusing on its over-hyped advantages. Although concentrating on only two parts of the food industry, the fairly unsurprising answer is that there is no 'one-size-fits-all' in terms of enforcement strategy. Thinking about enforcement beyond deterrence or persuasion has advanced towards a more refined view regarding mixed strategies. They offer more differentiated approaches towards the handling of different actors, given their different capacities and motivations. However, they place considerable demands on those that are doing the regulating and it is therefore important that the potential limitations of the different strategies be considered.

Conclusion: no, we can't?

Does all this mean that 'Amnesia belly' is an unsolvable problem? As noted at the outset, any discussion regarding enforcement needs to deal with regulation as a 'living system'. Enforcement cannot be 'automated' in most contexts. Instead, it requires choices in terms of both detecting information and finding ways to modify behaviours. These choices have to deal with the motivations and capacities of regulated entities on their own *and* as a whole. It also requires a view of what 'compliance' actually means (Yeung 2004). For some, compliance is all about following the rule. However, as noted in the previous chapter, following the rule may miss the point. Therefore, compliance may also be interpreted as following the 'intention' rather than the 'letter' of the law. Such distinctions do matter, as it already points to considerable demands on enforcement staff to interpret the motivations that might underpin observed 'rule-breaking'.

Empirical studies have noted considerable variation among approaches towards enforcement. To some extent, these reflect choices about enforcement strategy and also about the wider resources available to the enforcement agency. Its positioning within the wider political and institutional setting enables and constrains strategic enforcement options. For example, McAllister (2010, also Hawkins 1984) notes how different agencies in Brazilian states operate varying enforcement styles in the way they use formalistic and coercive approaches and how such choices reflect issues of resourcing and 'autonomy' within the wider political setting. As a result, one can distinguish between a variety of enforcement styles. These range from the 'retreatist' (poorly resourced enforcement agents that engage in mostly symbolic activities, Kagan 1994), to the highly resourced and less formalistic 'negotiated'. Among negotiated strategies, Hutter (1997), compares 'insisting' (pointing to clear limits of tolerance) and 'persuasive' (accommodating and educative) compliance-seeking approaches. Furthermore, there are the highly resourced but hardly autonomous 'token enforcers' (Braithwaite *et al.* 1987), and those highly resourced and highly formalistic enforcers that are seen as being over reliant on 'going by the book' (Kagan 1994). Offering advice regarding enforcement strategies requires a careful consideration of the administrative and political feasibility of executing particular options.

Such observations link to the type and organization of the regulated domain on the one hand, and to the resources and capacities available to enforcement agencies on the other. As we have seen, each regulatory strategy has its own prerequisites in terms of capacities and motivations among regulators and regulated. Furthermore, as a 'living system', any choice of an enforcement strategy will have its own impacts. Enforcement, therefore, is far from a machine where we can choose a few settings and observe intended effects. Inspection and enforcement are inherently about interpretation: why does this rule-breaking occur? What are the motivations and capacities of regulated entities? What kinds of sanctions are likely to provide for sustained voluntary compliance? Such questions are at the heart of enforcement and they cannot be answered in any automatic or one-size-fits-all way.

Persuasion-oriented approaches facilitate those that seek to follow the law, but fail when encountering 'amoral calculators' and lead to uneven outcomes. Deterrence-based approaches may provide for credible threats against wrong doing in some cases, but they require careful calibration in order not to appear unnecessarily punitive, thereby turning organizations into risk-averse and non-cooperative actors. Relying on responsive regulation and the enforcement pyramid might offer a useful way of considering different approaches, but they require considerable analytical capabilities within enforcement agencies, and it requires continuous interactions with well-resourced (i.e. large) organizations.

Chapter 5

Alternatives to Classical Regulation

There is growing concern about lemonade binge-drinking. People are getting so high on the sugar content of the drinks that they have started late-night rioting in cities, leading some newspapers to suggest that inner cities have become 'no go' areas. At the same time, there has been concern about the long-term health effect of lemonade drinking and complaints that lemonade has been marketed to young children in particular – and teenagers, especially girls, have been prominent in late-night rioting. Lemonade cafés are a particular feature of Amnesian society and appear prominently in tourist guides, although their economic significance has suffered since the introduction of anti-smoking legislation. Supermarket sales of lemonade have increased. Tax rates for lemonade are lower in Amnesia's neighbour country, Dezertia.

Amnesia wishes to address the problem of lemonade binge-drinking. It also is committed to an approach that favours 'alternatives' to regulation over 'classical regulation' (defined as legal standards backed by sanctions). This follows an international trend in advocating 'alternatives to regulation' (BRTF 2000; OECD 2002, 2010a; Department of Treasury and Finance 2007). Alternatives include exemptions, market-based solutions, design-solutions and self-regulatory options, and also the 'do-nothing' option. So what would you advise? What do we know about the regulatory tools available and how they would deal with the problem of lemonade binge-drinking?

Classical regulation and its limitations

Classical regulation is often described (somewhat dismissively) as a 'command and control' approach (Baldwin 1997). This would include a clear fixed standard backed by criminal sanctions. The law would therefore be used to set demands, prohibitions or conditions for particular activities to take place. Should there be an infringement of the rules, then the aggrieved party is able to seek legal redress and receive compensation. The arguments in favour of command and control arrangements are that passing a law or introducing a regulation offers an immediate signal that something is being addressed by marshalling the force of the law and that (to an extent) it reduces uncertainty by setting a standard that is applicable to all.

As we have seen in previous chapters, the way in which standards are set and how sanctions are executed is far from straightforward. A discussion of 'alternatives' to regulation is therefore closely linked to previous discussions regarding different standard-setting approaches (such as performance- or management-based approaches) and enforcement strategies (i.e. 'responsive regulation' and risk-based regulation) (Ayres and Braithwaite 1992; Coglianese and Lazar 2003).

The so-called command and control approach is said to be affected by a number of problems.

- Problems with standard-setting in terms of over- and under-inclusion, the rigidity of rules once set and therefore the potential lack of 'innovation' and flexibility to accommodate social and technological change. Indeed, it might be argued that the demand for regulation follows the political instinct to 'hit them all' and thereby failing to target regulatees in a proportionate way. Furthermore, once established, standards are unlikely to be withdrawn or scaled back, instead it is likely that standards will witness further amendments and growth.
- Problems with regulatees being motivated to comply in that a set standard will be seen as a 'minimum' compliance target without any incentive to improve beyond that particular standard.
- Problems with enforcement in terms of overzealous and/or uninformed enforcement (e.g. 'legalism'), uncertain effects of enforcement actions, and difficulties in terms of capacities, motivation, and knowledge/understanding among regulators and regulatees alike to achieve intended objectives. As noted previously, 'hierarchical' forms of enforcement are likely to encourage creative compliance and other forms of gaming and cheating.
- Problems of 'cost'; one of the key criticisms has been that state-based regulatory strategies are highly costly regarding the time it takes to formulate a standard, but also in the cost of bureaucracy, both in terms of requiring an inspectorate and concerning 'form filling' and other compliance activities.
- Problems with 'decentredness'; if we accept that regulatory authority is distributed across different parties, then any attempt to control regulatory activities via one centralized approach and one standard is likely to be limited.

To illustrate these points and reflecting on Amnesia's problem with lemonade binge-drinking, a range of approaches would qualify as 'classical regulation'. Table 5.1 provides examples of a number of such command and control approaches and also points to potential limitations that might give rise to calls for 'alternatives'. Any attempt to deal

TABLE 5.1 *Command and control regulation and lemonade binge-drinking*

'Command and control' type	Prerequisites	Limitations
Prohibition of sale of lemonade to under-age individuals	Requires identification system and credible sanctions against shops and cafés selling lemonade to the under-aged	ID 'theft' among siblings, parents/over-age individuals will purchase lemonade for the under-aged; difficulty of monitoring domestic consumption
Restricted opening hours for cafés/hours during which shops are permitted to sell lemonade	Requires monitoring and sanctions against potential 'lock-ins'.	Might facilitate binge-drinking to 'beat the clock'; might facilitate imports and domestic consumption; harm 'café culture', encourages café 'lock-ins'
Tough penalties against rioting/intoxicated individuals	Requires reliable means of identification, a credible sanctioning regime, and capacity to 'hold' individuals in 'sobering up' cells	Penalties might become 'badges of honour' in youth culture; requires willingness to provide resources to enforce provisions
Automatic penalties against rioting individuals	Requires identification regime and capability to impose immediate penalty (i.e. force individuals to pay on the spot via ATMs or credit card)	Requires individuals to be able to provide for immediate payment; difficulty for enforcers to deal with rioters
Prohibit the sale of lemonade	Requires monitoring system and ability to clearly identify lemonade	Might encourage illegal imports and brewing of lemonade; potential shift to 'harder' drinks; financial losses faced by cafés, loss of tourist attraction
Limit sale of lemonade to registered 'users'	Requires identification system and clear eligibility criteria; monitoring of compliance by cafés and shops	Encourages ID-theft and excludes tourists
Only permit the sale of 'healthy' lemonade	Requires monitoring of compliance to prevent illegal imports	Might encourage illegal imports and domestic consumption; reduced consumption might cause financial losses to café owners
Limit sale of lemonade to state-owned cafés and shops	Requires state infrastructure to facilitate restrictive sales	Might encourage domestic consumption of imported lemonade: high cost of running specific state-owned operation

with lemonade binge-drinking through 'tough' measures is likely to face considerable constraints, due to the capacity requirements of these 'command and control' strategies, and due to the motivational impact of these strategies on regulatees that are likely to encourage gaming and avoidance.

The various 'command and control' options appear rather costly (in the sense of being prohibitive and requiring administrative effort). They rely on considerable state enforcement activity and are likely to shift lemonade binge-drinking to private places that are even less easily controllable. Prohibitions are also likely to encourage illegal imports (or even illegal private production) that would require further administrative controls.

Given the widespread acceptance of these limitations, it has become commonplace to suggest that the search for approaches to deal with any particular economic or social problem should start with a consideration of 'alternatives'. So-called 'classical' regulation should only be considered as an option of last resort. For advocates, this search for alternatives encourages a more creative approach towards the consideration of different strategies that also consider the benefits and costs of different techniques of regulatory intervention (including the option of non-intervention). Such considerations supposedly avoid the negative consequences of traditional regulatory approaches (Black 2002a: 2). For critics, the limits of classical regulation have been over-emphasized by those special interests and ideologues who wish to advance a 'light-regulation' agenda of minimal state interference in economic and social affairs. The words 'classical regulation' and 'command and control' are therefore, according to this view, devices by opponents of regulation to highlight the inherent shortcomings of regulation.

Overall, it is important to see these different options as complementary and any debate should view the search for different regulatory strategies as one that deals with complementariness rather than competing and exclusive options. Furthermore, any discussion of 'alternatives' is inherently based on three value-driven choices: first, the way we understand the definition of the underlying basic problem; second, the balance of assumptions regarding the significance and the likelihood of market failure versus 'regulatory failure' (i.e. unintended consequences), and, third, underlying assumptions regarding the capacity and motivation among state, market or associational actors to address a particular problem in a satisfactory way.

The two previous chapters have already touched on a range of different approaches that are seen to move beyond the limitations of 'command and control' regulation, especially in terms of performance- and management-based standards. These both seek to make organizations responsible for finding ways of complying with set objectives rather than regulators prescribing such instruments or procedures. The

Architecture Relies on structures and other devices to steer behaviour or make particular behaviours impossible	Variants of classic regulation Relies on exemptions and relaxations of 'traditional' command and control regulation
Market-based regulation Relies on incentives and self-interest to steer behaviour	Self-regulation Relies on industry self-regulation and other forms of delegating regulatory power to the regulatee

FIGURE 5.1   *Four alternatives to classical regulation*

discussion in this chapter draws on these considerations, but takes on a more regime-wide perspective by considering overall approaches that include standard-setting, information-gathering and behaviour-modifying components. The rest of this chapter considers four logics of a range of alternatives to classical regulation. They share a common rationale in that they all claim to be able to avoid the supposed shortcomings of 'command and control' regulation. However, they disagree when it comes to their underlying causal mechanisms that achieve the facilitation of compliance. We distinguish between four logics, although hybrids and sub-categories can be imagined. Figure 5.1 summarizes these four approaches.

In the following chapter, we will expand these four basic types, including various sub-types and empirical examples, and discus the dominant logic and inherent weaknesses. Most real-life applications display a degree of mixing and matching among different alternatives. However, in order to explore such mixtures, it is important to discuss 'pure' versions first. The concluding part returns to the different options regarding 'alternatives' to regulation that could be considered in Amnesia.

Variants of classical regulation

The first type of alternatives seek to address diagnosed problems with command and control, but through the use of exemptions or modifications. Therefore, the primary intention is to reduce the potential costs of command and control regulation by considering compliance costs and by facilitating regular reviews. We consider here one strain of variants in particular, namely those variants that emphasize the importance of granting exemptions and limiting the scope of particular provisions. A second strain, one that emphasizes evaluation and review via 'sunsetting' is discussed in Chapter 10.

The strain that emphasizes the importance of differential treatment focuses on limiting the scope of command and control type provisions and on tolerating certain deviations. Limiting the scope of regulation includes exemptions for specific groups. For example, small- and medium-sized enterprises are often exempted from particular regulations in the field of workplace health and safety or labour law – such as restricting the establishment of mandatory workplace councils to firms with more than a certain minimum number of employees. Related initiatives have sought to reduce the administrative burden for small enterprises by exempting certain businesses below a particular turnover threshold from completing particular tax-related paperwork. Granting exemptions assumes that compliance cost, especially in terms of administrative cost, is relatively far more costly and difficult for smaller companies with fewer employees than for larger companies with their own compliance units. In smaller companies, these compliance costs are said to deviate attention away from economic activity and, even worse, to stifle potential innovation.

Furthermore, it is often said that small market entrants in electricity retail markets should not be burdened with the same kind of climate change-related provisions as large retailers. Here, the policy conflict is between the aim of reducing the cost of market entry and the aim to establish a 'level playing field' by addressing the need to deal with environmental objectives. Attempts to alleviate the 'regulatory burden' on small- and medium-sized enterprises has become a contemporary key policy theme, but not always with the desired results (especially as these enterprises often demand the removal of 'all' regulation rather than a relaxation of particular administrative costs). For example, in the United Kingdom it was feared that the attempt to remove the requirement on small- and medium-sized enterprises to file their accounts with the official government register would restrict the affected companies' access to credit as filed accounts were used by credit-rating agencies to assess companies' credit risk (*Financial Times*, 11 June 2011). Exemptions are however also often granted to those 'large users' who might be particularly affected by a specific regulatory intervention (such as an energy consumption tax on high energy users). In other words, the politics of exemptions very quickly turns into a process that resembles the world of capture and other special interest politics rather than a public interest world of seeking to alleviate disproportional burdens. Even if one believes in the benevolence of political choices, the politics of exemptions requires tricky choices between those benefitting from exemptions and those that do not.

A related variant is to tolerate certain degrees of non-compliance or to allow regulatees to justify their non-compliant behaviour. Especially the latter approach is said to facilitate discretionary enforcement rather than unreasonable 'going by the book' (Bardach and Kagan 1982) and to encourage responsible behaviour among firms that goes beyond mindless compliance with the rules. Such a system, however, requires informed inspections and a willingness and capacity among firms to engage constructively with regulatory intentions. It therefore arguably also encourages the abandonment of a supposed 'level playing field' and might be seen as being too vulnerable to special interest influence.

Variants of self-regulation

A second set of alternatives to classic regulation addresses both the problems of lack of 'intelligence' and 'motivation' of command and control regulation by delegating rule-making power to the regulated company/industry sector (Coglianese and Mendelson 2010; Rostein 2010). The idea here is that the state deliberately chooses to rely on a close connection between regulator and regulatee to deliver public goals. This means that the state negates on its potential authority to act on its own and shares public (or regulatory authority) with other social interests.

Self-regulatory alternatives are said to reduce the level of rule-prescriptiveness by state-based regulators and to rely on group-based or associational arrangements. The broad argument in favour of such decentralized regulatory strategies repeats the arguments against command and control regulation noted in previous chapters. In brief, the inherent information asymmetry between state regulatory and regulated entities makes any regulatory strategy not just outdated and enforcement 'unreasonable'. It is therefore more advantageous to rely on 'reflexive' devices that allow regulated entities and systems to develop self-regulatory processes in the light of wider public policy goals and, thereby, to steer behaviour indirectly. At least three broad, albeit overlapping variants of self-regulation can be distinguished (1) professional self-regulation, (2) (enforced) self-regulation by industry associations and (3) voluntary agreements and other forms of 'soft law' (also known as co-regulation).

Professional self-regulation

Self-regulation has been a well-established mode in the regulation of professions. In particular, the focus here is on the regulation of individual behaviour. Professions usually operate in areas that make their operations difficult to measure (medics in the operating theatre, armies in war, lawyers in exchanging legal documents), and they usually also seek to develop autonomy from other areas by establishing high barriers of 'entry' (e.g. through training qualifications). Professional self-regulation relies on the development of ethical and procedural standards ('codes of conduct') and enforcement strategies within the regulated domain, often operated by professional bodies that enjoy exclusive status within the profession.

Professions are said to 'know best' in terms of developing reasonable regulatory strategies and are assumed to be behaving responsibly in seeking to advance the quality of individual conduct. As professional associations control qualifications and training, professionals are educated within a particular normative framework that guides professional self-regulation – thereby arguably limiting enforcement problems as professionals are guided in their behaviour by these normative frameworks. For example, in the past, carpenters were required to move between different towns and different 'master craftsmen' as part of their so-called journeymen years in order to acquire broad skills before being allowed to settle down and become member of a guild. In the present day, medical associations design standards of good practice and sanction malpractice. Similarly, bar associations develop codes of practice for lawyers and enforce compliance.

Self-regulation is said to encourage the application of professional expertise, especially as the motivational problem of having to comply with rules set by state-based regulators does not exist. At the same time, the mechanisms of sanctioning, in particular the threat of exclusion from the profession, establishes the professional group at the centre of accountability relations. Therefore, the individual professional is bound by the code of the profession. However, such codes may clash with other loyalties, such as those to the management of particular organizations and its concerns regarding financial viability (i.e. it raises the question whether a medical code of conduct can be aligned with the managerial and financial priorities of a hospital at all times, and how potential conflicts are resolved).

Self-regulation of individual conduct through professional bodies represents a long-established mechanism. Such regimes are usually employed to control discretionary activities that are inherently difficult to monitor from a distance. Wilson (1989) suggests that 'craft' and 'coping' organizations, that is, those where only outcomes but not individual or organizational outputs can be monitored, or where neither outcomes nor outputs can be measured, need to rely on professional codes of conducts and other norm-driven devices to ensure a certain degree of consistency across activities that are difficult to monitor, let alone measure. Similarly, Herbert Kaufman (1967) noted how one particular type of bureaucrat, the forest ranger, displayed a remarkable consistency in problem-solving. He argued that such consistency was achieved through a system of training and professional norms (and reinforced by other mechanisms) given that formal oversight was near impossible given the nature of the task.

Professional self-regulation is, however, far from unproblematic – as the growing caseload regarding medical malpractice has suggested over recent decades. First, there is the problem of close relational distance that might facilitate lenient enforcement practices and a reluctance to account for self-regulatory activities to the outside world. Thus, self-regulation requires legitimacy and the attribution of legitimacy by outside bodies. Second, powerful professional bodies are required that actively pursue self-regulation (i.e. thereby removing incentives for individuals to shirk). Professional self-regulation is therefore challenged where no such bodies exist, or where practices are disputed and where there is limited opportunity to seek redress in case of wrong doing. For example, it is often argued that alternative medicine suffers from a lack of professional self-regulation in contrast to more 'orthodox' medical practice. Related to this, professional self-regulation requires a professional identity that does not tolerate non-compliant behaviour. Indeed, the breakdown of such existing understandings is said to have been at the heart of the transformation of professional regulation over the past few decades (at least in the United Kingdom, see Moran 2003). In the context of declining public trust in professional self-regulation and increasing calls by state-actors for formalization, professional domains such as medicine, law and accounting, but also areas such as finance and sports are said to have witnessed an increasing formalization and growing organizational and instrumental similarity with state-based regulation.

Industry self-regulation

The previous section dealt with professional regulation of *individual* conduct. A second key theme has been self-regulatory arrangements that focus on the *organization* or firms (Ayres and Braithwaite 1992: ch. 4). Again, such regimes have been a long-standing feature across national systems of regulation. Broad distinctions between self-regulatory and meta-regulatory approaches can be made in terms of agenda-setting power: in self-regulatory systems, the regulatees impose their own commands and their inherent consequences upon themselves, whereas in meta-regulatory systems the imposition of commands by regulatees follows broad instruction and guidance by outside regulators (Coglianese and Mandelson 2010: 150; see also Braithwaite 2000; Courville 2003; Parker 2003). In other words, although the exact boundaries are likely to be blurred, the key difference between self-regulation and meta-regulation is one of separation of regulator from regulatees.

Self-regulatory schemes have developed at the national (for example, movie rating systems and advertising), international or global level (for example, the Forest Stewardship Council, international standard-setting bodies, nuclear reactor operator associations) in which various industry participants establish self-binding standards and (to some extent) commit to a degree of monitoring and self-enforcement. Similarly, the emergence of risk-based regulatory systems, such as HACCP, that also are part of international (*Codex Alimentarius*) and EU provisions require organizations to develop regulatory systems of 'self-control'. The level of government involvement varies, ranging from requiring indus-tries to develop these responses, to the incorporation of existing volun-tary industry-standards into state-based regulatory provisions. Meta-regulatory strategies benefit from being directly applicable at the firm level therefore, they do not require any industry-based agreement *per se* (in contrast to co-regulation).

So-called meta-regulatory regimes or systems of 'enforced self-regulation' (Gilad 2010) are primarily distinguished not by the degree of state involvement, but by the extent to which they prescribe organiza-tional conduct. Regulatory standards, for example food or environmen-tal standards, are set in performance-based or management-based terms, and organizations are legally required to develop their own responses. In some cases, these standards are self-binding and therefore are hardly enforced by external regulatory bodies. In other cases, there is a close connection between state-based standards and the way in which industry translates these requirements into industry-wide codes of conduct. As noted in previous chapters, this strategy requires credible enforcement mechanisms, suffers from accountability deficits (especially at the level of industry-wide regimes), and therefore might potentially also suffer from a lack of effectiveness. Indeed, as discussed by Gunningham and Sinclar (2009), meta-regulatory strategies require complex organizations to 'sing from the same song sheet'. Anyone who has ever worked in an organization will realize that interests across various operations across different sites, between managers and workers, and even between differ-ent professions are unlikely to allow for a consistent interpretation of meta-regulatory strategies.

Co-regulation

Whereas the previous two sections discussed self-regulation at the indi-vidual and the organizational level, this section moves to so-called co-regulatory regimes. These kinds of regimes are characterized by an intermeshing of non-state and state authority. Ayres and Braithwaite also include the recommendation that such co-regulatory schemes should involve public interest groups (Ayres and Braithwaite 1992: 102). Co-regulation can be defined as an explicitly specific non-state regulatory regime set up as part of a (inter)-governmental strategy. In short, they are directly linked to public policy goals (reduced emissions, for example) and are supported by state-based legal frameworks. In other words, the state grants discretionary power to industry (and indus-try associations) to develop their own regulatory standards, while the state backs these regimes with its authority (the so-called 'shadow of hierarchy'). Such a strategy has become widespread in EU environmental regulation and is said to have also increasingly informed approaches to media regulation.

The advantages of such a regime are, on the one hand, the reduced decision-making costs for state-based regulators, as the costs for standard-setting and initial monitoring are incurred by industry. On the other hand, they also promise a 'reflexive' strategy in that these strategies employ industry to reflect on state aims and to act purposefully to comply with them. Otherwise the threat of direct state-based regulation looms. As with the previous two variants of self-regulatory strategies, such regimes arguably suffer from a legitimacy deficit and depend on the capacity and motivation among industry actors to develop and comply with such regimes, even if backed by the threat of state intervention. This raises the further issue as to the credibility of the 'threat' of state regulatory intervention should 'self-compliance' not be forthcoming.

This section has accentuated difference. Most regimes that rely on delegated or associational self-governance are characterized by a mix of different aspects. For example, international business agreements are often based on management-based strategies. In short, it is 'sequencing' between, and combination across, different variants that matters rather than 'pure' strategies, and such variants include different degrees of 'shadows' of hierarchy, that is, the presence of (the threat of) state involvement (Gunningham 2007).

Marked-based alternatives

A third 'alternative' to command and control regulation is to rely on market mechanisms and economic incentives (Grabosky 1995b). By appealing to individual and organizational self-interest (via the price signal, for example), the achievement of regulatory goals does not require reliance on formal regulatory regimes. Market-based incentives are said to allow for flexibility and efficiency, while encouraging organizational innovation. Indeed, incentives are said to allow organizations to go beyond minimal levels of compliance – if it is profitable to do so. For example, green taxes or emission trading schemes might facilitate an ongoing attempt to cut the consumption of fossil fuels (if the price for trading CO_2 is sufficiently high), whereas the setting of emission levels might merely encourage a minimal compliance response. Insurance requirements may offer effective alternatives to risk regulation, as the price signal may deter certain economic activities. For example, a provision that would require all homeowners to acquire flood insurance would quickly reduce the demand for houses in flood areas, in contrast to a regulatory approach that might rely on building specifications and flood controls. Equally, compulsory dog insurance might reduce the attractiveness of some types of dogs, at least for those dog owners willing to comply with insurance obligations. A number of different market-based alternatives can be distinguished, ranging from market incentives, information provision and certification effects to direct monetary incentives.

The use of market mechanisms to achieve regulatory objectives comes in many forms, and has become most well-known in the context of the Kyoto Protocol of 1997 that sought to establish binding targets on the emission of greenhouse gases (Breidenich *et al.* 1998). Among the most well-known types are *tradable permits* or *cap and trade*, especially in the form of emission trading regimes. The general idea is that, usually, a public authority (government ministry) sets particular limits in terms of pollution. Companies purchase permits (emission allowances or 'carbon credits' in the case of CO_2) that fix a particular volume of pollution. As the total number of permits is restricted (representing the set level of overall pollution which, over time, is to be reduced), permits are traded on a market with companies that exceed their permitted pollution level having to purchase from those companies with emissions below their permit level. Indeed, environmental organizations may choose to enter the market and purchase (carbon credit) permits and decide to 'retire' them, therefore driving up the price for permits. The key principle, therefore, is to rely on market-based mechanisms, in particular the price signal, to incentivize industry participants to reduce their emissions, but granting them flexibility in terms of the way they seek to do so.

A reliance on such trading regimes is seen, by economists in particular, as a 'light touch' and a low-cost alternative to the supposedly prescriptive nature of command and control regulation (Baldwin *et al.* 2012: ch. 10). Such a mechanism, however, introduces considerable transaction costs between market participants. It requires a 'strong' price signal to motivate actors, and it requires government commitment to maintain such market-systems over time. Concerns regarding price volatility emerge when permits set particular quantities rather than price levels. The governmental capacity to allocate permits is then likely to turn into a game of picking winners. A different instrument that would avoid such political choices would be to set a particular emission tax. However, such a strategy would not automatically translate into an interest in reduced emissions (as outputs would depend on overall economic activity). As a result, much emphasis has been paid on 'mixed systems' such as a quantity-based emission system that nevertheless allows for maximum and/or minimum price levels to reduce price volatility.

Such mechanisms also raise considerable political problems; for example, how large users who also happen to be large employers should be handled under such regimes (usually, these industry lobby successfully for exemptions). It raises issues as to whether 'grandfather rights' should be granted, or whether initial permits should be allocated through auctions. Both of these starting positions are likely to favour the resource-rich and are therefore likely to prolong existing power asymmetries. Indeed, setting up such regimes in one single jurisdiction may encourage 'jurisdiction shopping' (or 'carbon leakage' in the language of environmental regulation) in which firms move to jurisdictions that do not apply similar regulation (similarly, firms may vary forms of pollution/pollutant). If one introduces international trading regimes, then further questions as to fairness arise. For example, it raises the question whether the industrialized world should be in a position to purchase a clean conscience on the basis of purchasing permits in non-industrialized countries. More generally, the trading of permits and allowances requires conditions of measurability and enforceability; in other words, the market requires considerable bureaucracy to make the effective buying and selling of permits happen.

Besides the international arrangements surrounding the Kyoto Protocol, a range of smaller and larger emission trading systems have developed over the past 10 to 15 years, many of them organized by private associations. The most important example is the European Union's CO_2 emission trading scheme. Here, the trading scheme is combined with targets for overall reductions in greenhouse-gas emissions. How effective emission trading schemes are in practice or theory, is a contested matter (Baldwin 2008). What, however, is evident is that trading schemes do require a regulatory bureaucracy to monitor and enforce markets, and they are far from politics-free zones.

A different market mechanism is a reliance on *consumer information*. Accordingly, poor choices, or, as Akerlof (1970) names them, 'lemon choices', can be avoided if we are properly informed about the goods that we wish to purchase and/or consume. Therefore, it is suggested that consumers can make informed choices if they are properly informed (and are able to act easily on such information). In other words, the importance of providing information, possibly in standardized form, and provided in a range of ways, such as through government websites or labelling, has to be mandated through disclosure legislation. Apart from requiring mandatory information, this approach relies on 'choice'. And, as one would expect in market-based systems, choice by consumers will make providers responsive to these revealed preferences. For example, Fung and colleagues (2007) assess 18 cases of such 'transparency policies'. They find that the required disclosure of information regarding car accidents, especially in terms of 'rollover ratings' had a specific effect on so-called SUVs (sport utility vehicles). These cars were revealed to have a higher rate of 'rollover', leading to a high number of mortalities. In response, car manufacturers started to update their SUV designs. Consequently, accident rates dropped rapidly between 2000 and 2005. It was argued that consumer choice was influenced by the disclosed safety provisions and that manufacturers responded accordingly.

Information disclosure requirements – and wider attempts at steering behaviour through 'publicity' (Yeung 2005) – are closely related to market-based mechanisms in that they enable 'choice'. There is potential scope for application of consumer information requirements in a wide range of markets, ranging from cars, food and financial products to public announcements (such as the publication of criminal 'hot spot' maps). Particularly influential are league-tabling or benchmarking exercises that allow the consumer to make comparisons between different products and services. Similarly, disclosure allows for a 'naming and shaming' approach that might encourage attempts at improving organizational performance.

A reliance on disclosure requires the ability to find the appropriate mix between the required complexity of information for the information to be meaningful, and the kind of information that is easy to understand (i.e. information disclosure often requires a third party, such as the media, to translate or digest a range of information into simple indicators). Moreover, the use of information disclosure requirements requires 'rational' consumers who are able to respond correctly to the information (i.e. they take notice of this information, they are able to understand probabilities and risk, and disclosure does not lead to a moral panic or witch hunts). Information also needs to be consistent and displayed in places where actual choices are made, whether this is on websites, in showrooms, or on the front of entrance doors. Furthermore, a star rating system that requires restaurants to publicly display the results of their latest hygiene inspection might inform consumer choice. However, such schemes require some degree of consistency (across UK local authorities, there are star rating schemes that rely on a three, four and five star ranking for their hygiene score, thereby sending confusing signals as to whether, for example, a 3-star score is the optimum or just a mediocre result). Furthermore, businesses have been complaining about the potential 'lynch mob' attitude that such a publicly disclosed 'shaming' could trigger, especially as displayed inspection results are said to hardly reflect 'real' performance. Instead, critics suggest, such public disclosure systems provide outdated and uninformative results. This is especially the case when publicity about a bad inspection score is followed by a long time-lag until the next inspection, thereby leaving a restaurant with a poor result despite having potentially rectified the original concerns and having improved its actual performance record. As a result of these concerns, Fung *et al.* (2007) argue that it is important to engage nongovernmental organizations to monitor disclosure provision, facilitate dissemination, and also actively promote qualitative enhancement. In general, however, such systems are built on the idea that information facilitates a 'certification effect', which we discuss in more detail below.

Disclosure requirements are also constrained by a fear of potential maladministration in the case of over-hasty publication. That is, the urge and demand to inform quickly and widely (for example, about food scares) is likely to conflict not just with the need to establish conclusively that a particular wrong doing has occurred, but also with the legal rights of those accused who might potentially be innocent but who will nevertheless, through the court of disclosure requirements, be tried in the court of public or media opinion.

As already noted, a third type of market incentive is provided by *certificates* (Bartley 2011). Such schemes are often run as part of self-regulatory regimes operated by industry associations or NGOs, although state-run certificate-based schemes also exist. Membership is often non-compulsory. One example would be so-called eco-labels such as the 'blue angel' in Germany where state institutions work together with industry and other public interest groups. Certificates seek to exploit consumer interest and incentivize choice. This means that the certificate signals an improvement in the quality of the good, such as by offering enhanced energy efficiency or the comfort of having purchased a 'green' product.

Such mechanisms are said to be less effective when the quality of the good is not visibly 'improved' (Scharpf 1996). Consumers are unlikely to fork out more for any particular good if it is not evident what the 'quality enhancement' is. However, although therefore the effect of certificate-based schemes has often distinguished between product-based and process-based standards (the former allows for certificate-based schemes as the quality of goods is visibly improved, the latter has more difficulty in establishing such effects as the approach merely affects the process, not the quality of the product). Later research has, however, shown that certification schemes that do address process-based issues (such as the labour standards affecting wood-based products, cocoa bean plantations, or factory-standards for sports shoes or children's toys) have an effect in that consumers express a preference for 'certified' goods (see Abbott and Snidal 2009). Thus, a certificate that points out that a particular good fulfils the criteria of the forest stewardship council, or fair trade standards, adds a 'premium' to the price of the good, but one that (wealthy) consumers are willing to pay.

Differences exist in the type of standards that such self-certification schemes adhere to (usually they are of the management-based or performance-based kind). There are also differences in the degree to which enforcement is conducted by third parties, through 'participatory guarantee systems' (in which producers, consumers and others might directly participate in the regime) or simply taken on trust. Furthermore, many of these self-regulatory systems are contested, that is, they do not enjoy monopolistic status (unless there is some state-centred standardization process). It is therefore not always transparent to consumers what a particular standard actually represents. For example, a range of certification schemes for organic food exists, leading to considerable consumer uncertainty about what is meant by any one standard and how 'organic' is defined in the first place.

Finally, *direct financial incentives* offer a further market-based mechanism to achieve desired policy objectives. For example, governments offer subsidies or set additional charges or taxes to encourage or discourage particular market developments. A prominent example is the widespread use of 'guaranteed' feed-in tariffs. Similarly, unleaded petrol was introduced by a tax subsidy in order to shift consumer preferences away from leaded petrol. The idea therefore is to find ways to internalize costs that otherwise remain external to the production of the good.

A different example is the use of the *price cap* mechanism in utility regulation. The simple idea of this mechanism (where prices were adjusted by the formula of inflation minus an efficiency factor, set by the regulator) was that this offered companies an incentive to be as efficient as possible. If they were able to reduce production costs further than the prescribed 'X'-factor, they could keep these profits given a regulatory 'promise' not to revisit the price cap outside formal review periods (see Chapter 8). However, establishing strong incentives to be efficient might come at the expense of long-term investments and 'asset sweating' (Helm and Tindall 2009). Similarly, the use of taxes and direct subsidies has been widely criticized as a method of picking winners (or losers), while also providing no real long-term commitment, as governments may decide to withdraw particular schemes at any given time (unless some contractual arrangements are provided for).

Taxation is used as a tool to decrease demand via the price function. It enjoys widespread use as a means to deal with cigarettes, alcohol, petrol consumption or other aspects of environmental pollution (although the gained tax revenue is not usually used to address the kind of problems that these 'pollutants' trigger; rather, they are usually absorbed into the overall revenue base of the state). Some studies have argued that alcohol taxes might be an effective tool for reducing overall consumption of alcohol. However, such approaches often lead to a deflection effect in that alcohol consumption moves to other jurisdictions and forms of illegal imports become widespread. Similar taxation on cigarettes has been widely used, although reduced consumption has arguably more to do with social norms than taxation.

Indeed, a further question is how long such financial schemes should operate as there is a risk that such incentives create dependency relationships when such schemes should alter basic market dynamics (such as the 'infant industry' argument) and allow particular industries or products to establish themselves. However, often subsidies and tax systems become objects of convenient state revenue raising and special interest politics. In addition, they require bureaucracy that distributes, collects and manages these payment streams.

Finally, there might also be an argument in favour of a reliance on general competition law provisions and other legal measures that govern economic transactions and employment relations. This form of 'do nothing' option would therefore argue that economic regulation, such as decisions about interconnection prices, could be dealt with through general competition law with competition authorities and courts in the driving seat. Similarly, employment law could be used to force employers to deal with 'safe' conditions at work, placing a premium on legal remedies and the like to deal with particular problems that might also be regulated through other means.

Architecture and nudging

Attempts to change behaviour through design, for example, by changing the physical environment (to reduce traffic speed) or via 'codes' (Lessig 2000) provides a further (and final) 'alternative' to command and control regulation.

Among the most insightful examples of using architecture to advance detection is the so-called panopticon effect. The design was first put forward by the philosopher and social reformer, Jeremy Bentham in 1785. It was used in 1842 for the Pentonville Prison in London and, later, in the construction of the Dublin Kilmainham jail in 1864. The design allows an observer to view all prisoners from one single point – without the prisoners knowing that they are being watched. In the wider sense, the panopticon effect describes a way through which regulators can insert themselves into a central nodal position that efficiently allows them to monitor regulatee conduct, with the regulatees being unsure as to whether they are being watched or not.

It is not difficult to find means by which states 'discipline' individuals and organizations through architecture, even if such means rely less directly on detection, for example, speed bumps or other road construction measures that seek to manage traffic flows. Detection and behaviour modification are, however, central to other ways of controlling behaviour: electronic turnstiles might be a way of containing crowding, which also allows a clear idea of who has entered a venue, and potentially reducing the possibility of illegal ticketing (Jennings and Lodge 2011). Another example is the widespread use of widely visible speed cameras to control traffic speeds, CCTV cameras to monitor spectators during sporting events, or helicopters with high resolution cameras during demonstrations.

More recently, the idea of 'nudging' via 'choice architectures' has become an increasingly prominent policy tool in diverse areas such as health, crime, energy consumption or pensions. A reliance on 'nudges' has been promoted as a low-cost middle way between supposedly intrusive government regulation and laissez-faire liberalism. A nudge, 'any aspect of the choice architecture that alters people's behavior in a predictable way without forbidding any options or significantly changing their economic incentives' (Thaler and Sunstein 2008: 6) requires a 'choice architecture' that moves 'people in directions that will make their lives better' (Thaler and Sunstein 2008: 8).

This strategy is therefore less interested in information gathering, but seeks to use incentive structures to modify behaviours. Thaler and Sunstein argue that applying nudges comes at little or even no direct cost (for government, consumers or industry) and preserves the autonomy of consumers/citizens. Choice architectures establish the incentive structure for individuals (by framing the 'default position') and individual behaviour will follow in the desired direction, as the incentives exploit individual decision-making biases and therefore appeal to self-interest. Examples of such nudging strategies include the design of urinals in public lavatories (to reduce spillage), the change of the default option on organ donations and pension plans from 'opting in' to 'opting out', establishing 'civility checkers' on email systems to reduce potential irritations and health insurance requirements that encourage the use of bike helmets (by requiring those who explicitly refuse to wear helmets to take out extra insurance cover).

As these examples illustrate, nudging draws on market-based strategies by exploiting information and disclosure requirements (energy efficiency indicators) or through the price signal (insurance premiums). The basic assumption is that individuals make decisions (or non-decisions) without fully reflecting on their actual long-term consequences. This might be because of inherent decision-making biases (risk aversion and optimism bias) or because of the inherent limitations that define individual (and corporate) decision-making (Simon 1947). For example, individuals regularly over-estimate their future retirement pension income and also make limited provision to deal with the potential costs of care in old age. Equally, individuals may not be fully informed about the degree of trans-fats (hydrogenated oils and fats) in their food or be aware of the (contested) implications for their health. Similarly, we drive too fast because we assume that we are 'in control' as conditions appear familiar.

The central assumption underlying 'nudging' is that these behavioural decision-making limitations can be usefully exploited through careful design. This includes the design of cafeterias (placing the 'healthy food' in key areas, banning unhealthy snacks from the cashier area, or the requirement that shop-keepers place unhealthy food on the top shelf next to adult magazines), the design of roads (painting lines on the tarmac that induce lower traffic speed), or the design of school attendance programmes (requiring parents to pay for their child's school attendance, but to return all the money plus interest should the pupil attend school on a regular basis). Similarly, the coverage of individual pension plans can be enhanced by imposing a scheme that relies on regular payments, unless individuals explicitly 'opt out'.

However, nudging places a particular emphasis in the central role of 'choice architecture' and those who design such architectures. Nudging therefore combines a highly technocratic view of life with one that relies on markets. So-called 'choice architects' or experts are assumed to be able to devise straightforward, and uncontroversial, nudges in different policy areas to influence our individual choices. They would act in our own interest, and also for the public good (as people eat more healthy food, reduce energy consumption, drive more carefully and so on). One could also argue that designing 'choice architectures' is also highly interventionist and resembles 'herding'. Advocates of nudging (e.g. Thaler and Sunstein) would suggest that the emphasis is placed on *choice* and that 'opting out' should be designed to be relatively cost-free and simple and that therefore individual liberty is not constrained through prohibitions.

However, such a distinction between prohibition through command and control and choice through nudging is highly problematic. Intervening in choice architectures might still be seen as interventionist (is there a straightforward definition of 'the good life'?), while allowing for choice might still incur considerable social costs that might be seen as requiring prohibition (such as nuclear safety). Put differently, nudging is about experts manipulating individual choices, thus raising issues of transparency and accountability (or the potential lack of them). It is not clear why particular experts should have the legitimacy to design choice architectures in a non-transparent way, especially when these choices include highly value-laden issues and might be considered as highly intrusive into private decisions; in other words, 'libertarian paternalism' might be considered to be an oxymoron.

Finally, nudging clearly has its limitations and therefore behaviour change might require more than nudging. Individuals might not be willing to be incentivized to eat more healthy food, even if nudged to do so. Parents similarly may not wish their children to be nudged to eat different food. In such cases, the costs of refusing to be nudged need to be set at a punitive level (and there also needs to be a threat of detection). Nudging therefore very quickly turns into shoving. Nudging is also limited in that it targets individual behaviour, whereas most decision-making takes place within an organized and organizational context. This means that any attempt at altering a 'choice architecture' will face potential competing demands and priorities (let alone commercial interests). Indeed, to use the bike helmet example noted earlier: even if the wearing of bike helmets is incentivized by mandatory insurance requirements for those refusing to wear a helmet, it does not solve the problem of damages incurred to potentially innocent third parties when involved in major accidents caused by those explicitly refusing to be nudged (i.e. car drivers might be found to be responsible for the death of a cyclist where the likelihood of fatal injuries would have been significantly reduced if a helmet had been worn). It is also questionable whether nudging will deal with the ill-intentioned rather than the merely ill-informed. It is unlikely that an airport security screening system that relies on nudging would be able to detect, let alone deter, those willing to provoke security incidents. In other words, a nudging kind of approach is highly limited, although it deserves careful consideration when seeking to develop approaches that aim to modify individual behaviours in choice situations.

What choice?

By now, the representatives of the Amnesian government are confused. What started as a straightforward dismissal of command and control-type regulation and a strong advocacy of alternatives of regulation has turned into long lists of advantages and disadvantages. Each of the different strategies starts from different assumptions, and the different alternatives also have different ideas about the problems with command and control approaches. Furthermore, each alternative requires its own set of bureaucratic information gathering and enforcement strategies, and is open to capture and political manoeuvring.

An approach that relies on 'variants of command and control' assumes that the key issue with command and control is that some regulatees are more affected than others and that therefore these asymmetric effects can be dealt with through exemptions and modifications to the initial regulation. Self-regulatory systems are based on the assumption that any attempt at hierarchical control and punishment is limited and usually ill-informed and makes regulatees 'irresponsible'. Therefore, delegating regulatory responsibility to regulated entities (in various ways) enhances expertise and flexibility in dealing with diagnosed problems. For market-based approaches, competition and self-interest are the best way to achieve behaviour-modification. For architecture-based views and nudgers, the central assumption is that regulatees are generally ill-informed and can be manipulated into doing 'the right thing' despite being lazy, emotional and short-sighted. Information is not a particular problem in this case as choice architects ensure that the right choices are taken. In other words, while official guidance encouraging thinking about alternatives suggests straightforward choices, a contrasting of these different alternatives points to competing understandings regarding the significance of failures, both in terms of 'market failure' and in terms of 'regulatory failure' (Bloor *et al.* 2006).

A la carte regulation?

So what can we do with the lemonade-binging youths in Amnesia? How should we consider the different options and in what order? Should we just leave things as they are and consider command and control as the last resort? Or should we start with command and control and only opt for 'alternatives' once we have persuaded ourselves that an alternative or a mixture of alternatives might be superior? Without claiming to be exhaustive, Table 5.2 offers an overview of some alternatives considered above and how they might be applied to lemonade binge-drinking concerns.

So what is the Amnesian government to do with their lemonade-binging youth? It might first consider relying on a 'drink responsibly' information campaign by the lemonade industry itself. Such an approach may however be seen as hardly discouraging consumption. Similarly, a reliance on architecture that requires all lemonade to be sold under the counter is unlikely to have much effect if lemonade drinking is regarded as fashionable, and indeed, as an essential part of the tourist appeal. Similarly, a reliance on cameras and sprinklers might be seen as an approach that fails to engage with the underlying problem.

Each of these options, or a mix between them, further requires an administrative apparatus that monitors compliance (regardless of regulatory alternative). Even market-based mechanisms require oversight over price mechanisms or disclosure requirements. Such regimes can operate at the level of the industry itself. However, it is likely that potential escalation is required, not just in terms of sanctions, but also in terms of threatening a potential application of state-operated classical regulation.

So, should Amnesia adopt a single instrument-type approach or a 'have it all' smorgasbord-type approach towards lemonade binge-drinking? Or how should it seek to apply different approaches as any single approach is unlikely to address every aspect of a regulatory problem, such as lemonade binge-drinking, especially as there is a potential threat of leakage towards consumption in Dezertia, illegal imports and/or a shift towards private speak-easies. Such an approach would also align with the OECD's recommended response to obesity. In 2010, the OECD argued that the health impacts of any single policy intervention, on obesity levels, was small (OECD 2010a: ch. 6). One way, advocated by those following Gunningham and Grabosky's smart regulation approach (Gunningham and Grabosky 1998; Grabosky 1995c), would suggest that the option should be to opt for less intrusive approaches in the first place and thereby appeal to individual and business self-interest to (over-) comply, rely on detection by third-parties (rather than state-based regulators), and only in the final instance, rely on an escalation of sanctions and an escalation towards increasingly formalized and punitive classical regulatory approaches.

TABLE 5.2 *Regulating lemonade binge-drinking*

Approach	Application to lemonade binge-drinking	Rationale	Limitation
Variants of command and control	Exemptions on closing times for cafés	Allows some cafés to remain open to attract tourists; licence can be revoked if it encourages rioting	Difficult to monitor and enforce; does not deal with private drinking
	Exempt particular cafés from overall prohibition	Allows some cafés to attract tourists; licence can be revoked if it encourages rioting	Difficult to monitor and enforce; does not deal with private drinking and illegal imports
Market-based	Disclose lemonade-sugar indicators	Seeks to 'inform' drinkers of likely impact of their consumption	Relies on lemonade becoming 'unfashionable'; might encourage search for 'hardest' lemonade
	Tax sugar content/ subsidize low-sugar lemonade	Price high impact lemonade out of the market	May encourage illegal imports/ flourishing duty-free trade, and search for even more high impact/addictive ingredients. Subsidies require financial commitment and attractive alternatives
	Allow lemonade producers to 'trade' lemonade-production quotas	Cap permissible production levels and encourage shift to other drinks	Encourages illegal imports from Dezertia and duty free trade; might encourage search for cheaper, more high impact drinks; requires policing of quotas and 'attractive' price
Self-regulation	Encourage industry code to encourage responsible drinking	Allows industry to develop approach towards binge-drinking without intervention, most likely through advertising	Industry does not commercially benefit from reduced consumption; unlikelihood of an immediate impact

(Continued overleaf)

TABLE 5.2 *continued*

Approach	Application to lemonade binge-drinking	Rationale	Limitation
	Encourage code of conduct for shopkeepers and café owners to sell 'responsibly'	Allows shops and café-owners to display their own professionalism in selling lemonade	Very difficult to enforce; limited likelihood of immediate impact
Nudging via choice architectures	Devise 'self-binding' schemes that restrain youths from drinking through small-scale incentives	Follows 'nudge' fashion; individuals can 'buy' high interest 'bond' that commits them to non-binging/rioting, financial loss if found rioting	System requires detection and enforcement – highly complex; unlikely to change behaviours
	Require shops to remove all public promotions of lemonade	Reduced visibility will reduce demand	Does not deal with displays/advertising in Dezertia; unlikely to reduce drinking in cafés
	Install cameras and sprinklers to contain rioting and 'cool down' rowdy binge-drinkers	Visible detection and automatic behaviour modification instruments deter disorder	High cost of installation; might be seen as infringement of personal freedom, potential injuries from sprinklers

Conclusion

An account that compares alternatives to regulation, in particular that contrasts 'law' with alternatives is likely to face criticism for failing to understand the normative power of 'law' in contrast to the signal sent through prices. It is argued that law has a normative appeal and that most people comply, given the normative obligation to obey the law. This contrasts with behaviour in the market-place where the price signal is the all-important information that signals whether compliance is in one's self-interest or not. A reliance on market-based or self-regulatory alternatives might also be limited given the type of incident: day-to-day problems might easily be accommodated by voluntary arrangements, but such mechanism might be less effective in the case of one-off large-scale accidents where mandatory insurance mechanisms might offer a better alternative to the likely under-insuring by individuals and firms against low probability, high-impact events.

Our example of lemonade binge-drinking provides one core case of the kind of problems that debates regarding regulatory alternatives seek to address. Other types of problems, such as environmental pollution or other kinds of common-pool resource problems (that broadly suffer from characteristics which others call 'tragedy of the commons', Hardin 1968), or moral issues (e.g. example, whether the keeping of wild animals in travelling zoos or circuses, should be regulated, prohibited or left to zoos to decide) need to be investigated in terms of their problem specificity. However, ultimately, any such discussion will return to variants considered in this chapter.

Such choices are based on underlying assumptions regarding human behaviour and decision-making, and the likelihood of particular types of pressure. Most of all, any of these 'alternatives', like classical regulation, requires a bureaucracy to monitor and enforce. Furthermore, each one of these alternatives is open to the kind of political processes that lead to capture or other expressions of special interest or political involvement. In short, the attempts to perform smart regulation through the intelligent combination of different alternatives to regulation needs to consider the inherent limitations of any of the approaches (such as side-effects through adjusting behaviour to regulatory strategy, and administrative costs to operate the specific regulatory regime), *and* it needs to consider the likelihood of special interest politics perverting the intentions of the initial regime.

Chapter 6

Regulation Inside Government

The Amnesian public prison system is in crisis. After a series of escapes and reports about the widespread abuse of prisoners by staff, the Amnesian government is concerned about the way in which prison directors exercise their authority. Amnesia's prisons are overcrowded. In addition, prison officers and prisoners have formed networks to supply televisions, cell phones and drugs to the wider prison population. At the same time, the finance minister complains about the considerable cost of rehabilitation programmes, especially as reoffending rates are high.

Amnesia's government would like to know what kind of control strategy it should adopt regarding its prisons. What control strategies are available to assess a prison director's management? Is the application of tighter and more intense controls on prison directors the only available strategy?

What is regulation inside government?

The regulation of government by itself differs from the more generic setting of regulation in terms of its distinct setting within the public sector and the multiplicity of policy objectives. In relation to prisons, key questions are how to improve control over the Amnesian prison sector, how to assess whether different values, namely efficiency, security and rehabilitation, are met, and how control strategies are chosen that facilitate cooperation from prisons rather than suspicion and gaming.

Such questions are not unique to the prisons domain. They equally apply to domains such as childcare facilities, schools, hospitals, or nursing homes, and arguably also to the wider regulation of state-owned enterprises, such as ports or utilities. For some of these domains, a specific feature is the vulnerability of their clients who are unlikely to be able to act as 'fire-alarms' (i.e. dementia patients are unlikely to call regulators or other public officials about standards of care). In other areas, regulation inside government focuses on areas of key economic and social significance, or on the procedural aspects of the exercise of governmental power (such as through procurement or appointment).

In general, regulation inside government relates to three fundamental activities (Hood *et al.* 1999):

- the *quality of service* offered during the delivery of services within set policy objectives, with examples including the inspection of hospitals, the military, prisons and universities;
- the *audit of public expenditure* by using a court of auditors and other financial watchdogs that seek to scrutinize whether public monies have been used in an efficient and appropriate manner, leading to wider interests in 'value for money' studies that have become commonplace since the 1960s in the United States and in the United Kingdom since the 1980s (Pollitt *et al.* 1999); and
- the *ethical conduct* of those in public office, especially in terms of conflicts of interest (for example, in the allocation of public tenders), or other bodies that process complaints regarding alleged irregularities in official behaviour (for example, the 1978 US Ethics in Government Act).

These functions have been at the heart of traditional public management and are far from being a merely contemporary phenomenon. For example, the Chinese Imperial Censorate conducted regulation inside government over 2000 years ago, the oversight of local government activities was commonplace across European countries, such as Tsarist Russia or Napoleonic France or early 19th-century Germany in the wake of the French Revolution, and Nationalist China created a whole separate constitutional branch for oversight and inspection in the 1931 Four Power Constitution (Lodge and Hood 2010: 591).

The three broad activities noted above are an inherent part of public management. In relation to our prisons example, the quality dimension relates to issues of care (cells, meals, facilities, rehabilitation), the audit function refers to issues of expenditure and contracting for services (such as the contracting out of laundry, kitchen or transport services), and the ethical function focuses on the appropriateness of appointment processes or the award of particular tenders). Central to contemporary discussions has, however, been the somewhat new trend, accompanied by a growing heterogenization of service providers, to grant regulators of government activities the power to monitor and ensure competition, for example, between providers of public services.

More broadly, the development of standards for regulatory regimes governing public services and other government activities (such as public appointments) is, of course, dependent on wider decisions regarding the availability of particular services. For example, regulators may be able to condemn the quality of rehabilitation-related activities within particular prisons. However, such condemnation reflects wider policy decisions that may restrict the availability of such programmes, for example, by cutting expenditures. As a result, quality-checking needs to consider the wider resources available to those delivering particular services. For example, if public services are cut to such an extent that elderly people in need are no longer in a position to receive heated meals or support with their personal hygiene, and, as a result, these patients die, this might be interpreted less as a failure in regulation, but an outcome of policy decisions. The delivery of policy and its control are therefore two separate but related activities that are inherent to public management.

The debate regarding regulation inside government has emerged as a key feature in the late 20th century as part of wider reforms within public management. One key change has been the growing diversification in ownership in the delivery of public services, especially the use of private providers. This trend is said to have encouraged a growing formalization and contractualization in relationships, making rules more explicit as former informal administrative relationships are no longer seen as effective devices to guide interdependent relationships. In the area of Australian prisons, for example, John Braithwaite (2008) has illustrated how the need for formalized and explicit regulatory regimes emerged as a response to the demands of (new) private providers. This demand resulted in the adoption of contemporary regulatory thinking and concepts in the Australian prisons domain. According to Braithwaite, private organizations demanded the same 'level playing field' in terms of standards as their public counterparts. In addition, prisoners' rights groups supported the extension of formal rights. As a result, regulators extended their new style of regulation to include both private and public providers for prisons. In short, the growing heterogeneity of relationships within the provision of public services is said to have led to an increasingly formalized control style.

A second, related theme has been the prominence granted to freestanding regulatory bodies within government that check on governmental activities. This relates to diverse phenomena such as the strengthened role of audit offices that goes beyond traditional 'beancounting', the creation of specific 'ethics watchers', ranging from ombudsmen to freedom of information commissioners, to the creation of specific domain-related 'quality' checkers, such as education-related regulators. The common feature of these bodies is that they, at least to some extent, operate outside the normal chain of command within governmental organization. More traditionally, regulation inside government was conducted by units within normal ministerial organizations (checking on compliance of other governmental actors, both horizontally and vertically) and by bodies set up by the legislature to oversee the executive, such as audit offices, or special inspectors, in particular for the military (in Germany the *Beauftragte*).

If these two trends of growing explicitness of rules and of freestanding oversight bodies offered potential solutions to the problem of Amnesian prisons, then what has been the problem? What makes the control of government by itself such a problematic activity? And how can such debates inform any discussion regarding Amnesian prisons in particular and the regulation of public services in general? The next section considers the traditional position regarding the 'problem' of regulation inside government. Then, the discussion turns to different ways in which control 'styles' within government have been conceptualized. We explore their specific strength and weaknesses, including side-effects. We then consider how these mixes between modes of control can be utilized and how they might be applied to Amnesian prisons. The conclusion returns to wider discussions regarding the control of government by itself.

The problem with regulation inside government

As noted in previous chapters, the regulation of any activity has to consider that compliance will not easily be forthcoming. However, as shown, the ultimate power of government is the use of coercive public force, namely the removal of civil liberties through outright incarceration or the revocation of a licence to trade. Of course, the exercise of such ultimate power might be limited because of processes such as capture, judicial obstruction or lack of resources to conduct such enforcement actions. Nevertheless, when it comes to the power of public authority over private activities, there remains, in principle, the power of the state to coerce individuals and organizations to comply with the law.

Within the public sector, such a reliance on a state's coercive power as *ultima ratio regnum* is more limited. There are only very few cases where a public sector body has taken another public sector body to court. Indeed, in their classic argument, Wilson and Rachal (1977) suggest that government is inherently less able to control itself than it is able to control activities by private actors; 'it is easier for a public agency to change the behavior of a private organization than of another public agency' (Wilson and Rachal 1977: 4).

Such an argument may appear surprising, at least at first sight. The supposedly hierarchical structure of governmental organization should facilitate compliance, for example, through the power to give direction or instructions, as well as the power to move public servants (and, in some cases, to dismiss them). However, even before an age of employment litigation regarding wrongful dismissal, the extent to which the hierarchical powers of the state could be used to control state activities has been limited (Wilson and Rachal 1977).

A number of reasons exist for this diagnosed problem of regulation inside government. For Wilson and Rachel regulation of governmental activities is fundamentally more problematic than the control of private activities due to the politics inherent in any government activity. These problems occur in relationships between horizontally equal organizations, such as ministerial departments, which draw on the same level of legitimacy as 'higher organs' of the state. There is therefore no automatic hierarchical relationship between 'superior' and 'subordinate' organizations.

Furthermore, control activities are often carried out by junior staff in one department (often with a brief that cross-cuts other departments' domain-specific jurisdiction). They then seek to modify the behaviour of senior management in other departments. Such attempts are usually met by resistance, both on the basis of seniority and a lack of subject expertise. For example, a former senior UK civil servant in the Department of Education, Michael Barber, publicly complained about the junior and non-expert nature of staff from the Cabinet Office's Regulatory Impact Unit (RIU) that sought to direct efforts in cutting 'red tape':

> what the RIU actually did was send people who knew nothing about education policy (the kind of people Nigel Lawson [a former UK Chancellor] might have dismissed as 'teenage scribblers') and had consulted a couple of union representatives, to ask me take the pressure off teachers! No chance. (Barber 2007: 63)

According to Barber, any attempt by such cross-cutting units to steer domain-specific departments is bound to fail. In addition, this lack of results also means that senior staff will eventually withdraw their support from their junior staff's activities. The solution to this diagnosis of seemingly inevitable failure is, according to Barber, to establish small controlling units containing highly qualified individuals at the heart of government (an approach he practiced when leading the UK Prime Minister's Delivery Unit between 2001 and 2005). However, it remains unlikely that low-ranking staff in regulatory oversight functions would be able to hold high-ranking officials (in their own or other departments) to account, even less so, when powerful ministers object to such controlling activities.

Apart from issues of seniority and expertise, a further problem affecting the ability of one government organization to modify the behaviour of another is that one departmental unit's key priorities are likely to be other units' and departments' least important items on the agenda. For example, if within one government department, one unit's priority is to reduce mental health problems within government (as part of workplace regulation exercises), then it is highly likely that this programme will be met with little interest among units in the same department that deal with, for example, terrorist threats or immigration. It will receive even less interest among other departments dealing with climate change, energy security or employment legislation.

Vertical relationships within government face similar problems. At least there exist clear lines of hierarchy regarding superior and subordinate authorities, or between levels of government. In other words, the ability 'to instruct' a subordinate body or to request information from a subordinate body offers the means to exercise formal control. However, there are also constraints on the exercise of formal authority. For example, the relationship within one administrative domain is often characterized by so-called 'vertical brotherhoods among specialists' (in German, *vertikale Fachbruderschaften*, see Wagener 1979). These 'brotherhoods' (that increasingly also include women) are formed by a common professional identity (or close 'relational distance', Black 1976) that may be facilitated by shared professional experiences. As a result, these vertical relationships are characterized by cooperative interactions, a shared interest in avoiding external criticism and surveillance, and a mutual desire to maintain informal control relationships where regulation is, at most, a soft and highly politicized affair (see Lodge and Hood 2010: 594).

In short, in the context of horizontal relationships, regulation inside government is hindered by the lack of clear lines of hierarchical authority, and the lack of interest in dealing with other departments' cross-cutting agendas. In the context of vertical relationships, regulation inside government is limited by issues of close social relationships or 'relational distance' (Black 1976).

More broadly, any exercise of government authority to control another arm of government is always a political act that will affect important political constituencies. Indeed, it might be argued that the operation of government is inherently about seeking to address competing objectives (such as in the case of prisons, the competing demands of efficiency, security and rehabilitation). It therefore makes, as noted already, any attempt at regulating public services problematic. Any attempt at control will be met with accusations of having ignored one particular value at the expense of others. It is therefore unsurprising that regulators of public services often face difficulties in operating a regulatory regime, with regulatees refusing to provide information or refusing to comply with enforcement requirements, often by seeking redress via political channels.

Therefore, the problem of regulation inside government is about the inherent political nature of governmental activities; it is about turf battles between organizations, and it is about the inherent inability to utilize hierarchical authority to an extent that supposedly exists in the context of private regulation. This world of regulation inside government where 'there is little sovereignty, only rivals and allies' (Wilson and Rachal 1977: 13) contrasts, Wilson and Rachal suggest, with the regulation of the private sector where the 'authority' of the state cannot be ignored or denied, and where the possibility of a regulatory body taking on a private entity is real.

In the next section we discuss four strategies that deal with these issues of regulation inside government. We then consider whether the empirical evidence suggests that the regulation of government by itself has indeed proven to be more difficult than the regulation of privately provided public services, as Wilson and Rachel suggested nearly four decades ago.

The public management of regulation inside government

As noted above, regulation inside government is said to face difficulties in applying the law, especially in terms of being able to escalate sanctions, or to require the provision of information. Instead, an adversarial relationship ensues in which public regulatees are aware that ultimately they are able to call in political favours to undermine regulatory demands. In the Amnesian prison case, problems in regulation may be based on widespread fatalism and cynicism as powerful unions that resist changes to work practices and limited resources hinder investment in security and rehabilitation, while the overall domain suffers from media feeding frenzies following scandals.

Such problems do not exist solely in the area of publicly-owned activities, but across all activities that involve politically well-connected business interests. After all, it is not difficult to identify examples where regulators abstain from using their 'big gun' sanctions in the face of sustained industry and political pressure, and the literatures regarding 'alternatives to regulation' and 'enforcement' point to the need to seek alternative ways of achieving compliance than through a reliance on tough sanctions.

However, there is a range of ways in which the problems of traditional control via reporting requirements, formal inspections and hierarchical sanctions can, at least to a degree, be mediated. The rest of this section points to four broad modes in which control over government activities can be supplemented. Table 6.1 summarizes these different views regarding modes of control. The views are informed by the cultural theory influenced approach towards control over bureaucracy (Hood 1998; Hood *et al.* 1999; Hood *et al.* 2004; Lodge and Wegrich 2005a, 2005b).

The *oversight* mode relates to the type of control criticized by Wilson and Rachal (1977). Oversight relies on close relational distance (a 'high group' feature, as considered by Black 1976) and attempts to exercise regulation through formal rules ('high grid') that leads to adversarial relations. Arguably, these diagnosed problems could be addressed by emphasizing a further reinforcing of oversight, especially by adding to formality (i.e. grid). For example, one hierarchical tool would be to increase relational distance to reduce the extent to which 'vertical brotherhoods' dominate regulatory processes. This could be done by introducing another level of regulation, bringing more outsiders into the control relationship, by reducing social contacts, or by enlarging the

TABLE 6.1 *Four modes of exercising regulation inside government*

	Control	*Standard setting*	*Behaviour modification*	*Information gathering*
Oversight	through hierarchy: monitoring and directing from a point of authority	by rules enacted by specific authorities and expert advice	prosecution and licence removal	obligatory information reporting
Competition	through choice or other forms of rivalry (naming and shaming)	competing standards, encouraging rivalry between providers	competitive pressures (league tables)	incentives to reveal performance information
Mutuality	through group processes: Mutual observation and embedding in group interaction	rules set through participative processes	persuasion	peer-review
Contrived randomness	through unpredictable processes	by volatile or inscrutable standards	uncertainty restricts opportunism	random selection of reporting requirements, surprise inspections

Source: Adapted from Lodge and Hood (2010: 599).

jurisdiction of regulators. The effect of such a jurisdictional extension would be to make regulators face a more heterogeneous set of regulatees, while regulatees would similarly face a more diverse set of regulators (see Lodge and Hood 2010: 602). A further strategy based on 'more' hierarchy would be to rely on a greater formalization of processes. Such formalization might be achievable through a reliance on enforcement by external actors, such as international organizations or the European Union, or other third parties, such as (international) non-governmental organizations. In other words, the strategy would rely on adding 'external' actors as an additional layer to the regulation inside government.

However, beyond the plan of adding 'more' hierarchy to respond to the shortcomings of hierarchy, Table 6.1 offers three alternative ways of thinking about how to structure control processes. One way, one presumably advocated by Wilson and Rachal (1977), is to rely on *rivalry*, namely the use of private and competitive providers of public services, and a more general reliance on processes of competition. Such control strategies became popular with the rise of the so-called 'New Public Management' (Hood 1991) in the 1980s. A number of rivalry-based strategies can be identified. One is a reliance on the comparative assessment of performance indicators, combined with market-like incentive or sanctioning mechanisms, such as direct financial incentives (performance pay) or naming and shaming (league tables). Such performance indicators could range from costs per inmate, to escape rates and incidents of violence or recidivism rates of released prisoners. The underlying view is that public servants will be motivated to perform through individual material incentives and 'public races' for positional advantages, particularly through league tables and other ranking systems.

A different option is to rely on *mutuality*, or group processes. Standards are set by consensus and are a result of a participatory process. Similarly, information-gathering and behaviour-modification rely on peer-monitoring and persuasion. A mutuality-based strategy reduces the problems of hierarchical oversight in that it relies on greater acceptability of regulatory processes, as enforcement builds on persuasion (rather than deterrence), information-gathering relies on a process of mutual learning and peer-review (rather than formal requests), and standards are negotiated as part of a professional community (rather than appear as bureaucratically imposed standard operating procedures). In other words, this strategy advocates a strengthening of 'vertical brotherhoods' as a regulatory strategy where the judgement of fellow peers becomes the primary motivation among staff (for example, prison directors) to improve their performance (see, for example, Finer 1950 and Heclo and Wildavsky 1974 who stressed the importance of such processes in other parts of civilian bureaucracy). Advocates of this mode of control would also argue that mutuality allows for a much more far-reaching 'in-depth' kind of inspection than inspections that rely on other modes. In particular, it is argued that complex public organizations, such as hospitals, prisons or schools, cannot be inspected without in-depth insights from those operating these particular establishments.

Participation, in this view, would also include the involvement of wider societal groups, in order to reduce potential distrust between the domain-specific processes of control and the 'outside' world. For example, the prison domain has traditionally relied on some system of participatory oversight through local 'boards of visitors' that consist of external 'interested parties' and that offer not just an additional source of scrutiny, but also a channel for prisoners to communicate their complaints about mistreatment.

The third alternative is to rely on elements of enhanced uncertainty and surprise, or *contrived randomness*. According to this approach, standards and approaches remain uncertain, or are acted upon in unpredictable ways, so that gaming actors – such as prison directors – are unable to foresee when and how the future will develop. Traditional career structures within various parts of traditional bureaucracy, such as military postings, policing, tax administration, and colonial administration, all relied on a degree of uncertainty, so that over-familiarity and therefore close relational distance could be avoided, or, at least reduced. A reliance on surprise (such as through postings or regulatory enforcement teams being allocated through lottery-type processes) eliminates corruption possibilities that require predictable and regular social interactions. Similarly, relying on information gathering through unpredictable, or 'surprise' inspections offers one way of reducing the outright gaming of information by regulatees.

In sum, if one accepts the argument that hierarchical ways of conducting control within government are faced with severe limitations, then it can nevertheless be argued that 'enriching' hierarchical controls through some alternative ways of conceptualizing control, namely through processes of mutuality, contrived randomness and rivalry, offers ways of alleviating the most intricate problems associated with 'oversight'. We now move to a discussion of the limitations of these strategies, and consider these in the context of Amnesian prisons.

Going inside: limits of competing control strategies

How, then, would these strategies 'translate' into the prisons domain of Amnesia. Each of these modes of controls has distinct implications as to the way in which control is to be exercised – and they offer contrasting diagnoses as to why the problems have arisen. Figure 6.1 offers a brief summary, translating the broad strategies introduced in the previous section to the specific context of Amnesia's prisons domain.

All four modes of control therefore address, in their own ways, the diagnosed deficits of Amnesian prisons, whether in terms of the decent treatment of prisoners, indicators of overcrowding, escapes and suicides,

Contrived randomness Use surprise inspections to reduce 'gaming' and to gain insight into operation of prison	Oversight Impose stricter and more extensive reporting requirements; bring in external and different inspectors
Rivalry Use league-tabling and benchmarking to assess prison performance	Mutuality Strengthen inspection and relationship with prisons by advancing professional conversation and by introducing third party (regime-outsider) audits

FIGURE 6.1   *Contrasting strategies for Amnesia's prisons*

and the overall effectiveness of expenditure on rehabilitation programmes. It is difficult to suggest any 'predictable' way in which secretive networks between prisoners and prison guards can be discovered. It is therefore likely that contrived randomness would offer an effective tool to exercise control (similarly, abuse may be most detectable through unpredictable means of control). The different strategies illustrated in Table 6.2 also point to some degrees of agreement. For example, both rivalry-based and mutuality-based approaches would emphasize the importance of not trusting centralized bureaucratic inspection and reporting regimes. However, they differ in their advocacy of particular interventions, one (rivalry) arguing for an exploitation of the 'competitive spirit' among different prison staff, the other (mutuality) arguing for an emphasis on professional collaboration and openness. Similarly, both contrived randomness and rivalry share a scepticism regarding the ability of 'vertical brotherhoods' to control themselves effectively. However, both approaches differ as to whether performance should be controlled through benchmarking and league-tabling, or whether this should be conducted through processes of surprise and unpredictability.

These four basic control strategies have their distinct strengths and weaknesses. The key (supposed) advantage of hierarchy, the ability to impose 'tough' information reporting and behaviour-modifying sanctions, is counter-balanced by the problems of 'command and control' regulation that have featured in previous chapters. Such a mode of control is likely to have a particular motivational (*de*motivational) impact on those who are being regulated, encouraging counter-learning and gaming. Prisons will therefore develop their own methods to counter information demands and to frustrate attempts at sanctioning. For example, a study of the German prison system suggested that both sides of the regulatory relationship, that is, regulators (prison units within government departments) and regulatees (prisons) regarded 'more' hierarchy as an unhelpful response to perceived failings. Instead, there was widespread support for what has been defined here as a 'mutuality'-based strategy. This strategy, according to this view, offered the advantage of mutual professional exchange that encouraged openness and trust (Lodge 2004; Lodge and Wegrich 2005a). As a consequence, the benefit of unannounced inspections was also discounted. German prison staff regarded the extensive application of a 'surprise'-based method as unhelpful as it facilitated further distrust between the different parts of the prison administration. This perception contrasted with an earlier study of the English prison system that found an extensive advocacy of contrived randomness to counter widespread gaming by prison directors and staff (Hood *et al.* 1999).

Mutuality-based controls are far from problem-free. In particular, these problems are closely related to criticisms pointed at self-regulation:

TABLE 6.2 Overview of modes of control in Amnesian prisons

Mode of control	Amnesian prison regulation	Expected benefit	Limitations
Oversight	Strengthen formal inspection requirements and establish further oversight functions	Allows for more and consistent information, more formal enforcement action	Gaming and output distortion, demotivation and problems of enforcement given 'politics' of regulation inside government
Rivalry	Rely primarily on competitive and comparative benchmarking, link career incentives to performance	Motivates rivalry between different prisons/prison directors and thereby improves overall performance/allows for yardstick competition and thereby reduces asymmetric information	Over-emphasis on competition and rivalry leads to gaming and output distortion, reduction in professional conversation, problems of being able to compare between diverse institutions
Mutuality	Strengthen 'professional conversation' between prison staff, introduce peer review	Appeals to demand for 'high trust' relationship across actors and exchange of professional knowledge, reduces distrust between regulator and regulatees (e.g. hiding of information)	Lack of accountability towards external actors; encourages lack of challenge within domain, no formal means of gathering information and modifying behaviour
Contrived randomness	Strengthen random surprise elements, such as surprise inspections	Reduces possibility of gaming system by reducing predictability	Reduces trust within system
Oversight-mutuality	Using peer-review to inform official inspections and reporting	Seeks to use professional judgement in gathering information and in executing enforcement	Tension between demands to perform peer-review and being part of formal hierarchical relationship

(Continued overleaf)

TABLE 6.2   *continued*

Mode of control	Amnesian prison regulation	Expected benefit	Limitations
Mutuality-rivalry	Using benchmarking to inform peer-review learning exercises	Reduces need for formal inspection as comparative performance information is used to inform professional conversations	Lack of central direction and enforcement possibilities, reduces information sharing
Rivalry-contrived randomness	Benchmarking on 'unpredictable' indicators	Reduces possibility for actors to game performance indicator 'game'	Reduces trust and reduces ability of overall system to provide for 'strategic' direction
Contrived randomness – oversight	Mix of predictability and surprise in information-gathering and behaviour-modification	Reduces ability to predict and game system, especially regarding information gathering	Increases distrust, and tension between formal procedures and elements of unpredictability
Oversight-rivalry	Oversight activities provide comparative information and encouragement of rivalry	Reduces information asymmetry by encouraging self-revelation of performance, allows a degree of prison director discretion to implement output/outcome objectives	Tension between conformity of oversight and emphasis on discretion, potential output distortion, might turn into 'target & terror' regime
Contrived randomness – mutuality	Blind (anonymous) or lottery-generated peer review processes	Reduces possibility of informal relations to subvert peer-review process (interactions based on blind one-shot games rather than interactive tit-for-tat)	Limited population reduces possibility of true 'blind' or unpredictable review process, tension between high trust and low trust mechanisms

mutuality-based systems are often criticized for discouraging open criticism and frank assessment. Mechanisms of peer-pressure have been seen to be strong and effective, such as in the world of academia or also within government (Heclo and Wildavsky 1974); but with respect to controlling public services, mutuality might lead to over-lenient practices. In other domains, such as the higher spheres of government and within academia, an emphasis on mutuality has either declined (higher civil service) or is seen as successful resistance to attempts to open up activities to managerial direction (academia). Similarly, an over-emphasis on professional conversations among peers within prisons is likely to restrict public access to information regarding the performance of prisons in general, and regarding the treatment of prisoners and prisons' disciplinary records in particular.

Rivalry-based strategies, for example, a reliance on league tables and benchmarks, allow for a comparison of performance. Such comparison may be conducted by either consumers of services or regulators, or both. As earlier discussions of incentive-based regulation have suggested, one motivation to encourage rivalry is that those entering the competition will seek to outperform each other. Furthermore, being able to compare performance, similar to the idea of 'yardstick competition', reduces inherent information asymmetries for regulators and consumers: instead of facing the information provided by one single monopolist, or receiving diverse and inconsistent signals, regulators are able to assess performance on the basis of consistent information. Similarly, a reliance on 'crime maps' (illustrating crime rates on a street-to-street basis) or 'food deserts' are said to facilitate local accountability and to offer overall information about the supply of policing and public health objectives (although citizens have been reluctant to supply information in fear of condemning their neighbourhood as a crime hotspot).

There are, however, problems with such comparative benchmarking exercises. For one, it requires indicators that offer robust and valid signals about the overall health of the system (i.e. are indicators about school-leaving certificate completion rates in prisons a good indicator for the overall rehabilitation programme?). In addition, the more the measurement of performance is linked to individual career advancement, the more such measurement exercises will be met by gaming and output distortion (see Bevan and Hood 2006; Hood 2006; but also Kelman and Friedman 2009). Gaming implies that institutions will meet demands for performance through 'creative compliance', whereas output distortions imply that rather than concentrating on 'really' strategic objectives, organizations focus on those activities that can be measured or are politically important (i.e. quality of prison inspections is measured in 'number' of inspections).

Examples of such gaming are widespread. In education, schools select students to fulfil particular criteria, decide to concentrate on selected pupils who will improve aggregate performance at the margin (or grade inflate everyone), and teach to the test. For example, Indonesian schools were condemned for discouraging teachers from speaking out against managerialist demands to allow students to copy from successful peers (*The Economist*, 7 July 2011). Performance management in the hospital sector will lead to a concentration on those activities that are being measured at the expense of others. In policing, performance measures, such as 'crime-solving success' measures, will encourage a focus on solving petty crime rather than difficult cases.

A further problem is comparability. Prisons vary in their 'customer' profile (high-level terrorists versus tax dodgers, male versus female versus young offenders' prisons), and in their locational attributes (rural prisons are likely to have different procurement costs than urban ones). The more general point, therefore, is that a reliance on comparative performance assessment as a means to encourage rivalry-based modes of control requires broadly comparable performances that also need to be measurable in a way that does not allow extensive gaming.

As a result, the main problem if rivalry is used for prison control is that prisons are not production organizations for which the outputs (what is happening in the prisons) and the outcomes (security, crime prevention and fighting, rehabilitation) are easily observable and where a causal connection between some type of output and an outcome can easily be established (Wilson 1989). Some measures are easily quantifiable, such as the cost per inmate, but the contribution of a good or bad educational programme in prisons to low recidivism rates is almost impossible to establish, given the range of context variables shaping the lives of released prisoners (cf. Lin 2000). Hence, using such a control style comes with the risk that prisons will be treated like production organizations and the emphasis put on those aspects that can be measured, while those activities that cannot be measured or only with great difficulty will be crowded out (Wilson 1989). Indeed, such a strategy might further reduce professional standards by forcing a managerialist 'code of silence' on organizations where potential dissenters or 'whistleblowers' will be discouraged from revealing any gaming or other output distortion activities (as in the case of Indonesian schools, see above).

One way to counter such negative effects across all four modes of regulation is to rely on combinations or hybrids. Such ideas of hybridization are said to offer stable and advantageous solutions to the problems of control (Hood 1998). Equally, Verweij and colleagues (2006) have suggested that 'clumsy solutions' offer beneficial outcomes to, what they call, elegant solutions. Examples of such hybrids are the combination of announced and unannounced inspections, or of rivalry-based performance assessment and 'hierarchical' inspections. Similarly, inspection results could be used to rank performance. For example, German nursing homes have been given individual 'care grades', with the results being published in the internet (www.pflegenoten.de). Furthermore, rivalry-based performance comparison could also be combined with mutuality-type peer-based conversations in order to advance 'learning'.

At the same time, such attempts at hybridization are not without their own tensions. For example, an emphasis on rivalry is likely to run counter to any attempt at encouraging mutuality and peer-review as individual advance is unlikely to be facilitated by partaking in group-based activities. Encouraging rivalry at the organizational level is also likely to encourage gaming, therefore reducing the ability to compare and assess the quality of the gathered information. Similarly, an emphasis on contrived randomness is unlikely to advance trust within the domain. At the same time, with too much emphasis on 'peer-review' and mutuality, there will be difficulties in encouraging formal enforcement or in encouraging a basic degree of 'distrust' that keeps regulatees 'on their toes'. Finally, an emphasis on standardized (oversight) reporting duties is in tension with (rivalry) attempts to delegate discretionary managerial power to regulatees, such as prison directors.

In the prison domain, therefore, a number of solutions to the diagnosed problems of Amnesia can be put forward. Table 6.2 provides a summary of the different modes of control and their implications for Amnesian prisons. This discussion also includes two-way hybrids between the four modes of control.

In short, an emphasis on bringing together a range of modes of control is likely to offer a remedy against the inherent weaknesses affecting the regulation of government by itself that were diagnosed by Wilson and Rachal. Comparative empirical studies have shown that different state traditions draw on somewhat different mixes across modes of control, but they do not draw on one single approach (Hood *et al.* 2004). Little, however, has been said as to how to design such 'hybrids' and how to maintain support for such intelligent designs. Similarly, it might be suggested that these hybrids emerge through a process of happenstance and gradual adaptation and 'layering', thereby leaving little space for regulatory design. Furthermore, while these mixes might be said to alleviate some of the key problems associated with pure strategies, it is not certain whether these mixed strategies will provide stability over time, or whether tensions between the components will lead to contradiction and/or break-down.

Conclusion: 'don't go to jail' cards in regulation inside government

We began this chapter by introducing the argument that regulation inside government is inherently problematic due to the limits of exercising hierarchy within a system where politics rather than formal authority matter. Such limits may be partially addressed by separating out control functions from the day-to-day running of a political ministry. However, such a strategy will hardly be a fully satisfactory solution. This chapter has sought to advance two points. One, there are more modes of regulation than hierarchy or oversight, namely mutuality, rivalry and contrived randomness. Therefore, the limitations of hierarchy can be overcome through the introduction of alternatives. Second, although these alternatives provide some answers to the problems of hierarchical oversight, they introduce their own tensions and problems.

The evidence suggests that countries rely on various mixes between modes of control – thereby overcoming the limitations of 'pure' control strategies. Indeed, the empirical evidence of an age of 'private' provision of public services does not suggest that 'public' ownership stands in the way of effective public regulation. In other words, the importance of ownership might be over-rated. Instead, the key impediment to regulation is the complexity and competition between values that affect regulated activities. Competing values mean that the regulation of public services – such as prisons – needs to find an (often uneasy) balance between emphasizing the values of efficiency (financial resource use), equity (the fair treatment of prisoners) and security (the absence of security incidents, such as suicides, riots or break-outs). It is unlikely that any regulatory regime will find a perfect balance between these three values and that 'perfect' implementation will ever be feasible. Incidents will therefore always occur, and therefore criticism will always occur. Regulation inside government thus deals with complex problems that involve inherent trade-offs that have little to do with 'public' ownership. Instead, when regulated actors are powerful, where issues are complex and involve trade-offs and value-choices, any regulatory strategy will be faced with inherent limitations. However, by mixing regulatory strategies across modes of control, it is less likely that such limitations will become particularly prominent.

Chapter 7

International Regulation

Imported Akunam honey has become highly popular in Amnesia and other countries. It is valued for its nutritional health benefits, and it is also used for the treatment of skin diseases. Akunam honey can only be harvested in the few areas where the Akunam tree grows. Recently, some disturbing reports have emerged that point out the poor conditions in which bees and beekeepers are being treated by various producers. In addition, contaminated and fake Akunam honey has emerged on the Amnesian market. In response, demands have been made for a stricter regulation of Akunam honey, possibly at the international level. Retailers and non-governmental organizations are proposing to establish a certification scheme (using a bear called Hans as a mascot). Some producers have created a different self-certification scheme, called Bruno (also using a bear as a mascot). Critics suggest that these two schemes lack credibility in terms of enforcement and inspection. Consumers are said to be confused between the two schemes, especially given their similar-looking mascots.

What would you advise? What would be a rationale for having an international regulatory regime? How would such a regime be justified? What kind of regime(s) should be established? Should private regulatory regimes be encouraged? What kind of mechanisms should be put in place?

Why have international regulation?

Demands that 'something' should be done about an international problem are widespread, especially in the context of the perception of existing or potential 'transboundary crises' whose impact inherently crosses jurisdictional boundary lines (Boin 2009). Phenomena that classify as potential transboundary crises include: climate change, declining fish stocks, epidemics, the protection of tropical rain forests, radio-spectrum allocation, food safety, small arms, narcotics and 'blood' diamonds. More generally, the growing importance of international regulation is said to be a consequence of the internationalization and the growing complexity of economic relations. These changes to the economy potentially pose a challenge to the credibility and efficacy of national regulatory regimes, thus opening a window for the advocacy of international regulatory regimes (supplied by international organizations (as noted by Majone 1994 in the case of the European Union). Furthermore, as international regulation and its impact on national regulation lead to an ever more pronounced system of multilevel governing where 'simple' hierarchical relationships are largely absent, a key emphasis has been placed on cooperative and collaborative modes of regulating, often building on the concepts considered in Chapter 5.

International regulatory initiatives, involving different organizations and formations, have therefore become a prominent feature on the regulation agenda (Koenig-Archibugi 2010). Examples include traditional international governmental settings that deal with issues such as trade, labour, telecommunications, pharmaceuticals or pesticides. 'Old' regimes have, however, not always been purely governmental. For example, private standard-setting regimes for electrical and electronic engineering were set up in 1906 (the International Electro-Technical Commission (ETC) (Mattli and Buethe 2003). Similarly, the regulation of food has become increasingly internationalized. For example, EU level inspectors inspect food hygiene in third countries that seek to export to the European Union. Various private certification schemes supposedly certify particular production standards, such as in organic farming (for example, the 'Principles of Organic Agriculture' of 2005). In addition, international standard setting (ISO) has become also more prominent, at the expense of the earlier dominance of national standard-setting bodies, in particular the German DIN (Deutsches Institut für Normung). Furthermore, international regulatory regimes involve 'common pool resource'-type problems, such as the challenges of over-fishing or climate change. In this section, we consider the rationales of why regulatory regimes should be allocated at one level of government rather than another. The subsequent section considers differences in regime types.

So why have international regulation? Why not regulate at the national level and rely on 'proper' national regulation? After all, national regulation is legitimized through control via national politicians, it is able to reflect national administrative and political constellations and it is 'closer' to the regulatory problem. International regulation may appear to suffer a legitimacy deficit: it may be accused of lacking due process (especially if negotiated between private interests), lack enforcement and moral obligation. So how can 'global' regulatory regimes be justified, especially in the case of Akunam honey?

At the heart of most arguments calling for an international regulatory regime are suggestions that national-based regulation cannot deal with particular *externalities*. For example, transborder air pollution or maritime pollution would qualify as such an externality. It is unlikely that a national firm regulated by a national regulator would fully consider the wider international effects of its polluting activities. Equally, if some countries were to engage in so-called 'geo-engineering' to deal with climate change, then such interventions (sails in the sky, for example) would require some degree of international agreement to reduce free-riding or mitigate potential side-effects of manipulating weather patterns.

Similarly, maritime incidents, leading to, for example, large-scale oil contamination and the killing of maritime life require international coordination regarding compensation and clean-up activities. Furthermore, it might be argued that international shipping standards are essential to avoid the negative aspects of a 'race to the bottom' (Vogel 1995). According to this argument, ship owners are likely to register their ships in low-cost locations (which involves labour, construction and maintenance standards as well as taxation) in order to obtain a competitive cost advantage over those shipping companies that are based in 'high-cost' locations. To stop shipping companies from moving to such low-cost locations, different jurisdictions will seek to reduce the level of their regulatory standards to maintain their industry and possibly poach other shipping companies.

Jurisdictions, accordingly, are engaged in a competition over regulatory standards and enforcement practices. In some circumstances this can lead to a 'race to the bottom'. National regulation which bans ships that do not conform to particular standards from docking in one country's harbours is likely to be of limited effectiveness. After all, competing harbours (in neighbouring jurisdictions) might still attract traffic, thus also taking further economic activity away from 'high-regulation' jurisdictions. Furthermore, maritime incidents causing pollution are not addressed by a prohibition against docking in national harbours, in particular when it comes to seeking payments for cleaning-up operations and other required compensation.

If, however, the international economy is shaped, if not dominated, by the 'high-regulation' jurisdiction, it is likely that companies will internalize the cost of having to comply with higher standards as this is in their economic interest: the benefits of being able to trade with and dock in 'high-regulation' countries outweigh the costs of improved shipping standards. The overall effect might be a quasi-voluntary adoption of higher standards across jurisdictions, or a 'race to the top' (see Vogel 1995). Such a 'race to the top' can only occur when the compliance with higher standards can be certified and tested (as in the case of ships). With other goods, the (visible) quality of the good is not affected by imposing particular regulatory requirements (such as the imposition of minimum-space requirements on chicken farms which makes no visible difference to eggs). As a result, there is little incentive to comply voluntarily with raised standards.

This argument about 'racing' is informed by Tiebout's seminal contribution on so-called consumer-voters 'voting with their feet' (Tiebout 1956). According to Tiebout, efficient outcomes are achieved when 'consumer-voters' are allowed to move to locations that offer preferred 'bundles' of goods (i.e. attractive parks and higher taxes or no public libraries and lower taxes). Local governments, run by city managers, are therefore engaged in a process of product differentiation, and the outcome leads to an efficient distribution. Tiebout's basic argument was that decentralized production of public services was preferable to large-scale 'coordinated' production systems. In the areas of regulation, this would translate into a general preference for localized and flexible regulatory systems (given the likelihood of a higher responsiveness to local requirements) than for international 'fixed' standards. Centralized (or international) binding standards would be accused of lacking flexibility, suffer from information asymmetries and will therefore be characterized by a lack of reasonable enforcement.

The specific assumptions underlying Tiebout's model (which he openly acknowledged) highlight why coordinated regulation rather than the regulatory equivalent of a 'voting with your feet' arrangement can be justified. In Tiebout's world, there are no transaction costs, information is perfect, movement costs are zero, income is independent of location, and externalities do not occur. However, the world of regulation is one characterized by transaction costs, information asymmetries and externalities. In the 'real' world, transaction costs are asymmetrically distributed (labour is less mobile than most businesses, for example, an argument made by the International Labour Organization in 1919; see Koenig-Archibugi 2010: 407). In other words, international regulatory responses are said to be required in cases where capital is highly mobile (while other factors of production, particularly labour, are not) and is therefore able to 'threaten' particular jurisdictions with 'exit'.

A related 'undesirable' outcome is the 'tragedy of the commons' (Hardin 1968) and wider problems with governing so-called common pool resources (Ostrom 1990). Specific examples here are fisheries (i.e. the prevention of over-fishing) and pollution (for example, of river basins). In the absence of the ability to monitor and enforce the compliance of other parties, it is not in the self-interest of anyone to comply with common standards.

Regulatory regimes at the international level further deal with issues of compatibility. In these cases, the key issue is to find common standards that facilitate trade or expand potential markets. It is therefore in the interest of economic producers to come to a shared solution. However, up-front investment in particular technologies may create potentially high switching costs and therefore entrenched negotiation positions. Examples of such regimes that have been central to international trade and communications include the use of radio-spectrum or of standardized equipment for communications. In these cases, the role of regulation is to resolve particular coordination problems that are somewhat different to those noted above (Werle 1995).

Whereas in the earlier examples of 'racing' jurisdictions there was no incentive to 'cooperate', in the case of international standards that seek to establish compatibility, producers 'save' by having a unified standard (especially where the costs of incorporating technology capable of coping with different standards are high). Such 'battles' between different technological standards might be resolved in the market-place (as has been widely reported in various disputes over technological standards applicable to recording technologies, such as VHS versus Beta-systems for long-forgotten video-recorders; more recently, conflicts over recording standards existed between Blu-ray and HD DVDs). In other words, international regulation here is about facilitating coordination where the underlying constellation resembles a 'cooperation game', whereas in the case of 'racing' jurisdictions, the underlying constellation more closely resembles that of a 'prisoner's dilemma'.

There are also transaction-cost based rationales for international regulation given the international nature of a particular 'trade'. For example, international telecommunications require agreements between different providers as the 'termination' rate requires a regime to reduce potential transaction costs that might emerge if each call or relationship between operators had to be negotiated individually.

Highlighting transaction costs as a rationale for the establishment of international regulatory regimes points to further administrative aspects. Bilateral and multilateral regulatory regimes require a system of information-gathering and behaviour-modification. Without any form of oversight, regimes that rely on national or private corporate regulatory conduct alone are open to variations, if not gaming and outright cheating. Establishing some form of international oversight therefore allows for the creation of a supposedly neutral referee (see Pollack 1997) and also provides for a separate authority that is able to process information-gathering and behaviour-modification activities. National or individual corporate interests are said to be more likely to comply with such 'neutral' third party oversight than with bilateral regimes.

Such arguments are linked to issues of *institutional capacity*. An international regime may offer a set of standards and an associated information-gathering and behaviour-modification 'machinery' that particular national jurisdictions are unable to provide on their own. In other words, an international regime is likely to be more credible if certified by reputable actors rather than by local actors from highly contested jurisdictions that are poor in administrative capacity (such as war-torn countries). Similarly, it might be argued that a sole reliance on national standards is likely to be insufficient, as those responsible for the undesirable production patterns have a considerable influence on domestic politics. Furthermore, a unilateral approach towards imposing particular standards on international private organizations is problematic as even the most developed national regulator is unlikely to be able to monitor activities by non-national subsidiaries in different markets (and indeed, it is unlikely that workers in these non-national jurisdictions would be in a position to hold the company to account by going to court; see Abbott and Snidal 2009: 539).

In sum, there are number of reasons why one may advocate the creation of an international regulatory regime. However, as noted throughout this volume, the functional justifications that have featured in the above discussion are hardly uncontroversial. Whether or not a particular issue is seen to attract a 'race to the bottom' is a matter of weighting different issues, for example, whether the costs of moving are high, whether other benefits outweigh the costs of higher regulatory 'burdens' and whether such burdens actually constitute a cost base that may make particular goods and services less competitive. Answers to such questions are inherently contested.

These traditional arguments are also challenged by regimes that deal with issues such as Akunam honey that do not create 'externalities' as traditionally defined. The treatment of bees and beekeepers is unlikely to trigger a 'race to the bottom' as the honey can only be produced in a small number of jurisdictions. Unlike other goods, such as 'blood' diamonds or the small arms trade, Akunam honey is not linked to criminal networks. Therefore, the presence of this honey in Amnesia or the import of 'fake' honey do not cause negative externalities in terms of affecting other bees, other types of honey or other goods and services. However, one key challenge relates to institutional capacity: are the producers of Akunam honey capable and willing enough to establish an acceptable regime as Amnesian consumers may otherwise punish them by withdrawing their custom? Additionally how can international regimes benefit those producers that might be willing to improve their production standards, but whose efforts might be undermined by the presence of producers unwilling to comply? Such choices relate not just to the type of standards that specify under what conditions Akunam honey should be produced, but it also requires arrangements to facilitate information-gathering and enforcement. Whether a reliance on private certification regimes, with or without involvement by NGOs (such as offered by the 'Hans' and 'Bruno' schemes), will therefore offer a credible regime remains an open question. At the same time, whether arrangements between states will provide sufficient flexibility and enforcement and monitoring capacity is similarly debatable.

As a consequence, it is not just a matter of controversy as to whether there should be a regulatory regime at the international level. Similarly controversial is the question of how such a regime should be established, and with what consequences. Of course, whether or not an international regime (of any kind) emerges largely depends on institutional politics and decision-making rules rather than the presence of particular externalities. If international regimes require extra-large majorities as part of their decision-making procedures, it is less likely that an international set of rules will emerge than under systems where some resourceful actors pushing for such a regime are able to impose their preferences on others. Similarly, if dominant retailers are concerned about the viability of their profitable honey-sales, they are likely to push for a strong regime that certifies the whole honey production chain (as happened elsewhere in food regulation, as illustrated by the traceability principle 'from field to fork'). Equally, the presence of well-mobilized advocacy groups has been said to shape the extent to which certain issues emerge on the agenda and how they are reflected in international regulatory regimes (Braithwaite and Drahos 2000).

Furthermore, international regulatory regimes are also associated with dominant states which benefit from the presence of particular rule systems. For example, it is often said that the world trade system was 'secured' by the hegemonic interest of the United States (under the GATT system). In financial regulation, Beth Simmons (2001) argued that hegemonic states would seek bilateral solutions if the source of the 'negative externality' was clearly identifiable. However, where such a source was difficult to establish, pressures to establish multilateral regimes would be exerted. Such dynamics might be less relevant in our case of honey, but if powerful constituencies exist in dominant states, then pressures to establish an international code for the production of Akunam honey are likely to emerge.

Variations in international regulatory regimes

Having decided that something should be done about honey, what kind of variants exist? As already noted at the outset, international regulatory regimes are not merely about relationships between states. Considerable differences exist in terms of who should be involved (states, firms, non-governmental organizations, unions, industry associations), how specific the standards are and what kinds of certification and enforcement machinery exist.

In this section we illustrate four ideal types to distinguish between different international regulatory regimes. Figure 7.1 contrasts governments and non-governmental actors as regulators and regulatees (for a different approach, see Abbott and Snidal 2009). This categorization is only a starting-point for illustrating the diversity of different potential regimes. It cannot, for example, account for dynamics that make an initially 'private-to-private' regime turn into a regulatory approach that is also applicable on a 'state-to-state' basis. As noted already, the *Codex Alimentarius'* 'Hazards and Critical Control Points Analysis' (HACCP) approach towards food safety was initially developed by a private company (under contract from NASA). It was subsequently endorsed by

		Regulatee	
		Government	Non-government
Regulator	Government	A: state-to-state	B: state-to-private
	Non-government	C: private-to-state	D: private-to-private

FIGURE 7.1   *Forms of international/transnational regulation*

the World Health Organization, and then became part of the formal GATT and EU food safety regimes. In other words, states control private organizations according to these principles. These principles, however, also require states to be checked as to their compliance with the particular regulatory demands.

The traditional understanding of international regulation is represented in box A of Figure 7.1. It concentrates on those international agreements that bind states to particular standards and focus on the behaviour of governments. Such international treaties and other agreements (or 'regimes', Krasner 1982) include the World Trade Organization (WTO) or the Kyoto Protocol (the international agreement linked to the United Nations Framework Convention on Climate Change). Another prominent example of box-A type international regulatory regimes is the OECD initiative to reduce the ability of particular jurisdictions to provide tax havens (Eden and Kudrle 2005). The key emphasis here has been on 'naming and shaming' rather than on legal provisions to enforce behavioural codes. An interest in 'naming and shaming' also informed other OECD and European Union processes that sought to rely on benchmarking and peer-pressure.

Traditionally, telecommunications was governed through intergovernmental relations (through the International Telecommunications Union (ITU)). However, technological change and liberalization have brought about the emergence of a multiplicity of new actors and different standard-setting bodies that have changed the role of the ITU towards one that facilitates 'networking' between private and public actors and also private participation (i.e. a shift from box A to a mixture of boxes A, B, C and D).

More broadly, one of the key disadvantages of state-to-state regimes is said to lie in their intergovernmental character. It is maintained that such regimes have difficulty in generating compliance (as any violation immediately becomes a matter of cross-state conflict). In addition, their ratification requires consent in national legislative arenas. Intergovernmental regimes are further said to suffer from poor expertise and a lack of flexibility. The lack of expertise is because state bureaucracies lack the kind of information enjoyed by participants in the production chain. The lack of flexibility originates in the nature of intergovernmental conventions and their decision-making rules. One may therefore argue that for such regimes to operate, a certain degree of delegation to an 'autonomous' international body or secretariat will be required to undertake the necessary monitoring and to facilitate further delegated rule-making.

As noted, the nature and significance of box-B type (intergovernmental regimes focusing on private firms) has witnessed considerable change in the light of changing international markets. Older examples of such regimes, according to Abbott and Snidal (2009: 514–17), include the 1976 OECD guidelines for multinational enterprises that sought to facilitate a code for transnational enterprises in the face of sustained criticism of their conduct, and the 1981 WHO Code of Marketing for breast-milk substitutes. In these cases, international principles are further elaborated by secretariats and networks of actors (see Baccardo and Mele 2011). As Baccardo and Mele (2011) suggest, the OECD guidelines for multinational enterprises have become increasingly formalized, leading to quasi-tribunal hearings about corporate conduct. According to their study, compliance also has influence on procurement decisions. In other words, even without direct legal 'force', the effect has increasingly become quasi-legal, with direct legal consequences occurring in some national contexts, but not in others (Baccardo and Mele 2011: 455–7).

In response to the perceived limitations of 'state' based international agreements, increasing emphasis has been placed on 'private' and mixed forms of international regulatory regimes. In particular, it has been argued that national regulatory approaches, based on 'state'-centric regulators are unlikely to cope with global firms and their highly decentralized and flexible supply chains (Cashore 2002; O'Rourke 2003). According to Abbott and Snidal (2009: 509), such regimes are characterized by their 'decentralized' range of actors with different sources of expertise, the role of the state being one that 'orchestrates' self-regulatory regimes by utilizing 'soft law' (or 'alternatives to regulation') rather than 'command and control'. Such a shift is said to reflect the increasing interest in non-state based alternatives to 'command and control' regulation.

The regulation of private regulators overseeing private regulatees (box D) occurs across a variety of regimes that seek to develop binding codes of conduct and monitoring systems. One key motivation is the protection of reputation – global brands do not want to be associated with the sale of unethical products. More broadly, Abbott and Snidal (2009) distinguish between regimes that are dominated by NGOs and other associations, and those that are dominated by the industries themselves. Most regimes, however, include some degree of mix between internal monitoring and reporting, 'fire alarm' mechanisms by affected workers and other parties, and external validation by NGOs (see O'Rourke 2003).

Turning to 'industry self-regulation' first, firm-based approaches have included attempts by firms to regulate themselves and other firms through voluntary self-reporting exercises, especially also involving their subsidiaries and other units critical to their production chain. This field of private self-regulation is shaped by debates about 'corporate social responsibility', that is, the recognition of non-commercial norms and objectives in companies' production and work arrangements. One key example, representing a 'multi-stakeholder approach' that also involves the United Nations, is the 'UN Global Compact' (see Baccaro and Mele 2011). This 'Compact' emerged in response to the limited resources available to the United Nations to initiate an 'intergovernmental' process, but in its first decade (until 2010) had only a limited impact on corporate behaviour (Baccaro and Mele 2011: 460–1).

Private regimes to deal with forestry issues emerged in the context of the failure of intergovernmental negotiations (as part of the 1992 Rio UN conference on environment and development). For example, the well-known Forestry Stewardship Council was created in 1993 involving green interests (such as the World Wildlife Fund and Greenpeace). It operates a performance-based system, with external validation schemes and support by international retailers (Meidinger 2007). Competing standards also exist, whose emphasis is more on management-based standards. For Meidinger (2007; see also Brown 2001), competition between the different standards has led to an increasing similarity between the different private schemes. In addition, these private international standards have been adopted by national state-based regulators.

A similar failure in intergovernmental international enforcement motivated the so-called Kimberley process. The Kimberley process seeks to deal with the sale of 'blood' diamonds (i.e. the mining and sale of diamonds from civil war territories) (see Jojarth 2009). When faced by organized consumer boycotts, the most affected state, South Africa, initiated the Kimberley Process to protect the market for 'legal' diamonds. The regime depended on the expertise of one dominant firm (De Beers), but also involved a degree of external validation and monitoring. However, it is debatable whether the Kimberley Process managed to address the problem of 'blood' diamonds effectively (see *Financial Times*, 15 June 2010; Baldwin *et al.* 2012: 430). After all, one of the key NGOs involved in the process, Global Witness, walked out of the scheme in late 2011, claiming that it did not provide sufficient assurances that 'blood' diamonds were no longer being sold (*BBC*, 5 December 2011). Older examples of similar regimes include retailers establishing 'conditions' on their producers in order to protect their reputation as 'ethical' shopkeepers (such as the Body Shop chain: Abbott and Snidal 2009: 517).

Similarly, disasters can bring about private international regulation. In the field of risk regulation in the chemical industry, the Bhopal accident in India from 1984 played a critical role. The accident – involving a gas leakage in a pesticide plant – killed 3,000 people and caused the death of another 8,000 (due to gas-related diseases). In the face of the reputational and financial disaster for Union Carbide Corporation (who ran the plant in co-ownership with the Indian government), it introduced a system of industry self-regulation to manage the risks not only of its own subsidiaries and plants, but also of upstream subcontractors and component suppliers. Known as 'Responsible Care', this approach to risk management became a widespread standard in the global chemical industry. According to Braithwaite (2008; see also Gunningham 1995: 94), industry self-regulation has played a more important role in establishing risk regulation in the chemical industry (and beyond) than regulatory approaches of individual national governments. Governmental or intergovernmental responses to the Bhopal disaster were, in contrast, very limited.

A different type of 'private' regulation of private activities is represented by the international standard setting that affects professional activities. For example, the International Accounting Standards Board (IASB) has issued standards that are non-binding on its members. Instead they operate through their adoption into national accounting practices and they have become critical in shaping national accounting practices that previously reflected national varieties (in addition, the international standards were issued to prevent the adoption of European Community-based standards).

Finally, private regulators also regulate states (box C). The most well-known case here are the credit rating agencies, whose downgrading of sovereign debt shaped the evolving financial crisis in the late 2000s and early 2010s. Other examples include private accreditation agencies that regulate public (as well as private) university programmes. These private ranking exercises were taken increasingly seriously by universities as part of their drive to attract a growing international (and self-paying) student body. For example the ranking of business education programmes by the *Financial Times* was said to influence curriculum development.

In sum, this section was intended to offer a brief overview of different regime characteristics. One key argument has been that recent decades have witnessed a move towards 'network-type' regulatory regimes that include a variety of state and non-state actors. This move is said to be partly motivated by the growing complexity of international production chains that have made 'state-centric' regulation increasingly problematic. At the same time, it is said to reflect the power of transnational corporate interests and their interest in protecting their reputations (whether such reputational concerns can be seen as a sufficient motivator to 'open up' production processes is a matter of debate).

The changing character of international regulatory regimes has, however, also highlighted two key aspects. One is that despite the significance attached to the private regulation of private processes, the 'state' still remains an important actor. For Abbott and Snidal (2009), this role can be best described as an 'orchestration' role and it is the absence of capacities to orchestrate that is said to have caused regulatory regimes to lack effectiveness. Information-gathering represents the second key challenge. On the one hand, highly diversified and flexible production chains make information gathering inherently difficult, as is information gathering in highly contested (civil war) territories. On the other hand, there has also been only limited self-interest in openly reporting and allowing

TABLE 7.1   *International regulation regime variants for Akunam honey*

Regime-type	Rationale	Pre-requisite	Limitation
Reliance on self-regulation	Retailers' self-interest will establish credible certification and internal control mechanisms; rivalry will lead to a 'race to the top' in regulatory standards	Requires ability to control production chain (i.e. conditions for bees and beekeepers as well as inability to subvert quality control)	Complex production chain causes information-gathering problems; consumer confusion over different schemes may lead to overall distrust and market collapse; lack of legitimacy
State-orchestrated self-certification schemes	Facilitate information-gathering by whistle-blowers; facilitate communication between different private certification regimes	Requires state capacities to facilitate communication, willingness of NGOs and industry to participate	Limitations on information-gathering and behaviour-modification given complex production chain; non-participants may undermine 'official' schemes
Inter-governmental agreement for honey producers	State-based regime offers legitimate and binding standards backed by sanctions	Requires 'importing' country's ability to monitor and enforce standards	Problem with potential non-signature states; ability of producers to 'cheat' and undermine regime
Inter-governmental agreements on national honey regulation	Legitimate exercise of state power to establish binding agreements on honey production standards	Requires state capacities to monitor and enforce standards	Lacks flexibility and depends on willingness to cooperate; difficulties in establishing regulatory regime in contested territories

external certification in private regulatory arrangements. Such concerns also relate to the openness of enforcement actions.

Returning to our honey case, the emergence of the Hans and Bruno accreditation and industry certification schemes therefore seem to follow a wider trend. As in the forestry example, noted above, it might be suggested that the two regimes will vigorously compete and thereby become increasingly similar. At the same time, it might be argued that the role of the state in terms of 'orchestration' is critical – for example, by incorporating the industry standards into their own national provisions and in facilitating (and funding) external inspection visits by involved advocacy groups. Similarly, orchestration may be relevant in preventing confusion among consumers confronted with the similar mascots of the two private regulatory regimes. Others might argue that only a 'state'-based solution involving Amnesia and other importing countries together with the states producing Akunam honey would be sufficient. A third view would call for state-based agreements that would be binding on private producers of Akunam honey. A fourth view might suggest that letting private regimes seek to control themselves would offer the least intrusive way of regulating the honey production chain. Table 7.1 offers an overview of these different regime types.

In the next section, we discuss rationales for choosing between these different regime types and turn to some key design dimensions that shape international regulatory regimes.

Regime choice and design of control

Amnesia may therefore not wish to develop a wider international response to the problems associated with honey. At the same time, a pure reliance on private forms of regulation also appears to be problematic, as it raises issues about legitimacy (should private actors take on 'regulatory' functions, and, if so, what should the appropriate due process requirements be, apart from imposing moral obligations on actors to comply?) and participation (who should be involved in monitoring and enforcement?). Key questions are therefore: What are the key institutional design dimensions and what characteristics shape institutional choices? What modes of control should dominate control activities?

One of the key arguments in international regulation has referred to 'legalization' (Abbott *et al.* 2000; Koremenos *et al.* 2001; Brütsch and Lehmkuhl 2007). It is argued that tough international regulation is characterized by binding agreements that are backed by sanctions. As noted, such highly legalized regimes are far from being the norm in international regulation. It is also questionable whether they represent a more effective solution to international problems than other cases. Problems with highly 'legalized' regimes, which are those that seek to establish precise standards with clearly defined obligations, are described in Chapter 2 on standard-setting. These are the inherent difficulties in defining a precise standard, the ability of different affected parties to game and cheat, and problems in terms of establishing compliance and receiving appropriate information. Highly 'legalized' international regimes are also said to lack sufficient flexibility as extensive intergovernmental bargaining is difficult to revise in the face of key resistance, while concerted opposition is likely to undermine any attempt to achieve international collaboration. In other words, international regulation, just like domestic regulation, is about considering different mixes between modes of regulation.

For Christine Jojarth (2009: ch. 3), the key issue that influences decisions regarding the type of regulatory regime is the 'problem constellation'. She suggests that such problem constellations can be defined by the 'asset specificity' of the particular problem (i.e. the likelihood of other parties to the agreement cheating and the costs incurred by such cheating), the opportunity of states and actors to cheat in terms of the ease of observability of their behaviour and, finally, the wider environmental uncertainty (i.e. the likelihood of changes in the context of the policy domain that will shift the distribution of costs and benefits between different participants). Translating these aspects to the fourfold classification of different 'opportunity costs' as introduced by Murray Horn (1995), we can note the following key aspects that influence considerations regarding international regulatory regimes:

- *Decision-making costs*: the more costly the negotiation and renegotiation of standards, their enforcement and information-gathering for national political actors, the more likely it is that they will seek to shift standard-setting to private participants. At the same time, if these activities are seen as critical for national governmental authority, then regimes will be 'state-based' (i.e. intergovernmental).
- *Agency costs*: the more complex and difficult information-gathering is, the more likely a reliance on private self-control over the production chain and the active sponsoring of third parties (such as NGOs) to act as whistleblowers and fire-alarms.
- *Commitment costs*: the more likely it is that different regime participants will 'cheat' and thereby undermine the regime, the more likely it is that participants will demand 'binding' agreements backed by sanctions rather than self-regulatory regimes.
- *Uncertainty costs*: if the dynamics of the domain are likely to change, through technological change, or a change in customer preferences, an emphasis will be given to 'flexible' rather than 'legalized' standards.

For our honey example, certain key implications arise from such calculations. For one, bees are unlikely to act as whistleblowers.

Nevertheless, beekeepers and NGOs may be able to act as additional controls apart from industry self-reporting activities. Similarly, decision-making costs to politicians are likely to be such that they prefer to rely on private regimes. At the same time, private parties may see a purely 'self-regulatory' system of private self-certification as insufficient to overcome potential cheating by other private providers. Such problems emerge in particular when it comes to observing the 'quality of care' granted to bees. However, as studies on Europeanization have noted, the degree to which EU member states comply with transposition requirements stemming from EU-level provisions largely depends on domestic considerations (Falkner *et al.* 2005). Such considerations also have distinct implications for the kind of regime we expect to emerge, as illustrated in Table 7.1. It further highlights that simply suggesting that 'state involvement' equals a higher degree of 'hierarchy' or 'legalization', as put forward by Tanja Börzel (2010) is a highly questionable assumption.

In addition, the challenges of dealing with 'agency' and 'commitment' costs in international regulation also highlight the advantage of viewing modes of control through a diversity of perspectives rather than relying on a 'hierarchy versus non-hierarchy' perspective. Indeed, returning to our discussion of cultural theory influenced perspectives on regulation, we can distinguish four distinct ways in which international regulation is shaped and put into operation (see Lehmkuhl 2008 for an alternative account). As with domestic regulation, these modes are associated with distinct advantages and disadvantages. In addition, they also point to the way in which international regulatory regimes influence national and sub-national regulation through systems of 'multilevel governance'. They shape the way in which goals, institutions and responsibilities are allocated. Figure 7.2 offers a brief overview of these four different modes of control in international regulation. The rest of this section considers these modes in more detail.

A reliance on *hierarchy* reflects a preference for 'legalization'. As noted by Lehmkuhl (2008) the formal power to 'enforce' international standards can, in some cases, be granted by state actors to private organizations. For example, in the field of Internet regulation (domain name registration and conflict settlement), a non-governmental organization (ICANN) with authority delegated by the US government exercises hierarchical powers over private and public actors alike (in a wider setting that is characterized by community-based forms of governance). However, as noted throughout this chapter, a reliance on hierarchy is particularly limited in the international context given problems with information-gathering and behaviour-modification.

Given these limitations of hierarchy, a major interest has been placed on ideas of *mutuality*, in a number of ways (Mayntz 2010a). One mutuality-based argument stresses the importance of professional norms, as represented by international expert bodies (so-called 'epistemic communities',

Contrived randomness	Hierarchy
Emphasis on whistleblowing, NGO reporting and potential reputational damage of establishing incidents of malpractice	Emphasis on legalization. Reliance on formal subordination and reporting with mandated sanctions. Private authority to act granted by state-powers
Rivalry	**Mutuality**
Self-certification schemes reflecting the self-interest of economic (private) actors. Reliance on competing standards leads to a race to the top with different producers wishing to appear particularly compliant. Reporting allows for benchmarking exercises	Emphasis on standards and practices of transnational 'epistemic communities' and other 'communities of practice' that 'pollinate' regulatory approaches both across jurisdictions and also within national jurisdictions. Emphasis on peer-review mechanisms

FIGURE 7.2   *Contrasting international modes of regulation*

Haas 1992). These expert bodies, shaped by shared worldviews (or 'belief systems') are not just international in character. They also shape national and international standards and their operationalization, through direct participation, through agenda-setting in research and advocacy, and through shaping media-discussion (largely by a shared interest in a topic, not necessarily by universally agreeing on every single issue). In many ways, the rise of international advocacy-groups might be said to mirror such international epistemic communities. These bodies however represent not just a cause for international regulation, but also a resource for conducting information-gathering and behaviour-modification through deliberation and negotiation. Indeed, it has been suggested that such kinds of mutuality-based capacities are critical in advancing capacities in the global south (i.e. the less-developed world). Such capacities are arguably more important in their long-term effect than the immediate, possibly limited, outputs of international regulatory effects.

A somewhat different mutuality-type argument refers to 'communities of practice' (Wenger 1998; Feldman and Khademian 2007; Mayntz 2010a). It is suggested that shared international practices lead to a particular kind of 'on the job learning'. Such a shared, even loose exposure to similar requirements and technologies creates an international 'community of practice', which, through their informal accumulation of knowledge, discussion and exchange, in turn, shapes the operating procedures and technologies. Mayntz (2010a: 46) points to currency traders as an example of those who have a shared understanding of what the currency market 'is' and how trading is to be conducted. Particular positions in firms (e.g. company secretaries) expose particular individuals to challenges that they share with other company secretaries and that lead, in professional fora, to exchanges over practices and informal learning. This particular mutuality-based argument therefore suggests that a considerable resource in international regulation lies in the exposure of different participants to similar requirements and challenges.

A final mutuality-based argument relates to the increasing importance that has been attached to peer-review and learning exercises as part of international regulatory regimes and international organizations. For example, the OECD's regulatory reviews might be said to seek to contribute to a professional conversation about regulatory practices in particular jurisdictions in the light of OECD guidelines (Lodge 2005). Similarly, the European Union's interest in the so-called 'open method of coordination' (an approach that emphasized jointly agreed standards, national responses and reporting and a belief in peer pressure) was seen to foster an interest in learning across countries within particular domains. This approach, which was particularly prominent in social policy areas had, however, only limited effect (see Lodge 2007). In sum, these mutuality-based arguments emphasize the importance of learning and professional norms diffusing 'good practice' throughout regulatory venues.

Rivalry-based regulatory regimes are based on economic self-interest. For example, industry self-certification schemes might be seen not just as an avoidance of more demanding state-based regulatory attempts, but they also seek to signal a 'certification effect' by signalling that a particular good or product is of an advanced quality. Self-certification modes come in many variants (see Lehmkuhl 2008), with different degrees of voluntariness and NGO participation, as noted above (Abbott and Snidal 2009). An emphasis on 'racing' via competing private certification schemes is a further way in which rivalry can be incorporated into international regulatory regimes, although, as noted at the outset, a 'race to the top' is most likely to occur in those areas where the quality of the good is visibly altered.

Contrived randomness components largely relate to the way in which NGOs and whistleblower arrangements can be designed so that they provide an element of unpredictability in the control system. Of course, granting access to NGOs as part of an international regulatory regime is somewhat difficult to conceptualize as a 'surprise inspection'. However, the sponsored support of external verification mechanisms and 'fire alarm' resources could provide ways in which companies and states are shamed in unexpected ways. In other words, offering third-party access institutionalizes a distrust component within the regulatory regime.

Figure 7.3 applies this perspective to the honey case. It notes how states may be able to orchestrate regulatory regimes and it also points to the contrasting bases on which different regimes would be seen to be

Contrived randomness Establishing mechanisms that allow NGOs and beekeepers to raise 'alarm' in cases of ill-treatment. Facilitate whistleblowing throughout production chain to deter cheating *Effectiveness measure*: examples of 'naming and shaming'	**Hierarchy** Creating legal obligations and reporting duties via binding agreements. States may delegate private authority to provide for regulatory regime activities. States and producers legally obliged to protect bees and beekeepers and safeguard production process to avoid fake honey entering chain *Effectiveness measure*: compliance
Rivalry Emphasis on encouraging economic self-interest to provide self-certification schemes. Make 'Hans' and 'Bruno' schemes comparable and facilitate transparency regarding their operation *Effectiveness measure*: 'racing' of standards upwards	**Mutuality** Emphasis on creating and building on a community of professional practice (beekeepers, honey producers) and reliance on peer-review *Effectiveness measure*: strengthening communication-rich community

FIGURE 7.3   *Honey and modes of regulation*

effective. Each of these modes has its own measure according to which its success is measured. The variety of measures, as suggested in Figure 7.3, highlights the fact that the different modes have different objectives and it is therefore not feasible to compare their performance directly.

This is not to suggest that any one regime will be characterized by a sole reliance on one mode of control rather than on others. Drauth (2010), for example, notes how different codes governing 'corporate social responsibility' (the International Labour Organization's declaration, the OECD's guidelines, and the UN Global Compact), rely on different 'logics', ranging from an emphasis on 'naming and shaming' to an emphasis on peer-review and learning. These different regimes assume the presence of particular preconditions. For example, learning processes assume fully engaged actors. As noted throughout this volume, a perspective emphasizing variety allows an enriched view regarding the different logics that might be present in any one international regulatory regime. In addition, it points to potential interventions that might be used to advance the effectiveness of a particular regime. And finally, it further highlights the limits of hierarchical ways of thinking about regulation, and the potential of other modes of control to offer viable alternatives and complements. It offers a further perspective as to how states might wish to 'orchestrate' international regulatory regimes without having to resort to the kind of 'legalized' systems that have shaped traditional intergovernmental treaties.

For the regulatory analyst such a perspective may (hopefully) not come as a surprise. However, the literature on international regulation more generally endorses broad concepts without paying much interest to the administrative mechanisms and prerequisites. A perspective that emphasizes the importance of the variety of potential modes of regulation allows the discussion to move beyond a mere listing of various issues that might count as 'orchestration' (see Abbott and Snidal 2009).

Varieties in international regulatory regimes

International regulatory regimes offer a particular challenge for regulatory analysis. Some of the questions that have characterized debates in domestic regulation, namely questions about institutional design and the limits of hierarchical control, are replicated at the international level. In addition, questions about whether a particular aspect should be regulated at the international level rather than at the national level can also be translated into the domestic context, namely whether a particular problem should be regulated at the local, state or the national level. In the United States, much of federal enforcement of food regulation has been moved to the state level, leading to considerable concerns about the resources available to state-based inspectors to perform federal functions (Atlas 2007). In other words, debates about international regulation, and especially about what level of government should be responsible for a particular task in terms of standard-setting, can be informed by discussions drawn from domestic regulation. Furthermore, such debates also reflect the inherent multilevel character of regulatory activities, where standards might be of an intergovernmental origin, require enforcement activities from one part of government and information-gathering activities from another.

However, international regulation is also 'different'. It raises particular issues about legitimacy. These issues refer not just to the way in which particular international standards are agreed upon, who participates, whether particular parties are granted sufficient representation, and whether a degree of procedural due process has been maintained. Such a definition regarding legitimacy represents only a limited perspective. More important is the moral dimension of legitimacy. According to Max Weber (1956, also Mayntz 2010b), the state's monopoly of coercion required legitimacy. This legitimacy was not merely based on procedural correctness, but a moral or implicit understanding that compliance is not just a matter of costs and benefits, but an obligation. In international regulation, such moral obligations are arguably far more diffuse and subject-specific. International regulatory regimes therefore highlight one particularly critical feature of regulation, namely that it is not just about legal or non-legal exercises in authorities, but that regulation is fundamentally about addressing values.

Chapter 8

Regulating Infrastructure Industries

Amnesia is widely criticized for its poor infrastructure. The water pipelines leak and the water quality does not comply with contemporary environmental standards. The railways – the vertically integrated national monopolist (publicly owned AmnesiaRail) – are loss-making. The sole profitable part of the railway network consists of commuter services to Amnesia's capital, Frenezia, on which commuters rely to get to work. Elsewhere in Amnesia, most citizens prefer to use private transport. However, it is politically impossible to close down railway services. Amnesia's government has committed itself to liberalization and competition, but also to maintaining railway services at the present level.

Advise Amnesia on how you would set up railways and the water domain in Amnesia and how you would regulate it. In particular, consider options for (a) the type of regulatory regime, and (b) the ownership and structure of the industry.

What is so special about infrastructure industries?

The regulation of infrastructure industries has attracted considerable attention over the past three decades, with countries witnessing considerable reforms in line with the wider trend that saw a move towards a 'regulatory state' (Majone 1994; Lodge 2008). As noted in the introduction, these industries, such as energy (electricity and gas), railways and other transport industries, telecommunications and water, have seen a broad shift from public to private ownership, a prominent role played by regulatory agencies, and a contractualization of relationships. Much of the debate regarding contractualization will be covered in the next chapter, and therefore in the following we concentrate on issues of industry structure and agency design.

There are a number of reasons for the particular attention paid to infrastructure industries (Newbury 1999; Gómez-Ibáñez 2003). First, infrastructure implies inherent natural monopoly components (see Chapter 1). This means that a strategy of seeking to introduce pure competition is unlikely to work. Such questions might have become less relevant in telecommunications (given competition between providers, type of networks, and even substitutable technologies). However, as yet, there is little to suggest that the economy of scale argument, regarding railway lines, electricity transmission networks or water pipelines, has lost any relevance.

Furthermore, infrastructure industries also have positive externalities (public health benefits, for example, in the case of access to water), as well as specific network externalities. The value of a network goes up the more connections are available. A phone (or virtual social) network benefits from having a maximum number of connections, as the availability of possible connections rises exponentially as the number of customers increases (a negative network externality would be congestion). The provision of infrastructure offers important advantages for the economic and social development of particular regions, in terms of access and production, and transport costs in particular. Infrastructures also raise planning concerns (the 'right of way'): roads, tracks and pipes require land, and they also require provisions to allow for their repair and modernization (i.e. the right to dig up roads to repair water pipelines).

Furthermore, the pricing of these 'essential' services has wide-ranging social and economic implications: high prices for electricity may deter industrial production (especially among large users). Equally, high prices for broadband (or lower speeds) might mean that populations are denied access to services that are regarded as normal elsewhere, thereby causing a so-called 'digital divide'. In other words, infrastructure industries have important social aspects attached to them. For example, cutting off a family from access to their source of heating (gas or electricity) or from their water supply as a result of non-payment of bills may cause significant social harm. It is therefore important to balance the principle that customers should pay for their consumption with the wider need to facilitate people's ability to function as economic and social citizens. Therefore, questions as to what is a 'basic service' and what kind of provision safeguards the vulnerable are key aspects that govern the regulation of infrastructure industries. Such debates fall under considerations of so-called 'universal service obligations'. These debates include broadband speeds, the availability of services (such as, the number of rail or bus services per day, the maximum distance anyone should be expected to live from a post box, a post office or, in the age before mobile phones, a phone box), and also disconnection provisions in case of non-payment. More widely, such universal services (or 'services of general economic interest', as defined by EU law) also raise issues regarding financing. Most universal services are not profitable and would, without regulatory obligations, not be provided, or at least not at the same cost. This raises issues of cross-subsidization and mechanisms of ensuring such redistribution from profitable services and markets to non-profitable ones that are deemed as being of an essential nature.

Therefore, the regulation of infrastructure industries is a highly political endeavour. It needs to deal with the interests of producers (i.e. those providing the infrastructure services), and corporate and private consumers. Moreover, infrastructure industries have also played a highly significant role in military planning. For example, the railways have, especially in the past, played a critical role in the movement of troops. Contemporary debates about future sources of energy generation have also direct implications for infrastructure regulation. A reliance on more volatile energy forms (such as wind power) requires considerable changes in transmission network capacity (and therefore the setting of the appropriate regulatory incentives to encourage investment).

Finally, there are also issues of security of supply. For example, surplus capacity is required in energy generation and network capacity to deal with very cold or very warm weather and other causes of unexpected peak demand. Another example is the requirement to provide for continuity of supply. The flooding of an electricity substation without back-up may require the mass-evacuation of large populations (as their electricity supply will be disrupted for a prolonged period). In addition, studies in emergency management have suggested that social anarchy is likely to occur should the supply of electricity be fully disrupted, as cash machines fail to function, communications collapse as phone batteries become depleted, food supplies run short, emergency generators run dry, and water pumps fail.

Infrastructure industries therefore clearly matter and require regulatory attention. What, however, counts as an infrastructure, utility or 'essential service' is contested: the extent to which a particular industry is defined by natural monopoly characteristics changes in the light of technological innovation. For example, technical innovation may enable the separation of potentially competitive aspects of an industry from those defined by monopoly characteristics (for example, energy generation can be split from the transport of energy through transmission networks). Similarly, any calculation as to whether particular services are economically or socially useful depends fundamentally on the way these benefits are defined. For example, the construction of a new railway line may be justified (or not) by the number of customers likely to use this particular line, or in the way in which this particular line also reduces overcrowding on other lines (in addition to the social benefits of reduced journey times).

In the regulatory context, the key problem for infrastructure industries is their asset specificity. This means that it is largely impossible to move the same infrastructure to another place (or at least it would be highly costly). Once we have placed railway tracks on the ground, it is very costly to remove them. The same holds for water pipes or electricity transmission networks. These industries are therefore especially prone to the *time inconsistency problem*. In short, should investors decide to establish a railway infrastructure or to replace water pipes, they will do so in view of expected returns on their investment.

Amnesia may offer potential investors in its water and railway industries the promise of 'lenient' regulation. However, once the investment has taken place and is largely irreversible, the investor is dependent on the Amnesia government and regulators to keep their promise. The question of potential time inconsistency, namely how regulatory regimes seek to ensure that certain benefit flows, as promised at one point in time, will be secure at a future point, represents the *commitment problem* in regulation. Variants of this *commitment problem* also concern those users whose existence is dependent on the availability and affordability of particular services. For example, water-intensive industries may not wish to invest in Amnesia if they have no idea how water prices are going to develop in the future.

The regulation of infrastructure industries is therefore about finding solutions to the *commitment problem* (see also Chapter 2). For observers such as Brian Levy and Pablo Spiller (1994, 1996) the commitment problem can be resolved through three devices: (1) substantive, written restraints on the discretionary action of the regulator, (2) restraints on the ability to reverse or amend the overall regulatory regime, and (3) institutions that safeguard these restraints. Ways to address the commitment problem could therefore range from legislation that sets out the provisions governing the regulated industry in great detail, the setting-up of a regulatory agency through legislation, or the use of legally-binding contracts or licences.

For Levy and Spiller, the key aspect that should inform institutional design is the reduction of unpredictable regulatory discretion. If we assume that Amnesia is a country where regulatory discretion is exercised in a 'responsible' way (i.e. where there can be an expectation of 'time consistency'), we are in a position to put our trust in regulatory agencies to take decisions. In contrast, if Amnesia's regulators have the reputation of exercising discretion in an unpredictable fashion, we should then advise that regulatory regimes should be 'hardwired' in a way that makes changes very difficult or politically costly. To some extent, therefore, the commitment problem is about the reputation of Amnesia's political and regulatory actors.

Furthermore, addressing the commitment problem depends on the characteristics of the political system, or, what Levy and Spiller call, the institutional endowment of a state. If Amnesia is a political system that is characterized by a single party in government with no second chamber of parliament that might over-rule the decisions of the majority in the first chamber, and by a judicial system that is unlikely to turn against the decisions of regulators or executive politicians, it is unlikely that this system will provide regulatory commitment. This is because discretion is unlikely to be controlled. The solution in these situations is to use devices, such as licences and concessions, that reduce the scope for discretionary regulatory decisions, and, if thought necessary, to make them enforceable in third-country courts.

In contrast, discretionary regulation is less affected by commitment problems in a system that places severe constraints on the regulators (for example, industry can rely on courts to address over-extensions in regulatory discretion) and on politicians in government who may be tempted to amend legislation (these constraints range from having to negotiate within coalitions, to receive consent in a second chamber of parliament and/or to be checked by an administrative or constitutional court).

The key message from the above discussion is that there is no one single solution to the commitment problem. How we address the problem depends on the institutional endowment of a given political system, and this endowment is both a result of the formal institutional features of a state and the reputation of its functioning. In those countries without institutional fixes to deal with the commitment problem, there may be no other option than to rely on state ownership. Such insights have been critical for the development of regulation in less developed countries, where the interest in the institutional design of regulatory systems has drawn heavily on this particular literature (Estache and Lewis-Wren 2010).

To consider further various institutional solutions to the commitment problem, the rest of the chapter considers some of the key institutional design choices. First, we consider questions of ownership and industry structure. Second we turn to the question of the organization of regulatory oversight, especially in terms of the dimensions critical for the setting up a regulatory agency. We conclude by noting some of the key tensions that emerge in attempts to address the commitment problem in regulation, in particular the tension between the principles of commitment and those of flexibility (to accommodate democratically-legitimized preferences and/or technological change).

Industry structure

The first choice facing Amnesia is to consider industry structure and ownership patterns for its water and railway industries. Questions of ownership have, in general, raised considerable political interests, with some seeing public ownership as a recipe for inefficiency, others as a way of maintaining social solidarity, and others as a way to protect essential assets.

In this section, we first consider questions of ownership and then move to questions regarding the structure of the industry. One insight over the past three decades of infrastructure regulation in the United Kingdom in particular has been that structural solutions seem to perform better in terms of reduced prices and greater customer responsiveness. This means that a reliance on private ownership on its own, without effective competition, is unlikely to provide superior results in comparison to a public monopoly. Moreover, liberalized markets, with a number of service providers active in these markets, also reduce demands on regulatory activities. Regulators are no longer faced with one single powerful interest, and they can rely on different sources of information, thereby somewhat reducing the information asymmetry between industry and regulator.

What kind of private ownership?

Much has been said about the potential benefits of private over public ownership in recent decades. As noted in Chapter 6, observers have argued that public agencies have (mostly political) problems in enforcing regulation against other public entities, such as state-owned enterprises. The history of state-owned enterprises was widely said to have been disappointing. For example, in the United Kingdom, they were said to have been characterized by under-investment and lack of efficiency (Foster 1992). Indeed, it has been widely suggested that the largely informal regulation of UK state-owned utilities was ineffectual, leading to capture and politicization at the same time (Tivey 1982; Thatcher 1998). Economists suggested that privatizing a monopoly would have beneficial effects in eradicating x-inefficiencies (see Button and Weyman-Jones 1993). However, these arguments reflect a particular set of views that became dominant in the 1970s. Earlier, in particular in the 1930s and 1940s, a different view about public and private ownership was prevalent: the model of the 'public corporation' was regarded as the efficient answer to the inefficiencies of private ownership (Robson 1960) (apart from the wider argument that key industries should be owned by the people and not by capitalists).

As noted, Amnesia's government has committed itself to privatization. However, what exactly is meant by privatization varies. Variants include:

• the partial or full transfer of ownership into private hands;
• a change in legal status without an actual change in ownership; and
• the use or market-type mechanisms, such as franchising and concessions (which will be discussed in the next chapter).

The railway industry has witnessed regulatory reforms of all three types, and the same has occurred in the case of water. At the same time, it is questionable whether ownership on its own is that critical for achieving regulatory objectives or improving industry performance. We may recommend splitting the industry into a number of public enterprises and have them compete against private utility providers, and even against other state-owned providers. For example (although possibly uniquely), publicly-owned electricity companies in New Zealand operate in a commercial environment. They compete against each other, cannot call on particular political favours, and do not enjoy a particularly constructive relationship with the similarly state-owned transmission company.

Those who contend that continued public ownership is a recipe for too much political interest or intervention might argue that a full transfer of ownership is required to improve private sector confidence (and, therefore, investment). However, a straightforward or partial sale does not necessarily offer a politics-free environment either. The question who owns key assets of the state is hardly a non-political matter. In general, the nature of private shareholders in infrastructure industries has changed over time, moving from private individuals ('Joe Bloggs'), to private investment funds and to, more recently, sovereign wealth funds (pools of money that governments use to invest for profit, especially in non-national companies). Especially in the case of foreign sovereign wealth funds (see Kimmitt 2008) political concerns have been raised about the potential implications of foreign ownership of supposedly key domestic assets (see Roberts 2010). For example, in 2006, there was widespread opposition in the United States to the transfer of numerous US port facilities to the ownership of 'Dubai Ports World' (which had purchased P&O – the previous owner). Dubai Ports World, however, was not a sovereign wealth fund, but a state-owned business.

The political fear has been that foreign governments might use their funds not as a means to maximize profits, but to use these resources to exercise political weight, gain sensitive information, or undermine corporate governance provisions. In other words, the political conflict over foreign ownership is about key assets being owned by foreign governments, and not necessarily about the degree to which shares are being held by 'non-nationals' (although some governments have required that the majority of shares should be held by 'nationals', leading to complex forms of gaming to get around these provisions).

Related debates have been conducted in the context of so-called 'golden shares'. Here, the state, as a minority owner (of the golden share), is granted particular veto-powers, for example over take-overs or other critical corporate decisions (Graham and Prosser 1991). Golden shares have, however, become increasingly contested, especially as the European Court of Justice has ruled a number of these constructions illegal (in cases affecting the United Kingdom, Germany, Portugal and Spain, among others). In these cases, golden share provisions were seen to be violating the free movement of capital within the European Union. More generally, European law does not prohibit state monopolies, but places restrictions on their scope (Art 14 TEU and 106 TEU; see Chalmers *et al.* 2010: 1030–8; Hancher 1998; Heritier 2001; Schwintowski 2003).

There are also questions regarding strategies of 'selling off' public shares. One strategy would be to sell the assets completely (by issuing shares on the stock exchange, or be selling the business to one investor). Such one-off decisions come with the risk of mis-pricing the asset which can lead to accusations that publicly owned assets have been sold too cheaply. Others would, however, suggest that any more gradual strategy runs the risk of political reversal and signals potential future governmental interventions that may depress the likelihood to attract the maximum private market interest. More gradual strategies would either rely on a timetable of gradual share selling or on a commitment to sell a majority or a minority stage in the infrastructure provider. Again, different variants exist. For example, Germany's constitution requires majority federal ownership of its railway infrastructure (Art 87e), but this requirement does not include the provision of passenger or freight services. Such gradual sale strategies are seen as more cautious, offering governments the ability to cash in on their assets at particular times of their choosing, therefore potentially maximizing their revenues. However, it opens the process to potential political blockages and it continues a potential confusion in the role of the state between those of being the regulator and those of being the owner (see below).

For Amnesia's water provider, if it was seen to be potentially profitable, one suggestion might be to advocate the transfer to private ownership – under regulatory oversight. As the railway industry is inherently loss-making even a full transfer to private ownership would require public involvement through the payment of subsidies. Moreover, as the possibility of bankruptcy has to be entertained and as continuity of service is critical, any full privatization also requires some provisions to ensure how services will be continued should private providers go out of business. From the perspective of potential private investors, full privatization might offer, at first sight, the reduced likelihood of state interference. However, as noted above, this still raises the commitment problem in terms of how regulatory oversight will develop over time. Should this be a concern, privatization may also involve the signing of particular licence-agreements, such as the guarantee of particular rates of return and other means that would reduce potential discretionary decisions by regulators.

Those privatization constructions that rely on 'mixed' ownership provide for distinct regulatory challenges. Such a construction requires choices as to how to handle potential conflicts between ownership and regulatory interests. The former is interested in maximizing profits (which would also guarantee a high sales price), the latter is interested in squeezing the regulatee to maximize efficiency gains through competition-oriented measures. In some countries, this potential conflict is handled by the separation of regulatory interests from ownership interests. This implies, for example, that the shareholder-interest of the state is placed with the finance ministry and the overall responsibility for regulatory oversight with the economics ministry. It is highly likely that the interests of the finance ministry will outmuscle regulatory concerns.

Finally, the past decade has seen a growing interest in 'mutually owned' or 'non-dividend-paying' companies. The argument in favour of these organizational constructions has been that privatization in terms of a full transfer of ownership has not led to sufficient interest in investment in infrastructure. Instead, it has been argued that the chief interest has been in satisfying the short-term interests of private shareholders. Especially when incentivized by the price cap formula RPI-X, firms have been accused of emphasizing efficiency through 'asset sweating' at the expense of capacity modernization. Mutualism and 'non-dividend-paying' organizations are said to offer a solution to this problem: as their directors and shareowners (the public) are not interested in their own financial return, they are likely to manage the company in the long-term interest rather than short-term shareholder interest. However, critics of this ownership approach argue that such constructions lead to confusion and inefficiency – as companies without motivation to maximize efficiency fundamentally violate principles of market-type economies.

How to open up markets?

Experience over the past three decades has shown that ownership *per se* is less critical than market structure and the way in which markets are liberalized. For example, it has been argued that the privatized telecommunications industry in the United Kingdom only developed once liberalization was gradually (and fully) introduced in the mid-1990s. Apart from competition awakening the 'competitive spirits' among firms, it is also argued that liberalized markets reduce the difficulties for regulators in exercising oversight. Competition reduces information asymmetry problems (there are competing sources of information to be submitted to regulators) and also reduces the likelihood of capture (because of competing concentrated interests).

For some, it might be enough to formally open markets. In other words, the presence of *contestable markets* is sufficient to make dominant providers efficient (Baumol *et al.* 1982). This would simply require the introduction of legal provisions that would allow market entry under the terms of general competition laws, for example. According to this argument, dominant providers or single service providers will behave as if they are in competitive settings, as long as the opportunity of (short-term) market entry exists. Should the dominant provider behave as a monopolist, entry by new providers would occur and drive down prices.

The idea of *contestable markets* is attractive – it assumes that once it is legally possible to enter a market and it can be assumed that some parties have an interest in facilitating this new entry, then markets are contestable. However, the idea is faced with considerable problems in particular in relation to infrastructure industries. It assumes a transaction cost-free environment in which market entry can occur quickly and easily and is not dependent on upfront investment or extensive supply chains. It is unlikely that market entry would be easily achievable when having to invest in, or negotiate access to, railway infrastructures, mobile phone masts, electricity transmission and distribution networks, or gas pipelines, especially when capacity is limited. In other words, ensuring market entry requires regulatory intervention to deal with matters such as access rights or price-setting.

It also may require more far-reaching and interventionist decisions in terms of the overall industry structure in order to allow equal access rights to the infrastructure: should a company be both owner of the electricity network and seller of electricity to consumers, then it is unlikely to welcome a new entrant wishing to purchase some capacity on its network. Similar concerns have also been raised in communications. For example, the United Kingdom communications regulator Ofcom (Office of Communications) considered whether competitors suffered from poor access to the broadband infrastructure (largely owned and managed by British Telecommunications (BT)). This led to a debate (in 2009) whether BT should be required to fully separate its infrastructure from its services, or whether a 'virtual' or internal separation would suffice (under the threat to enact full separation should continuing discrimination be observed). The latter option was chosen at the time. However, it might be argued that more structural solutions – namely those separating infrastructures and services – are required to facilitate the functioning of the 'contestable markets' idea.

So, how would we introduce competition into infrastructure industries, such as the water and railway industries in Amnesia?

One inspiration stemming from the advocacy of the 'contestable markets' idea is to encourage economic incentives that facilitate market entry. Therefore, one key decision is whether the industry should be *vertically and/or horizontally separated* or not. Vertical separation implies the parcelling out of different components of the industry, such as generation and transmission, or railway services and infrastructure. Horizontal separation implies the creation of different operators that provide similar (integrated) services. An example of the latter would be if we privatized the national petrol station monopoly by allocating petrol stations to four different companies (or sold them to four different companies).

The argument in favour of vertical separation is that monopoly (the infrastructure) and other aspects should be separated in order to allow competition in other markets. For example, electricity generation is potentially competitive, and so is the retailing of electricity, whereas transmission networks have natural monopoly characteristics. Similarly,

Amnesia's railways could be separated between railway services and the provision of infrastructure. The latter might be treated as a monopoly, whereas railway services would compete on the track (just as coach operators might compete on the same road). At first sight, this might be an attractive proposition: open the railway infrastructure to any provider who is willing to operate trains at particular times.

However, there are a number of objections to this basic principle. First, trains cannot compete on the same slot (one train can only be on one particular piece of track at any given time), decisions are therefore required on how to regulate the allocation of slots. Second, there are issues concerning the loss-making nature of the railway industry. In the Amnesian case, it is likely that a free access regime would lead to the provision of railway services around the capital (the commuter services) and the abandonment of most railway services in the rest of the country. This would contradict the government of Amnesia's policy. It is also argued that attracting passengers relies on providing regular services throughout the day rather than concentrating on potentially profitable services. Therefore, we may wish to recommend that certain profit-making and loss-making services should be 'lumped' together so that railway providers are required to cross-subsidize some of their services internally (we return to this point in the next chapter). This requires regulatory capacity to assess different bids for the running of particular bundles of services (for example, whether profitable commuter services should be bundled with services to other parts of Amnesia).

Furthermore, there are also suggestions that the railways are inherently an integrated industry (on technical grounds) and that vertical separation increases transaction costs unnecessarily (or that an internal 'Chinese wall'-type separation would suffice). For example, conflicts about causes of delays (is it a track-related fault or a fault caused by defective trains?) and the need to negotiate access to railway tracks are said to cause a costly liability management culture that is likely to displace the focus on the delivery of the actual railway service. This argument is usually supported by the examples of the perceived success stories of Japan and the United States that feature vertically integrated railway systems, whereas alleged failure stories, such as the United Kingdom, are associated with vertical separation (see Lodge 2002b). Such accounts therefore suggest that horizontal separation – the creation of different companies that may or may not directly compete against each other for customers – may offer an advantageous solution. Indeed, in 2012, some parts of the British railway system were moving towards creating joint regional structures to run franchise and infrastructure together.

So what can be said in favour of vertical separation, especially in the case of railways? One argument in favour has been that vertical separation concentrates management effort on very distinct services and also represents distinct investor interests: infrastructures require a life-cycle of 50 years or so, whereas rolling stock has a life-cycle of about two decades.

The other argument is one based on the cost of negotiating and agreeing access charges. That is, in systems where there is hardly any inter-running of train-services (e.g. trains just go up and down one single line) vertical separation is arguably of little value. This contrasts with systems where there is considerable 'inter-running' (where different train services cross a multitude of railway tracks, for example, services between A and B run on the same track as services that go from A and D, and between C and F). Inter-running raises issues regarding who determines access to the track and whether the presence of one vertically integrated operator leads to discriminatory behaviour. If the infrastructure is operated by the provider of train services between A and B, it is unlikely that other operators (providing the other services) will have access to the same attractive railway slots and on the same terms. At a minimum, such an arrangement would require regulatory oversight. If, therefore, the commuter services are to run on networks separate from other railway services, a case might be made for vertical integration (and, therefore, horizontal integration), if, however, there is widespread inter-running across different services, vertical separation may be more advisable.

The argument in favour of vertical separation, therefore, is that a separate infrastructure provider will offer track slots to the 'best' bid rather than be driven by the commercial interests of any one single provider, thereby reducing access negotiation costs and potential regulatory oversight costs. (Advocates of contestable markets would therefore also favour vertical separation: once the infrastructure provider's sole economic interest is to sell the maximum capacity at the highest price, the possibility of market entry should produce the kind of behaviour predicted by the contestable markets thesis, as noted above).

Discussions regarding vertical separation are even more problematic in the case of water (see Cave Review 2009). In this case, the water domain represents an integrated product, although some legal separation between network and retail activities may be entertained. Water industries typically appear as regional monopolies. For Amnesia's national water regulator this means that it is difficult to envisage vertical separation. How then could we introduce competition? One strategy may be to grant time-limited concessions, or the decision might to be sell-off these regional monopolies (i.e. horizontal separation). Neither of these options establishes competition 'in' the market. However, the former would allow competition 'for' the market (see next chapter), whereas the latter option allows so-called yardstick or benchmark competition. Accordingly, regulators assess the performance of individual providers on the basis of common benchmarks that permit a comparison between different firms. This comparison reduces the information asymmetry problem that regulators may face when facing a single provider of water services. Of course, the regional monopolies will all argue that their region is special and their inheritance peculiar. However, at least it would offer regulators the position to discuss a firm's performance.

There may, however, be questions as to how many regions we wish to establish in order to encourage yardstick competition. Again, there is a trade-off in terms of transaction costs: do the benefits from being able to compare performance by separating companies outweigh the additional costs that such a measure would cause, namely the need to negotiate relationships between networks? It might be argued that the more interconnected the different networks are, the less a case can be made for regional monopolies being regulated through yardstick-type measures.

Finally, given the loss-making nature of Amnesia's railway system, it may also be questioned how *subsidies* should be allocated. One way would be to subsidize the railway track, thereby cutting access charges and, in turn, reducing pressures on ticket prices. This supply-led system might be seen to encourage investment in infrastructure as the distortion of the network access price attracts extra demand. Critics would argue that such investment is likely to be 'wasteful' as subsidized operators do not allocate their resources efficiently (as the price signal is distorted). A demand-led approach would, in contrast, pay subsidies to those providing particular services that, in turn, pay fully commercial rates for access to the infrastructure. The advantage of this system is that subsidies are paid depending on consumer demand, therefore revealing preferences for particular services rather than others (this would also make the payment of subsidies more transparent, potentially allowing critics of railway services to use such transparent figures to campaign for the closure of (some of) Amnesia's railways). Critics argue that such a demand-led approach is costly – one transfers public money to railway companies that procure network access at commercial rates from a (potentially private) infrastructure operator who thereby profits from public taxpayer money.

The discussion in this section has been at a fairly abstract level. However, it highlights the kinds of choices that are involved in deciding on ownership and structural aspects of a regulated industry. It suggests that starting from the basic consideration of the commitment problem leads to a consideration of wider issues relating to ownership and, more importantly, industry structure. The key argument has been that transaction costs matter. One organizing principle has been that the costs of oversight for a regulator should be reduced by making regulatees behave as close to the competition-type arrangements as possible. However, as the cases of Amnesian water and railways suggest, such an arrangement is not necessarily easily obtainable and is likely to be highly controversial.

Regulatory agencies

As noted in Chapter 2, one of the key concerns in the regulation literature has been the fear of capture. In other words, setting up regulatory agencies is likely to make these bodies vulnerable to the interests of the regulated industry, especially when this industry consists of one firm, or firms with aligned commercial interests. The commitment problem also has direct implications for the extent to which regulators are delegated with discretionary powers. In contexts where investors believe that a regulator will treat them fairly and where political interference is unlikely, investors will have confidence in a powerful regulator with discretionary powers. In those contexts where regulators are on a political 'tight leash' or are not particularly well-resourced to undertake in-depth reviews, we may wish to rely on other devices than regulatory agencies. In other words, as noted in Chapter 2, regulatory agencies are vulnerable to three sources of drift: one is the drift away from initial intent through industry pressure ('capture'), another is drift because of political pressures. In addition, regulatory agencies may similarly drift because of typical bureaucratic self-interest: they may focus on those aspects that are popular rather than difficult and potentially politically unhelpful.

In other words, regulatory agencies might be a way to deal with commitment problems in some cases, but not in others. So if we wish to create regulatory agencies in Amnesia's water and railway sectors (rather than deal with the two industries through long-term concessions without regulatory oversight, or by relying on oversight by ministerial bureaucracies), what are the key features that characterize a competent regulatory agency? We use here the indicators that have been widely used to assess independence (Gilardi 2002; see also Hanretty and Koop 2011 for critical discussion of criteria of 'formal' versus 'actual' independence).

One key indicator is the *statutory basis* and the jurisdictional basis of the regulator. As already noted, having a statutory regulator may be a commitment device as legislative reversal takes political time and effort. However, how painful legislative reversal is for a particular government depends on the kind of political system it operates in. In some jurisdictions such efforts may be relatively cost-free (in the political sense). For example, British politicians have been accused of reminding 'their' regulators that the size of their parliamentary majority might be deployed to alter regulators' statutory remits. In such cases, regulatory agencies require a positive reputation among industry and media outlets, thereby making it politically problematic for governments to challenge a regulator's jurisdiction.

Finally, there is also an issue regarding the jurisdictional *status* of the regulatory authority. In Germany, regulatory agencies are subordinate administrative bodies (in terms of administrative law), accountable for their actions to a ministerial department. In the United Kingdom, the communications regulator, Ofcom, was created (in 2003) as a 'statutory corporation' rather than a non-ministerial government department (such as its energy counterpart, Ofgem (Office of Gas and Electricity Markets), or earlier economic regulators for infrastructure industries). This was to address a key problem of staff retention that had affected its predecessor, the telecommunications regulator Oftel (Office of Telecommunications). It was argued that one reason for the difficulties in staff retention was that the salary levels paid to staff were too low in comparison to those offered by the regulated industry (see Hall *et al.* 2000).

More generally, regulators' statutory bases also include the kind of 'reserve powers' that ministerial departments may wish to keep for themselves, such as the power to grant licences which regulators may then monitor and enforce. Furthermore, political powers to veto regulatory decisions or to issue 'directions' are usually also set out in statutory provisions. National regulatory laws (and competition laws) usually include clauses that set out procedures for ministerial interventions in particular areas (such as national defence) and establish the conditions under which a minister can intervene. In general, such ministerial powers are restricted to cases of 'national interest' or to giving 'general direction' or 'directions of a general nature' (such as 'consider the impact of all decisions on climate change'), rather than instructions on individual cases. However, the line between a 'general' and an 'individual' direction may become blurred in particular cases, and it is unlikely that regulators will take ministers to court for having overstepped their power to give 'general direction' (although the Jamaican Office of Utilities Regulation did so over a ministerial decision in 2002, and, on appeal, won its case in 2009) (*Mossell v OUR* 2009).

A further key aspect in institutional design relates to the *jurisdiction* of regulatory agencies. In the 1990s, one of the key arguments was that each domain required its own regulator to maximize industry focus and specialization. However, such a fragmented set-up has brought its own problems. In small states (i.e. those with small populations), having numerous regulators is particularly costly, leading to the duplication of, for example, human resource functions and spreading regulatory expertise rather thinly. Therefore, it has been argued that in these cases the putting together of regulatory functions is likely to create a powerful and well-resourced regulator that is able to draw on cross-sectoral expertise in its work.

A second problem with specialization has been changing industry structures and consumer preferences. For example, electricity and gas regulators have been merged in view of the substitutability of electricity and gas for domestic consumers, in particular as industry has turned towards becoming dual providers. In telecommunications, the merger with wider communications industries sought to reflect the changing nature of consumer and industry patterns.

Finally, continuous criticism has been directed at the consistency of regulatory expertise across regulatory industries. One criticism has been that fragmentation breeds over-specialization where different regulators treat similar problems in very different ways. One way to address such issues is to institute specific meetings between agency heads to consider and agree on common methodologies, for example. Others advocate a more formal organizational solution, namely the creation of an 'infrastructure regulator'. For example, Germany opted for the establishment of such a regulatory agency (the *Bundesnetzagentur*) to combine responsibility for energy, telecommunications, railways and postal services (where federal jurisdiction was granted). The functional justification was that such a construction would facilitate a consistent approach towards the regulation of infrastructure, which would stand side by side with the work of the competition authority. In contrast, critics of cross-sectoral regulators would argue that such a construction insufficiently reflects the varying dynamics across different regulated industries.

Related issues also affect the *funding* of regulatory offices. Most regulators finance their operations on the basis of levies paid by the industry and through budget-allocations from the national finance minister. A sole dependency on any one source may be seen as highly problematic from a commitment-based perspective. If regulators are dependent on financial support from the finance minister, especially when controlling state-owned enterprises, then budgetary allocations could be seen to be dependent on how well the regulator manages to be responsive to the government's overall preferences. If the regulator was solely dependent on industry funds, then similar dependency relationships might emerge. For example, if the regulator was financially reliant on the levy paid by one single firm, then any delay in this payment would affect the ability of the regulator to maintain its operation and to pay its staff (especially as legal proceedings to receive the required levy would take a considerable time). It has therefore been argued that a reliance on industry levies should only be entertained where there is no dependency on one single source of industry funding. This could be achieved in liberalized markets with a number of providers. Similarly, this might offer further support for the argument that a cross-sectoral infrastructure regulator should be established as this reduces the financial dependency on any one singly industry.

The final key dimension is concerned with the agency's *organization*, in particular in terms of the set-up and appointment of its leadership. One of the key institutional innovations (which reflected long-established British organizational tradition) was the United Kingdom's use of the 'director general' model. In contrast to the US model that relied on commissioners and collective decision-making, the argument in favour of such a 'presidential' agency leadership was said to provide for greater accountability and visibility. In particular, for regulators that needed to establish themselves in the public eye, it was said that a single director general would advance the public profile of the regulator and would provide for a visible counterweight to the organized interests of the regulatory industry (and, especially, the incumbent). In addition, having a single head was also justified by the traditional administrative doctrine that collective decision-making leads to a shifting of responsibility and a lack of transparent decision-making.

Since those early days of regulatory reform, the United Kingdom has moved towards more collective decision-making, with a board (led by a chairperson) overseeing the activities of the regulator (usually granting a prominent public profile to the chairperson and the agency chief executive). The justification for this shift in preference was that changes in individual regulators (director generals) brought too much change in terms of regulatory style. Thus, collective leadership structures were advocated to advance more stable and consistent decision-making. More importantly, it was argued that individual regulators had been difficult to handle politically, leading to conflicts between ministers and regulators, especially when the latter insisted on taking decisions that were not appreciated by their political masters.

The second key aspect is the type of appointment procedures that are used to select regulators. The most widespread indicator to highlight that the regulator is not directly dependent on politics is to decouple the term of office from the electoral cycle by choosing longer terms. As a result, an incoming party in government is not in a position to replace regulators (without having to claim that regulators have turned insane or are otherwise incapacitated), while a government facing an election is unable to ask for particular 'regulatory favours' to gain electoral benefits. Longer tenure also means that as regulators' careers are detached from those of politicians, they are less interested in being popular with the electorate or politicians in government.

A related debate questions whether regulators should be able to be reappointed or not. For some, the possibility of seeking reappointment creates a self-interest in being popular with those in political office who make re-appointment decisions. As a result, some regulators have sought to indicate their independence by stating early into their initial term that they would not be seeking a second period in office.

A third key choice is 'who' should appoint regulators. In some jurisdictions, the final choice, from a shortlist, is taken by the relevant minister. Other countries opt for committees representing majorities in different chambers of parliament. In other jurisdictions, the choice is in the hands of a particular committee or commission (such as the appointments panel for senior civil servants). Even here, though, it is likely that an equivalent of the old British 'face doesn't fit' convention exists, namely that regulators should be broadly agreeable to politicians in government, both in terms of their outlook and in terms of their personal fit. In appointing boards of regulators (i.e. a 'commission-type' model), countries have opted for varied terms of office, thereby allowing a rolling replacement of commissioners over time. In some cases, the membership of those in charge of regulators has been prescribed in statute. For example, such prescriptions could include explicit commitments towards including civil society, economic and engineering interests among the leadership team of regulatory bodies. Critics of such an approach would argue that seeking to make a regulator 'representative' violates a regulator's primary intention to be oriented towards economic efficiency, apart from violating the overall merit principle when it comes to appointment.

Amnesia's choices

Based on the above discussion, Amnesia is faced with a number of key choices, in terms of industry structure and ownership, and whether and how to establish a regulatory agency. These different choices, noted in the previous section, are summarized in Table 8.1 below. These choices suggest that advice such as 'privatize' and 'have a regulatory agency' is highly simplistic and unhelpful. Any discussion informed by a regulatory analysis perspective requires an interrogation into what kind of privatization and market structure should be applied given a particular context, and what kind of organizational principles should underpin a regulatory agency. Each of these options has distinct implications for the kind of regulatory regime for Amnesia's rail and water industries.

With rail, those who argue that railway systems are inherently vertically integrated will demand that all ideas promoting vertical separation should be excluded. Instead, they will consider the creation of regional monopolies that can be regulated via yardstick-type regimes. These advocates would also discount the extent to which access rights for outside parties would be open to discrimination. In contrast, those who favour turning infrastructure industries into markets would argue that vertical separation is essential: it would provide the infrastructure provider with the incentive to fill in infrastructure capacity and to seek maximum return, rather than discriminate in favour of one particular railway service provider.

In the case of water, such debates might be less heated, although attempts at introducing competition 'in' the pipe have been regularly made. Amnesia's key choice seems to be how to facilitate yardstick competition-type regulation, especially if the various regions have different investment needs. Regional monopolies would also face considerable negotiations concerning access rights should the different networks overlap and not be fully separate across different regions.

In short, Amnesia has a considerable number of options, in terms of ownership structure, of how to structure the two industries, and of how

TABLE 8.1   *Designing infrastructure regulatory regimes*

Dimension	Design debates	Amnesia's options
Ownership and market structure	Ownership distribution (debates about degree of transfer of entity from public to private sector, type of ownership transfer, and about degree of national/non-national shareholders) Structure of policy domain (horizontal fragmentation) (debates about degree of domain fragmentation) Vertical separation (debates regarding the fragmentation of the industry between different elements of the service production stages)	**Rail:** Choice of type of privatization and between vertical separation (infrastructure split off from services), creation of integrated companies, or maintaining one fully integrated company (with internal separation), requires decisions as to how to 'bundle' services to facilitate cross-subsidization and how to financially support loss-making industry, regulatory oversight over track-access and quality of services and infrastructure. Price control for commuter services, if dominant position diagnosed. **Water:** Choice of privatization strategy, problem with vertical separation, therefore potential to rely on yardstick competition between regional companies, or keeping one single integrated operator. Requires regulatory oversight over capacity, maintenance and pricing.
Allocation of regulatory authority	Authority and organization of regulatory agency (debates regarding whether regulator should be focused on sector, on industry or should be cross-sectoral; what type of leadership should be provided for (collective or individual), types of appointment procedures and how funding for regulatory activity should be provided (taxpayer and/or industry)) Distribution of regulatory competencies across actors (how resources are allocated across regulatory domain, their formal authority	**Rail and Water:** Creation of sectoral regulator (water and rail regulator), or placing regulatory oversight with existing regulatory authorities (i.e. creating an infrastructure regulator, or a regulator for 'public transport' and water).

Source: Adapted from Lodge and Stirton (2006: 468).

to channel regulatory and financial incentives. All of them are linked to particular outcomes – and weaknesses – and it is therefore difficult to suggest that any one system will provide a 'best in world' template.

Conclusion

This chapter has drawn on one particular approach towards the study of regulation, namely the institutional design perspective. As noted in Chapter 2, this perspective has enjoyed considerable prominence, as it suggested that countries could 'design' themselves out of their distinct commitment problems. This literature therefore offers countries with a weak institutional endowment the opportunity to intelligently structure incentives that would maximize private investment in the industry in question. However, just focusing on the commitment problem by itself might be seen to be problematic, and this conclusion focuses on the inherent trade-offs that any institutional design perspective has to face, especially with regard to the regulation of infrastructures.

First of all, as Table 8.1 has suggested, even if we agree on the broad contours of a regulatory regime, there are still significant 'second order' choices to be considered. Whether, for example, we approve of presidential ('director general') or collective decision-making appears to be less a matter of extensive analysis, but rather a reflection of some dominant arguments about recent regulatory experience. Arguments about institutional design mostly reflect an (over-)compensation to the latest events in relevant sectors.

Second, and related, the regulation of infrastructures is inherently shaped by the particular experience of those who are charged with developing regulatory regimes. For example, if Amnesia's railway reforms are driven by individuals with a sole interest in public transport, then the reforms at large will look very different from those that would be chosen by individuals whose sole experience has been in other infrastructure industries (see Lodge 2002b: 138–9). More broadly, what is regarded as legitimate and successful is a matter of perception and limited searches, and therefore highly contingent on the kind of worldviews that dominate a particular regulatory domain or the set of people involved in considering options for regulatory reform. It also has clear implications in terms of what kind of staff should be attracted to regulatory agencies, for example, whether this should include a dominance of lawyers, economists or engineers.

Third, even when considering the commitment problem as critical, as this chapter does, this commitment problem needs to be seen in the light of tensions with other potential problems. For example, there is an inherent tension between *commitment and flexibility*. We may regard the fixing of the terms of a licence for a prolonged period as a successful commitment device (especially if any alterations are associated with considerable penalties).

However, such long-term commitment comes at the expense of flexibility, in at least two ways. First, such commitments fly in the face of democracy and potentially changing popular preferences. One might argue that there are certain limitations to the extent to which current governments should be able to tie future governments' hands, especially when accusations are made that politicians provide 'cronies' with long-term contracts that are highly costly to reverse.

Second, long-term commitment, especially towards particular technologies, also faces inherent problems as technologies undergo change, consumer preferences adjust, and international agreements alter domestic benefit flows. For example, the Jamaican government granted the then Cable & Wireless a set of 50 year licences that granted C&W almost complete exclusivity over voice telephony in the late 1980s. The idea was to offer a maximum commitment device to facilitate private investment (and network extension) in a context that had had a poor reputation for maintaining commitment in previous decades. This licence might have been regarded as a 'commitment device' in the 1980s, but in the 1990s this licence was mostly defunct as a commitment device. Communications technologies multiplied, international agreements put private monopolies under pressure, and US regulators undermined the basis on which Jamaica and other countries financed their telecommunications services (the Federal Communications Commission required the gradual lowering of international settlement rates which had been a key source of revenue for a large number of operators, allowing them to cross-subsidize domestic services) (Lodge and Stirton 2006). In other words, there is no such thing as 'perfect commitment'. Everything, at best, is an incomplete contract.

A final trade-off is between *commitment costs* and *agency costs*. We may suggest that delegating regulatory powers to an agency is one way to signal commitment as it reduces the scope for political interference. However, as noted, empowering regulatory agencies with discretionary powers can lead to capture. In other words, political means to prevent capture (such as the 'police-patrols', 'fire-alarms' or 'deck-stacking' devices discussed in Chapter 2) may be seen as devices that challenge commitment. Equally, the more we emphasize 'commitment' in institutional design, the less feasible is the intensive scrutiny and potential for reversal that makes capture less likely. In other words, the consideration of so-called agency costs and commitment costs will rarely establish a solution that will not be faced by criticisms and trade-offs.

In sum, the commitment cost problem has been one of the most dominant ideas in regulatory thinking over the past two decades or so. With increased application has come a growing sense of the limitations of the belief that institutional design can solve all commitment problems. No institutional settlement is that bullet-proof or teflon-plated that it cannot be undermined by changing circumstances or determined political action. Nevertheless, when considering the regulation of infrastructures it is necessary to start somewhere, and to start with the idea of commitment costs and then to consider how to reduce the demands placed on regulators for dealing with particular industry structures offers one set of key principles that can guide regulatory analysis.

Chapter 9

<hr/>

Concessions and Franchising

Amnesia's final decision was to opt for a franchise model for its passenger railway services. Particular problems have emerged with the local railway system in Amnesia's capital, Frenezia. The incumbent was vested with a franchise for 15 years, and the franchising period comes to an end in seven years. The incumbent refuses to invest in rolling stock and makes any further investment dependent on an early renewal of its franchise. Faced with reduced services and deteriorating service quality, the mayor of Frenezia asks you to offer advice on how to improve the franchising system in order to prevent any repeat of this conflict.

Introduction

Franchises or concessions (we use these words interchangeably) are one of the key instruments in the contemporary regulatory state. They define a way of allocating the rights to provide services, usually involving a degree of exclusivity. These contracts are limited in their duration and at the end of a contract, a new auction is held to allocate the franchise for the next time period. Franchises or concessions are therefore somewhat distinct from other kinds of licence allocation decisions, such as the allocation of radio-spectrum, where the allocation is about input, allowing competition in the market and variations in the kind of services that are offered (although this distinction blurs at the margin in that allocated inputs may be required to be used for particular services or are essential for the provision of a particular service).

Whereas in the previous chapter we considered the design of regulatory institutions, this chapter looks at franchising as a regulatory instrument that relies on contractual devices. A reliance on fixed contracts is said to contrast with more discretionary regulatory arrangements, for example, a reliance on regulatory agencies to conduct price controls. Price-controls may be 'deck-stacked' in procedural terms, but the outcome of decisions is not fixed. Franchises or concessions rely on contractual devices that hardwire particular arrangements, such as the requirement to provide particular minimum services, to offer services at a particular price and/or the right to earn a particular rate of return. In general, a reliance on such contractual arrangements creates problems with flexibility, whereas more discretionary arrangements are said to trigger more problems with capture.

Franchises and concessions have attracted considerable interest: they have been used to allocate licences for TV broadcasting (and cable transmission), they have been applied to local and national public transport (such as the UK passenger railways and London bus services), and they have witnessed widespread application in the less developed world across all infrastructure industries. At the same time, there has also been considerable evidence of unhappiness, with a series of countries and sectors requiring renegotiations (76 per cent of concessions in the water sector in Latin America were renegotiated between the 1980s and early 2000s within the first three years of their signing: Guasch *et al.* 2008). Single case studies have also highlighted how problematic franchising contracts in water in the developing world have been (Nickson and Vargas 2002), given rebellions against contractually agreed tariff increases (especially as tariffs established during periods of public ownership are usually biased in favour of the wealthy-influential, and therefore easily mobilized, rather than the poor) and political contestation over allocation decisions.

To inform Frenezia's mayor, a number of questions need to be asked. Why have franchises in the first place? How should franchises be allocated? What can be done to deal with issues of monitoring and enforcement? What lessons can we draw from wider international experience?

Why have franchises?

In the previous chapter, it was noted that Amnesia's railway services were loss making overall, apart from the commuter services into Frenezia. The local rail services within Frenezia, however, are also loss-making. Their ticketing and timetabling arrangements are integrated into the wider metropolitan transport system, called TransFrenezia. Within the capital city, the rail system enjoys a near monopoly, as buses are no potential competitor but offer complementary services. It is argued that railways benefit from an integrated timetable that also offers regular rather select services during profitable times. It was a political requirement that there should be no changes to the timetable. The initial franchise contract therefore allowed cross-subsidization and for mechanisms that would provide a method for allocating subsidies. This means that subsidies are paid directly to the provider and no competition is allowed. Railway services are operated under a contractual framework with limited discretionary rights (on either side) and are monitored by a special unit (within the mayor's office), but the main threats are the termination of the franchise or the non-renewal of the franchise at the end of the fixed period.

Before moving to different design dimensions, it is worth stepping back to consider the rationale for relying on concessions. Apart from the usual arguments regarding 'natural monopolies' that require some form of regulatory approach, the rationale for adopting franchising in the case of railways is one of preventing 'cream-skimming' – if no monopoly rights were granted, competitors would undermine the financial viability of the overall product by offering services during profitable periods (therefore requiring higher subsidy payments or tariffs). An additional traditional justification for the use of franchising is to advance overall planning and to avoid 'excessive competition'. According to this argument, often made in the cases of bus services, competition would lead to unseemly races between different bus providers along high streets, while non-profitable services would be abandoned. In the case of Frenezia's railways, the argument would be that new entrants on the track would not just cause problems of network congestion, but also make integrated transport timetabling even more complex.

A different argument would justify the use of franchising or concessions with resource scarcity. This argument has been traditionally used in the case of broadcasting and other means of radio communications as the radio spectrum constitutes a scarce resource. Licences to operate on particular bandwidths are granted in order to address the problem of interference. Where scarcity is not a problem a licence would not have similar implications in terms of price and service obligations, but would be more generally understood as permission to operate *in* the market (and therefore also compete).

Of course, there is also an interest group or 'capture'-type argument for franchising arrangements. Accordingly, franchising offers a good basis for powerful interests to avoid competitive market arrangements, especially as the presumed benefits of competition *for* the market can be negotiated away once the initial franchising agreement has been signed. We return to this point below.

As noted already, franchising and concession devices have been particularly popular in less developed contexts. The argument has been that contracts offer a more credible commitment device than discretionary regulatory arrangements (see discussion in previous chapter). They seem to reduce the scope for political intervention, they appear to require no major regulatory 'intelligence', and they rely on judicial institutions (that appear less political than political or administrative actors). Government, according to this view, can concentrate on its role as an auctioneer and does not need to become a regulator. As already seen, such hopes have been dashed given the large number of reversals and renegotiations. Experience also shows that franchising requires considerable discretionary regulation on an ongoing basis. Opposition parties have used concession agreements as key platforms to attack incumbent governments. In the UK railway case, continued conflicts have emerged over the length of franchises, investment commitments and the relationship between infrastructure and franchise operators. Some franchisees have gone out of business, requiring the state to run particular railway services. Thus, concessions and franchises have most certainly not been 'non-political', although the degree of reversal and renegotiation that has been witnessed over the past two decades or so may have to do with the 'newness' of the initial contractual arrangements. Perhaps once international experience with franchising accumulates, more stability will be attained. At the same time, the core issues that affect concessions, and are discussed in this chapter, are inherently about political choices and therefore will always attract attention and criticism.

The intellectual attraction of franchising has re-emerged since the late 1960s with the seminal article by Harold Demsetz (1968, also Posner 1972). The original idea, however, is much older. The 'locus classicus' by Chadwick (1859) made the case for 'competition for the field' (Chadwick 1859: 385) for public utilities (such as railways), but also for other economic activities, such as funeral services (and the production and distribution of bread and beer) (see also Ekelund and Ford 1997). From a position of scepticism regarding the performance of US regulatory commissions, Demsetz argued that the benefits of markets and competition could be met by encouraging competition *for* the market, under particular conditions. This argument suggests that competition for a particular monopoly licence would 'compete away' the available monopoly rent, therefore leading to the same results as competition *in* the market.

However, this argument has also been contested, given the particular assumptions that underpinned Demsetz's argument (who himself highlighted the importance of all potential bidders having access to the same inputs, and collusion between bidders being unlikely, Demsetz 1968: 58). For example, it was argued that competition *for* the market would work in stable activities that required no investment. However, once franchise holders are supposed to invest, this raises issues regarding how to frame the duration of these concessions and how to compensate former owners for their loss of franchise, for example. Similarly, the inherent incompleteness of the franchising contract means that any franchise is open to tensions over demands for renegotiation, whether because of extraordinary events (recessions or natural catastrophes reducing demand) or because of service quality issues.

In cases of such non-performance, governments (such as Amnesia) are faced with a difficult choice between cancelling a non-performing franchise and potentially causing disruption and legal challenge, and having to negotiate with the incumbent provider from a position of relative weakness. This applies in particular to franchise agreements of prolonged duration. And, finally, there are also issues about the actual degree of *competition* for the market. For example, incumbents will always have an information advantage concerning the actual cost base compared to any new potential bidder (see Williamson 1976; Loeb and Magat 1979; Ogus 1994: 318–36; Gómez-Ibáñez 2003: 84–108). Furthermore, if there is very little competition for the market, then the supposed benefits of this arrangement will not be realized. It is these tensions that have shaped debates regarding the way in which franchises or concessions have been applied and that feature throughout the rest of this chapter.

How to allocate franchises

Frenezia's mayor has just entered office and immediately started an investigation into how the incumbent was granted its franchise. It has been established that the franchise was simply handed out to the existing publicly-owned provider in a non-competitive setting. At the time, this was seen as the easiest way to justify continued subsidy payments to the incumbent, especially as services were seen as broadly satisfactory. Conveniently, at the same time the incumbent promised to relocate its headquarters to Frenezia. Such decisions to allocate a concession non-competitively may have been relative common in the past, but more recently franchise decisions have usually relied on the actual implementation of Demsetz's recommendation to encourage actual competition *for* the market. The franchisee would bid for the award of the franchise and would carry (at least some of) the commercial risk if eventual performance was not in line with expectations. However, as straightforward as this advice might appear, the design of such a process depends on a number of key decisions – all of them with their distinct consequences.

The initial decision is to establish what is actually being franchised: is it one particular service, a particular bundle of services that can be regionally separated, or should the service be fully integrated? As suggested in the previous chapter, franchises may be allocated to service providers that use a third-party infrastructure (the choice taken by Amnesia and therefore also Frenezia), or to integrated providers that use both infrastructure and services. The second key choice regarding the content of the franchise is whether this is an 'operating' or an 'investment' franchise. An operating franchise separates between investment and maintenance activities. For example, it might be said that it would be more appropriate for the franchise-holder to concentrate on running services (i.e. running trains for passengers) and without having to bear any long-term investment decisions (such as investing in infrastructure or rolling-stock). This would remove some of the problems of re-allocating the franchise at the end of a particular franchising period (see below). It would also remove uncertainty about the value of the franchise if there were no substantial investment requirements in the future. At the same time, if the infrastructure is a central component of the actual service, then it could be argued that the benefits of allocating an operational franchise might be limited (as there is very little to do and all commercial risk is with the infrastructure). Operating franchises allow for smaller units to be 'parcelled out', thereby introducing the possibility of comparing performance ('yardstick competition'). For Amnesia, the use of an 'operational franchise' would mean that the railway operator would not be responsible for investing in rolling-stock, but would be only involved in its upkeep (at most). Ownership of the rolling stock could remain as a separate entity, for example, in a government-owned unit, or with leasing firms that compete against each other.

Investment franchises, in contrast, require a larger degree of involvement with (and ownership of) the facilities. The inclusion of investment in infrastructure or rolling-stock, for example, usually also implies that such franchises are of a longer duration. It reduces the contractual complexity that characterizes those operational franchises which depend on other parties to deliver critical investment (such as investment in infrastructure). It means, however, that there is a greater reliance on the financial resources of the franchises and therefore supposedly gives greater freedom to the franchise holder, such as Frenezia's rail provider (it does not just run services on tracks with carriages all owned by someone else).

However, investment franchises create considerable problems. Most of all, they raise an issue about the investment cycle. As illustrated in our vignette, towards the end of the franchising period, investment is likely to drop off markedly and/or will become part of a political battle between franchiser and franchisee (Williamson 1976; Laffont and Tirole 1988). Firms know that they can reap the early returns on their investment, but are reluctant to invest towards the end of the concession if others are going to benefit. (Early studies of the first round of UK railway franchises suggested, however, that companies invested towards the end of the franchising period. This trend was explained by an attempt to generate political support for renewal; see Affuso and Newbery 2000.)

This problem of how to handle investment in durable assets means that regulatory measures have to be found that will compensate the franchise holder in the case of a non-renewal or loss of the franchise (raising the credibility question of whether early commitments to compensate investment decisions fairly will be fulfilled). The problem of finding an appropriate compensation level and ensuring that this fair level sufficiently reflects future cost savings, such as reduced maintenance costs that have been directly generated by the asset-specific investment, are at the heart of the debate regarding franchising. These problems pitch the incumbent franchise holder (who will seek to overprice its assets) against the new entrant or the franchising authority (who will be keen to avoid any prolonged transition period), leading to a potential interruption of services (arguably a two-way and not just one-way 'hold-up problem' as arguably the incumbent can also be made to 'suffer' by the franchising authority: Williamson 1976).

Having decided on the type of franchise, Frenezia needs to decide on the type of allocation process it seeks to initiate. At one level, this leads to the distinction between 'beauty contests' and 'auctions'. So-called beauty contests allow for the submission of bids on the basis of (more or less) set standards. Some committee will then decide on who should be granted the franchise on the basis of these bids. Such bids may therefore not be allocated on price alone, but would consider issues such as 'legacy', the reputation of the firm to deliver, and other aspects. The benefits of such contests are said to lie in removing the potential optimism bias that may lead to over-ambitious bids being submitted (which then lead to financial trouble and the need for renegotiation). It also removes the pure 'price' signal in that other quality-type considerations can be favoured. In contrast, auction-type bidding processes generally seek to maximize the price paid or the minimum subsidy required. A different type of arrangement would be to accept that bid which offered to supply a particular service at the lowest cost to consumers.

At another level, different types of bidding processes can be distinguished (see Klein 1998: 49–51; Viscusi *et al.* 2005: ch. 13; Baldwin *et al.* 2012: 167–70). If the franchise is largely an operational one, the franchise could be allocated to the bidder who asks the lowest price from customers. Subsequent price changes will either be introduced through renewed bidding processes or by allowing for renegotiation (therefore introducing elements of discretionary regulation into the process).

However, once asset-specific investments are involved, different choices are required to account for the presence of these assets. One variant would be to allow bids to be submitted on the basis of asset value (which requires, however, specifications regarding future prices). A different variant is to allow bids to compete on lowest price to consumers as the overall value of the assets has been centrally valued. In the latter case, should assets be valued too highly, this will lead to unnecessarily high fees for consumers in the future; should they be valued too low, then the incumbents will have little incentive to invest and maintain the assets. Governments may also allow for so-called 'menu auctions' that suggest that franchises are usually complex sets of projects rather than a single product. In such cases, bidding may even involve a set of different options from which the unit allocating franchises may choose (Bernheim and Whinston 1986).

If a decision has been taken to auction the franchise, then the third dimension is about the conduct of the actual auction itself (for a survey see Klemperer 1999; for discussion of the auctions used for the allocation of 3G licences see Thatcher 2005). There are a number of types of auctions available, ranging from first-price sealed bid auctions (in which bids are submitted in sealed envelopes and the highest, or lowest, bid wins and pays the proposed amount), second-price sealed auctions (in which the highest bid wins but pays the amount of the second highest bid), to more dynamic auction types. Two key types here are so-called 'English auctions' (in which the bidding price is increased until only one bidder remains) or 'Dutch auctions' (in which prices are lowered until the bidder emerges). Various variations on these four key auction types exist (Klemperer 1999). Theory suggests that the various auction types lead to broadly similar outcomes (Armstrong *et al.* 1994: 125–9; but see also Klemperer 2002). However, it can also be suggested that such auctions lead to cases of over-bidding ('winner's curse') where soon after payment for the successful bid has been completed, the franchise holder realizes that they have paid too much (a phenomenon that is also widely diagnosed in the bidding for mega-events, such as the Olympics or Football World Cups). Especially as companies assume that a successful bid is of a 'once in a lifetime' or an 'essential for commercial survival' character, such over-heated bidding processes are likely to emerge.

One of the ways in which to reduce uncertainty about the value of franchises has been to rely on a gradual roll-out of different franchises, if such regional differentiation is possible. So, in the case of Frenezia, this would mean that its franchise for the Frenezia region would be auctioned after other franchises had been granted. This allows competitors to avoid over-enthusiastic bidding, provides for more experience and learning across all participants, and reduces the administrative cost to everyone. Such options would of course not be possible if the decision had been taken to franchise all of Amnesia's railway services to one provider. Furthermore, a 'one-off' or 'big-bang' franchising round may also deal with the political risk of eventual reversal: it is less likely that incoming governments will seek to reverse franchises once they have been allocated.

Finally, the design of any franchise also deals with issues of specification. It may be argued that specification is essential to hold the eventual franchisee accountable for their performance. In other words, such contracts would prescribe quality standards (such as service frequency and price levels and the like. This is also linked to the type of bidding one wishes to encourage). Again, the issue here is how much discretion is to be given to the eventual franchisee, or whether there should be tight control. The former is said to encourage 'commercial savvy' among franchisees, at the expense of having to deal with the 'cliff edge' problems that come with the end of a concession term. The latter increases the potential for a neutral competition *for* the market, but comes at a reduced opportunity for providers to develop distinct business plans. In addition, there are differences regarding duration. Maximum certainty would require the reduction of the franchising term to a minimum, thereby reducing the possibility that the contract will have to be renegotiated. However, the cost of potential renegotiation has to be contrasted with the administrative costs of devising franchises and their auctions (as well as the cost to potential bidders), and the cost of having to negotiate a franchise. Especially if the franchisee is expected to make some specific, long-term investments, a longer-term duration for the concession might be favoured (as noted), requiring, however, some clauses that allow for interim reviews after set periods. However, as suggested, once investments are required, the incumbent has an advantage (Williamson 1976): it is difficult to transfer all human and physical capital to the new entrant, and it is very difficult to price the value of the investments. Indeed, the overall benefits of competition *for* the market rely on the presence of actual competition. This means that certain aspects may have to be addressed, namely the costs of the actual bidding processes and the cost and service implications of the franchise. Indeed, it might be argued that in order to encourage competition, some potential bidders may have to be excluded in order to maintain a 'healthy' field of potential franchise bidders overall.

Monitoring, enforcing and terminating franchises

The initial concession contract between Frenezia/Amnesia and the local railway provider specified levels of investment as well as a minimum level of services. The contract also specified the terms and conditions of the contract and the way in which the contract could be terminated before the end of the franchising period. However, the problems that Frenezia is faced with are multiple: it has to assess whether the claims by the provider are particularly convincing or not. In many ways, therefore, this is a classic enforcement problem, as discussed in Chapter 4.

Monitoring or information-gathering problems relate to the way in which franchise holders supply information and agreement on the appropriateness of the standards used to hold a franchise to account. At the same time, performance information needs to be understood in context. If there are no comparative sources of information, it is hard to interpret performance in terms of punctuality or service quality. It also raises issues of interdependencies. As noted in the previous chapter, systems characterized by vertical separation are likely to suffer from conflicts and blame-games between infrastructure and service providers. Such interdependencies also make enforcement problematic. Similarly, those monitoring the performance of franchisees need to be able to distinguish between poor performance that is caused by the franchisee and that caused by wider trends beyond the control of the provider. For example, technical change may reduce demand for particular services, recessions may lead to a decline in usage and, therefore, financial viability (equally crowding may be caused by economic growth), while criminal aspects might also cause problems. For example, the theft of copper cables in the UK in 2010/11 caused 16,000 hours of delays on the railways alone. Between 2008 and 2011, the infrastructure provider, Network Rail, had to spend £43 million on replacing cables and compensating rail operators (the price of metals had increased to a level that made such criminal activities profitable: *Financial Times*, 10 September 2011).

These problems of gathering and interpreting information directly affect enforcement. The key issue is whether to regard the demands for renegotiation as credible (i.e. based on reasonable grounds) or as a typical attempt at lobbying by a strategic interest. Any bidding process encourages strategic behaviour in that there is an *ex ante* underestimation of costs or over-estimation of demand to obtain the bid while relying on a later renegotiation. Inevitably, the franchisee will suggest that unforeseeable changes have occurred that require a renegotiation (Zupan 1989).

As noted, punishing providers for poor performance requires a clear allocation of responsibility. A key example here is the prolonged conflict between the city government of Berlin and its local train provider over the latter's abysmal performance record throughout 2009, 2010 and 2011. Similar to our case of Frenezia, accountability was blurred because of ownership issues. Berlin's S-Bahn was a subsidiary of the national railway company, Deutsche Bahn, which was fully owned by the German federal government. Any 'attack' on the S-Bahn therefore threatened to destabilize the financial health of a state-owned company.

Taking enforcement action further requires the ability to measure performance on the basis of agreed standards. Even if the contractual basis of a franchise seems to include clear standards and criteria for enforcement, the extent to which any penalties can be applied depends on issues such as the direct responsibility of the provider for poor performance (rather than external reasons, such as recessions) and the absence of any interdependency effects. Furthermore, as Williamson (1976) noted, franchise termination (as the ultimate enforcement sanction) is inherently problematic: public officials will not be keen to expose themselves to public criticism for being associated with a poorly performing regime, and they will also wish to avoid the extensive administrative costs of having to deal with the likely challenges by the incumbent.

However, at a certain point, such reluctance may quickly turn into political demands for an immediate rectification of the situation. In the case of the Berlin S-Bahn, the city government's initial reluctance to engage with 'commercial matters' quickly turned into a hard-nosed threat to terminate the contract once angry public opinion started to blame politicians. In response to this threat, the S-Bahn agreed on a renegotiation of the franchising contract, which included both a more detailed specification of service standards, as well as an increase in potential penalty payments. Similarly, UK experience with railway franchising suggests that officials are indeed willing to remove franchises on the basis of poor performance or financial vulnerability, and to rely on statutory provisions to operate services as a government-run enterprise while a new franchise is being allocated. It might be argued that one of the reasons for less opportunistic or adversarial behaviour among incumbent franchisees has been the potential reputational damage to the firm. If the franchise holder is involved in other franchises, or is interested in bidding again, it will behave cooperatively rather than opportunistically in order to protect its reputation as a trustworthy franchise holder. Equally, reputation is said to hold governments in check: should governments be seen to overturn franchising contracts on regular occasions, it can be assumed that the willingness of private parties to bid for franchises will quickly decline.

Nevertheless, as stressed throughout the chapter, the termination of a franchise raises considerable issues, especially in terms of establishing processes that facilitate a renewed auction. As noted, there is the need to find an arrangement to deal with asset-specific investment either through set procedures, or by removing investment decisions from the actual franchise (a decision that was initially taken in the UK railways case where so-called rolling stock companies were established to provide rolling stock to deal with the 'cliff-edge' problems between two franchising periods).

In sum, the discussion of both information-gathering and behaviour-modification suggests that franchising or concessions require continued regulatory oversight (by whatever kind of organizational configuration). It has been suggested that the presence of regulatory capacity has been critical in explaining why some concessions in Latin America did not require renegotiation (Guasch *et al.* 2008). This contrasts with the widespread argument that concessions are particularly attractive as they do not require the capacity of a discretionary oversight body, as is supposedly the case in France.

In the development regulation field, the 'French' concession model gained considerable currency as a contrasting model to the more discretionary agency-model. The French concession model in the water industry is organized at the municipality level and a variety of concession models exist: a *gérance* (direct management contract in which the firm is paid a fixed amount for managing the service), a *régie intéressée* (where the firm's revenue is partly dependent on its performance), and the *affermage* (in which firm and local authority share in investment decisions). The *concession* contract allocates full responsibility for investment to the firm, and these investments are transferred to the public authority once the concession has ended. Such arrangements are however not 'regulation free'. Indeed, as Stern (2009) has suggested these arrangements operate within a well-established framework set out by the Conseil d'Etat (in its capacity as legal advisor to the executive and as highest

French administrative court in France). The Conseil d'Etat established key provisions for the transfer of investment to the franchising public authority. According to Stern (2009: 19), the Conseil d'Etat has also become involved in the modification of contracts (especially in water supply) and has taken on cases involving consumers challenging their municipalities. Even the French concession model, therefore, is not without its discretionary components.

Frenezia's choices

Having listened to all these complications, what is Frenezia's mayor to do? It is evident that Frenezia (and Amnesia) are experiencing something that writings on franchising have been predicting all along: the holder of the franchise will seek to renegotiate the conditions of the franchise and exploit its institutional position accordingly. Governments are only in the position to renegotiate the contract when the threat of contract termination is credible, that is, at times of severe service disruption caused by the decisions of the provider management (the equivalent of having the 'big gun' available in other areas of enforcement, see Chapter 4). Looking back, it might have been said that it was a poor choice in the first place not to allocate the franchise in a competitive process. Other systems have sought to deal with potential incumbency advantages by banning incumbents from bidding for franchises (British Rail was prohibited from bidding for passenger franchises in the UK in the 1990s) and by ensuring that particular new entrants are encouraged. In the present context, Frenezia's mayor needs to decide whether the basis of the service provider's demands are credible or based on strategic behaviour. In other words, the choice is between immediate termination, re-negotiation or punishment. This choice is further complicated by the ownership of Frenezia's rail provider as a publicly-owned entity.

Looking to the future, Frenezia's mayor also wishes to know under what conditions the oversight of future concessions could be improved. In other words, what are the conditions that facilitate an effective use of franchising as a regulatory device? Arguably, there are three key aspects. One is the availability of comparative information, either by using information from other franchises in Amnesia or by considering the splitting up of the Frenezia franchise. Furthermore, it requires the specification of particular standards, agreed provisions that deal with the valuation of assets, and the possibility of monitoring performance. This should then also facilitate the enforcement of franchise provisions. Indeed, this would also address, at least partially, the incumbency advantages that apply during renewal periods. In other words, what Frenezia and Amnesia need is the presence of competitors that can take on incumbents, but who, during the period of the franchise, are unlikely to undermine financial viability of the franchise by offering competing services. In other words, Amnesia requires a number of franchises being run by different companies that are likely to compete *for* the market, but whose services do not undermine the financial basis of the concession contract once the franchise has been allocated.

A separate issue is how the rolling stock should be organized. Some might argue that the rolling stock should be organized separately. This would create an entity that would be interested in modernizing and maintaining the rolling stock without being tied to the terms of the operation franchise. Such an entity could be placed in private hands or be publicly owned, for example, a Frenezia public enterprise. Hybrid forms of ownership may also be considered, for example, the UK railway infrastructure provider (Network Rail) was established as a non-dividend paying private company. Other views are likely to oppose such a separation of rolling stock and operational interests. The emphasis here will be placed on creating incentives for franchisees to invest and maintain their property.

Conclusion

The attraction of concessions or franchising has been that it promised to provide a device that mitigated issues of commitment credibility in contexts where there was weak administrative and political support for discretionary regulation. In addition, franchising was seen as a useful device to allocate temporary monopoly rights to deal with the subsidization (or receipt of lump sum payments) of public services in a way that promised allocative efficiency. However, in the case of developing country contexts, concessions rely on institutional settings that are extremely vulnerable as enforcement has proven to be highly problematic. This weakness is not only one of formal organizational competencies, but also one of the capacity of monitoring and enforcement agencies that appear powerless when faced with the organizational resources of often transnational providers of public services.

As noted, the attraction of the idea that competition *for* the market has been that it offers a convenient way of allocating the right to provide an efficient service, and, at the same time, effectively allocating the distribution of subsidies (in the case of loss-making services). The benefits of using such concession-type contractual arrangements have to be weighted against the considerable difficulties that go hand-in-hand with such arrangements. In other words, contractual relationships may not be a superior solution to discretionary – and agency-based – regulation at all. Most of all, franchising has proven to require considerable *ex post* discretionary oversight.

At the same time, the design of franchises, their auctions and their enforcement and termination offers important insights for the regulatory analyst, noting in particular the institutional incentives that arise from particular arrangements. Franchising also highlights the particular problems that apply to all regulation, namely the difficulties in prescribing particular standards and in enforcing them.

Chapter 10

Better Regulation

In response to a drop in the World Bank's 'Doing Business' ranking (www.doingbusiness.org), Amnesian business associations have been calling for an immediate response to the diagnosed problems with 'red tape' and the overall quality of regulation. Consumer groups similarly are complaining about a lack of a 'level playing field' in regulation, where business interests are accused of enjoying privileged access. The Prime Minister has therefore appointed a Better Regulation Czar to develop an effective approach towards 'better regulation' that will be supported by business and civil society groups. The Czar needs to develop a strategy towards 'better regulation' by choosing from the international 'high quality regulation' agenda. The Czar will also be required to monitor how ministries and agencies apply the chosen better regulation strategy. Finally, there is also confusion as to where the Czar and staff should be located within the overall organization of the Amnesian government: in particular whether the Czar should be located within the prime ministerial office or the economics ministry, or whether a free-standing agency should be established.

As an adviser to the Amnesian government, you are asked to prepare to set up the Czar and in particular consider:

- What are the key issues that impact on the quality of regulation?
- Which 'better regulation' tools are the most promising for improving regulatory quality?
- Within the overall structure of government, where should the Czar be located?
- What are the challenges the Czar is likely to face in developing and implementing the programme – and how would you address these problems?

What is 'better regulation'?

In Amnesia, as in any other country, accusations regarding the quality of regulation feature prominently in the press releases of business associations. Equally, regular calls for 'bonfires of red tape' repeatedly appear in ministerial announcements or coalition agreements. Businesses usually blame governments for regulating inconsistently or simply 'too much', politicians are accused of responding to demands for regulation in a knee-jerk, low-intelligence way, bureaucrats and regulators stand condemned for encouraging 'regulatory creep' by seeking to expand their jurisdiction and for 'going the last mile' to regulate against the risk of any potential incident (BRTF 2004). At the same time, business rather than regulators are the source of much regulation (and not just because of capture): instead of asking for delegated responsibility (as advocated by those in favour of principle-based regulatory strategies), businesses demand certainty about the intention and interpretation of rules, thereby expanding the rule-book through their own lobbying.

Such debates about the sources of 'too much' regulation are usually not confined to the regulation of particular domains, such as criticisms regarding inconsistent enforcement styles across environmental regulators when dealing with pollution. The debate regarding 'better regulation' has been directed at regulation more systematically, focusing on the quality of regulation across governmental bodies and seeking to establish principles that allow for a consistent approach towards standard setting, information gathering and behaviour modification.

Debates surrounding attempts to improve the quality of regulation in particular, and policy more generally, are certainly nothing new. Long-standing attempts at evaluating the costs and benefits can be traced back to large-scale infrastructure planning projects, such as flood control or road or railway building or closures and also to budget and project planning within government. Well-established debates regarding 'good regulation' have focused on various objectives, whether the demand to maximize efficiency or to meet alternative social objectives (such as environmental health) or, regardless of outcome, procedural justice (Prosser 1986; Baldwin 2010: 260–1). However, debates regarding better regulation have gained prominence over the past decade or so, as questions have been raised as to the justification of particular programmes that seemed to have hardly any positive impact, but appeared to impose considerable cost. One key factor for this growth in interest is the attention of international bodies that have increasingly moved into the study and dissemination of 'best practice' regarding 'regulatory governance', for example, the World Bank's *Doing Business* approach, or the OECD's interest in 'regulatory reviews' as part of its agenda to inform debates regarding regulatory principles (Lodge 2005; OECD 2010b, 2011). Similarly, the European Union (cf. for example, European Commission 2010: 543) has developed an extensive interest in 'better regulation' in response to demands from member states, especially the United Kingdom, Ireland, the Netherlands and Denmark.

The 'better regulation' agenda can be traced back to developments in the United States (with the rise of cost–benefit analysis) and the United Kingdom, especially the creation of a 'deregulation unit' in the then

Department for Trade and Industry. In the United States, interest in the cost of regulation has been long-standing and has spread across all aspects of US government, as exemplified by the introduction of cost-benefit analysis under President Reagan (Executive Order 12.291, 3 CFR 127(1982)). This executive order also introduced an oversight mechanism by granting the White House's Office of Management and Budget some (broadly defined) control over agency activities. Some years later (Executive Order 12.498), all agencies were required to submit annual plans, thereby establishing a system of virtual pre-clearance in the system (see Hahn and Sunstein 2002). Under President Clinton, greater discretion was granted for considering 'softer' aspects (such as equity), while the scope of the requirements was extended to independent agencies. Similarly, in the United Kingdom, various initiatives have come and gone, while the better regulation unit has moved from business department (the then Department of Trade and Industry) to the central government ministry, the Cabinet Office, and then back to the business department (at the time of drafting this chapter, the Department for Business, Innovation and Skills) (see Lodge and Scott 2003; Lodge and Wegrich 2009).

As noted, the 'better regulation' agenda is directed at all three components of regulation, namely standard setting, information gathering and behaviour modification:

- In relation to standard-setting, the 'better regulation' agenda is concerned with avoiding the problems of 'command and control', in particular in the context of 'alternatives to regulation' discussed in Chapter 5. In particular, the use of Regulatory Impact Assessments (RIAs) is advocated to inform rule choice (and the choice whether to regulate at all) and to avoid suboptimal choices, that is, adopting intrusive regulatory measures that will only produce limited benefit. Similarly, ideas of reviewing regulation or setting 'sunset' clauses are targeted to address issues of regulatory standard-setting.
- In relation to information-gathering, the 'better regulation' agenda has increasingly focused on inspection and information requirements that add to compliance costs. The introduction of the so-called Standard Cost Model in Europe has offered one device that seeks to measure and reduce the administrative cost of information-gathering. The aim is to minimize the administrative burden for business and citizens in complying with these obligations to provide information.
- In relation to behaviour-modification or enforcement, the 'better regulation' agenda has paid particular attention to compliance cost aspects, in particular regarding the conduct and consequences of inspections. As a result, ideas regarding risk-based regulation (Chapter 4) have emerged to justify the allocation of regulatory resources to those activities that are supposedly of systemic importance.

If one wanted to find shared themes across all three components of any regulatory regime, one could say that better regulation is about seeking to encourage the adoption of 'lowest cost' instruments that are least intrusive, evidence based and applied in a fair and consistent manner (OECD 2002, Baldwin 2010). However, such an agreement hides a much more significant degree of contestation regarding the justification of 'better regulation' approaches. As noted in our discussion of regulatory failure (Chapter 2), there are competing interpretations as to what makes for 'bad' regulation and how such failings should be addressed.

For some, improving the quality of regulation is about limiting or reducing regulatory activities. Arguably, the early approaches to presidential regulatory review in the United States (in the 1970s under Nixon and 1980s under Reagan) and impact assessment in the United Kingdom (in the mid-1980s under Thatcher) were about limiting regulation. For others, better regulation is about improving the rationality of decision making by requiring and ensuring that social welfare is properly taken into account. Attempts to improve 'rationality' are introduced by increasing the information on which regulatory decisions are made and by reducing the scope for arbitrary political interference. Such a view builds on the reform tradition of rational policy making that gave birth to approaches such as PPBS (Programming, Planning, and Budgeting System) and early forms of impact assessment (McGarity 1990). A third view regarding 'better regulation' aims to facilitate unbiased participation of all stakeholders and strengthen the deliberative element in regulatory design (Croley 2008: 61–8; Prosser 2010: 214). In other words, there is no single interpretation of what failings of better regulation are to be addressed, and as a consequence there is no uniform recipe for addressing these different interpretations of regulatory failings.

'Better regulation' instruments seek to improve regulation by using procedural means. This view of enhanced decision making through procedural devices therefore closely resembles those theories of regulation that emphasize the importance of 'deck-stacking'. Others call such imposition through procedural means 'meta-regulation' (the 'regulation of regulation'), or *second-order regulation*. Such second-order rules set standards that regulate specific aspects of the regulatory process – such as when, who and how other governmental units/levels and non-governmental actors should be consulted; if and what kinds of costs and benefits should be assessed; and how various alternative options should be considered to address a particular regulatory issue. Government departments are expected to comply with these standards and it is assumed that compliance with these procedural requirements will improve the quality of regulatory decision making, without requiring an assessment of the substance of the outcome for each individual law or regulation.

The rest of this chapter first provides an overview of the choices of better regulation tools (and their limitations) available to the Czar. We concentrate the discussion on 'better regulation' tools that focus on government-wide (or 'whole-of-government') regulatory policy, thereby mirroring the international regulatory reform discussion. The interest in 'better regulation' is therefore not in improving the regulatory quality in one domain or one agency/department, but in seeking to improve the quality of regulation across government. We then move the discussion to the governance of the better regulation agenda, that is, how and where the responsibility for better regulation should be located within government and how to monitor and enforce compliance.

Putting 'better regulation' tools to work

One initial question facing the Amnesian Better Regulation Czar is one of ambition. Should the Czar opt for an expansive agenda or concentrate on one single tool? Should s/he focus on the 'front end' of regulatory decision-making, namely prospective evaluations of proposals, or should s/he also consider the 'back end' of regulatory decision making, namely the existing stock of rules and regulations?

Focusing on one component or method would allow the Czar to develop a highly visible initiative that might increase the chances of developing a consistent reform programme. However, such a focused approach is likely to attract considerable criticism, ranging from those who are likely to accuse the Czar of a lack of ambition, of bias and of being the lapdog of some special interest or another. A comprehensive approach therefore would allow the Czar to please more diverse audiences at the same time, but such a strategy would potentially raise criticism that the Czar is seeking to please too many audiences at the same time, doing too many things badly, and therefore lacking any focus or agenda.

What tools are available to Amnesia's Czar? The toolbox offers instruments that affect different parts of the regulatory decision-making process: consultation is directed at the input stage, regulatory impact assessments (and various cost assessment exercises) target the policy formulation phase, while sunset clauses (time-limits placed on regulation) are directed at the evaluation stage of a regulation. Risk-based regulation (discussed in Chapter 4) targets the enforcement stage. Regulatory impact assessment is often regarded as the cornerstone of any better regulation strategy as it seeks to integrate different individual tools and structure the whole regulatory cycle (but the point of intervention is the input and design stage of the regulatory process).

In the following, we discuss the main tools that feature on the contemporary 'better regulation' agenda. Table 10.1 provides an overview of the different tools potentially available to the Amnesian Better Regulation Czar.

TABLE 10.1 *Overview of better regulation tools*

Tool	Procedural rule(s)	Implicit theory of cause and effect	Design choices	Unintended effects
Consultation	Publish draft regulation and invite societal actors to comment; need to take comments into account in final draft	'Level playing field' – unbiased participation Maximize input of evidence	Timing of consultation exercise	'Fig leaf' function; layering of formal and informal consultation; selective interpretation of input
Regulatory impact assessment	*Ex ante* evaluation of different regulatory options during drafting stage of regulation/policy	'Rational selection'; regulatory choice based on evidence of costs and benefits; separation of regulatory choice from political definition of goals	Inclusion/exclusion of dimensions of impact: breadth vs. depth of impact assessment; weighting of impact dimensions	'Box ticking' – formal compliance *Ex post* rationalization of prior policy choices
Cost measurement	Obligatory cost measurement during drafting stage; combined with an overall reduction target for administrative burden/compliance costs	'Objectivation'; quantification via target allows management of compliance cost reduction	Inclusion/exclusion of cost dimensions; ability to measure all relevant cost aspects	'Gaming' of data

(Continued overleaf)

TABLE 10.1 *continued*

Tool	Procedural Rule(s)	Implicit theory of cause and effect	Design choices	Unintended effects
Sunset clauses	Expiry date for regulations	'Reverse burden of proof'; burden of proof shifted to those favouring regulation; introduces critical evaluation of impacts at *ex post* stage	General versus selective time limits	'Rubber stamping'; automatism of uncritical extension
One-in, one-out	Termination of existing regulation for every new one	'Link stock and flow' Limiting knee-jerk response to regulate	Exceptions	'Gaming' of termination (zombie regulations, merging instead of termination)
Crowdsourcing	Online collection of proposals from all interested parties	'Wisdom of crowds'; counter-balance to inherent bias generated by consultation of entrenched interest groups	Need for moderation versus open bias, unacceptable comments	'Campaigning' Reinforcement of bias and power asymmetry

Source: Adapted from Wegrich (2011).

Consultation

A focus on 'stakeholder consultation' seeks to address the way in which departments and agencies conduct their consultation exercises, namely when, how, whom and in which form they consult throughout the various drafting stages of the regulatory decision-making process. For example, the 1946 US Administrative Procedure Act sets out consultation rules in the context of agency rule making. It contained the well-known 'notice and comment' procedure that obliges agencies to publish draft regulations in the federal register, invite comments and take these comments into account when drafting the final regulation (for a study of the interest group politics surrounding this procedure, see Yackee 2006). Such provisions could also include the obligation to place all hearings on public record. The general logic of the Administrative Procedure Act has been emulated by a range of governments, including parliamentary systems where consultation rules apply to the preparation of laws by ministries. Minimum standards of consultation (for example, minimum duration periods, the appointment of individuals responsible to oversee consultation exercises in departments and agencies) are regarded as a core requirement of any 'better regulation' strategy.

Such rules on consultation are supposed to create a level playing field between interested societal actors and thereby prevent biased participation in the rule-making process. Another rationale is that input from societal actors provides a critical source of evidence. A third rationale is to use consultation as a mechanism for controlling agencies and ministries, that is, by enabling diverse societal actors to monitor what agencies and ministries do. These three rationales lead to different prescriptions. Those who see the purpose of consultation as a means to ensure that further evidence is generated will see little value in supporting extensive citizen involvement ('why should we listen to ignorant laypeople?'). If consultation, then, is about gathering more evidence, the responsible agency should be the primary actor with full discretion as to which evidence should be recognized and which sources should be dismissed.

If, however, the primary interest in consultation is to ensure balanced interest representation, then the agency will have to show how it has sought to accommodate particular inputs (for example, how it has accommodated environmental interests when considering pollution limitations). We may even wish to use a different agency to conduct the consultation exercise; at a minimum, we may have to externally monitor the conduct of individual agencies' consultation exercises.

Among the critical design aspects of consultation procedures is the timing of the consultation. Consulting early in the regulatory process ensures that the information received will be processed when critical decisions have not yet been taken. However, such an early timing is likely to encourage highly diverse and unspecific comments that might be of limited use when it comes to the design of regulatory instruments and a consideration of potential unintended consequences.

In contrast, relying on consultation towards the end of the decision-making process means that early decisions that have already been taken will not be re-opened. It will particularly disadvantage those societal interests that may only be able to mobilize in the face of concrete proposals in contrast to those business interests that have been following the drafting process from the beginning. Indeed, it is likely that the generated evidence will allow the agency to re-interpret the submitted evidence in its own favour (i.e. the agency will stress supportive submissions to vindicate its preferred option).

Alternatively, a late consultation may force an agency into embarrassing public U-turns, climb-downs or other forms of fancy footwork to respond to those interests that are concentrated and well-resourced enough to call on favours at the expense of politically less useful interests (see Yackee 2006). Late consultation also means that agencies are likely to informally consult early in order to test the water. Thus, decision-makers shift the 'really important' consultation exercises to an earlier and informal stage, reintroducing biased participation in a more non-transparent arena.

In sum, there is a risk of consultation procedures becoming a fig leaf to legitimize options that have already been decided on. This risk has to be assessed against the opportunity of consultation procedures opening up the regulatory process at a relatively early stage and thereby introducing further elements of accountability. In addition, an argument has also been made that formal consultation exercises have proven to be 'too expensive' (they take time, attract the 'usual suspects' one already knows about or does not want to hear about and require staff resources, etc) and that they should therefore be turned into 'crowdsourcing' type activities in which interested parties comment on message-boards and other web-based platforms (discussed below).

Finally, there is always the problem of the 'staying power' of procedural means of influencing decision-making. If there is a demand for urgent action, are regulators and politicians willing to insist on a minimum 70 day consultation period (for example) before action? Will junior staff in agencies and ministerial departments, tasked with overseeing the procedural correctness of consultation exercises, be able to stand up to more senior staff should they diagnose errors on the consultation process? More importantly, such procedural guidance tells us little about 'who' should be consulted: should consultation include international as well as national actors, should it deal with 'unorthodox' scientific expertise or weigh differences between consulted parties (i.e. large companies versus small businesses)? In other words, consultation is certainly a critical component on any 'better regulation' agenda. However, on its own, it is unlikely to have much of a sustained impact.

Regulatory impact assessment

Regulatory impact assessment (RIA) procedures (also called impact assessment or regulatory impact analysis) are often regarded as *the* central better regulation tool (Radaelli and Meuwese 2010; Wegrich 2011). RIAs have therefore enjoyed widespread adoption across national and international governments and organizations (OECD 2002). RIAs are, at their core, an attempt to appraise the potential impact of regulatory interventions under consideration. This includes an assessment of different options, how compliance is likely to be obtained, what the impact on various parts of the economy and society is likely to be, and what the criteria for ongoing monitoring and evaluation might be. In short, RIAs are supposed to inform decision making. They are not supposed to determine which options are to be taken.

As noted, RIAs are seen as central to better regulation: they provide the evidence base for the rational selection of regulatory approaches, they encourage the avoidance of unnecessary regulation, and they offer a framework for the input of societal actors in consultation procedures. The basic appeal of RIAs is that they offer something for everyone in that they reduce information asymmetry problems: for those seeking 'better information', RIAs provide elements of prospective evaluation. For those seeking to 'control bureaucracy and politics', RIAs provide a constraining influence that reduce discretionary decision making (at least in theory). For those that demand more consistency in regulatory approaches, RIA procedures supposedly guide regulatory decision making and thereby make them more predictable. And, finally, for those that demand that regulation should be more transparent, RIAs offer the prospect of more transparent information provision that facilitates consultation and discussion regarding different options. In other words, RIAs offer everyone the promise of 'better regulation', but, in their application they are likely to favour some applications more than others.

In terms of procedural standards, RIAs prescribe discrete steps that agencies/departments have to follow when drafting regulation. The underlying problem and key regulatory objectives need to be presented in a transparent way and different regulatory and non-regulatory options should be considered (i.e. following the list of different approaches outlined in the chapter on 'alternatives to regulation'). In addition, external actors need to be consulted on the draft impact assessment. The procedural rules also direct attention towards particular types of economic analysis that are to be applied in assessing the cost and benefits of the different options and towards the various impact criteria that are to be included in the analysis (i.e. economic, social, environmental).

A major cross-national difference exists as to who is required to apply RIAs to their decision making. In the United States, the frontrunner of RIA regimes, RIAs are primarily used as a tool to control delegated rule-making of agencies (of the executive branch). In contrast, across European parliamentary democracies and the EU Commission RIAs are used to structure the preparation of laws and policies by ministerial departments (and some countries, such as the United Kingdom, apply RIAs to both, departments and regulatory agencies).

The initial popularity of RIAs in the United States and the United Kingdom was based on the promise of limiting regulatory activity (i.e. they were a tool to foster deregulation). Since the 1990s, the dominant interpretation of RIAs is to see them as tools to advance 'rational' decision making. RIAs are primarily all about basing regulatory choices on the systematic assessment of the impact of various options. In other words, the dominant underlying theory of RIAs is that they separate the setting of regulatory objectives ('we should do something about the quality of chocolate/the problem with lemonade binge-drinking') and the choice of regulatory strategy ('we should prohibit chocolate/rely on self-regulation to deal with lemonade binge-drinking'). Therefore, once a decision has been made that 'something' should be addressed the analysis underlying RIA is to illustrate the advantages (benefits) and disadvantages (costs) of different strategies (including the 'do nothing' strategy). Based on this analysis, and the input gathered through consultation exercises, the final choice of regulatory strategy can be taken. RIAs therefore supposedly force politicians or agency heads to choose between different options on the basis of an explicit comparison, while also requiring bureaucracies to consider a variety of strategies rather than follow fashions or well-established strategies in an unreflective way.

A series of problems have affected the way in which RIAs have been operationalized. One is the trade-off between depth and breadth in the required analysis. Breadth is achieved by including a variety of assessment criteria. However, if the analysis requires the comprehensive assessment of all potentially relevant dimensions, the resources required for such an undertaking will overwhelm any agency or department. As a consequence, any agency will have to make choices, opening them up to criticisms of bias. For example, those systems that do rely on a broad range of supposedly equally weighted assessment criteria, such as those of the EU Commission, have been criticized for placing their emphasis on economic impacts, defined in terms of compliance costs imposed on business, rather than social or environmental aspects (European Court of Auditors 2009: 36). At the same time, any clear commitment towards a single set of criteria (i.e. a sole focus on cost on business) would equally attract criticisms regarding bias.

A second problem, related to the problem of weighting, pertains to the demands for the extensive monetization of costs and benefits. Such monetization is practised most extensively in the US system of cost–benefit analysis (Shapiro 2011) and also in the insurance business. For example, the idea of 'value of (a statistical) life' is inherently linked to any calculation that seeks to understand whether the imposition of particular regulatory tools is justified in the context of lives saved. Thus, questions can be asked whether the imposition of an estimated US$ 1 million compliance cost burden on industry is justified in the context of the estimated numbers of lives saved per annum, which might be 3 or 3,000,000 lives. Such calculations should, in principle, easily inform decision making as to whether a particular measure 'makes sense'. However, the results of such quantification exercises are prone to considerable variations due to factor loading. Small changes in the factors lead to considerable changes in the results of cost-benefit calculations. A related question links to the differential distribution of costs and benefits. For example, the impact assessment that underpinned the federal Canadian government's discussion as to whether polar bears should be granted 'at risk status' noted that those communities that were actually exposed to polar bears were generally opposed to any protective status. This contrasted with those living in 'polar bear free' areas that were in favour of protective measures (Government of Canada 2011). In terms of costs and benefits, the study noted, among others, that polar bear subsistence hunting generated a total economic value of somewhere between CAN$ 245,545 and CAN$474,635 to Canada (pelts added CAN$1.16m), whereas polar bear viewing (eco-tourism) added CAN$ 7.2 million. Outweighing all these active values were 'passive values', namely the 'existence value' and the 'bequest value'. Here, it was estimated that the passive value amounted to CAN$6bn to Canada for the preservation of polar bears in Canada. The overall effect of granting 'at risk' status was 'likely to result in net benefits to Canadians' (Government of Canada 2011).

In short, the definition of costs and benefits turns into an arena for political contestation; for example, environmentalist groups (after dismissing the method for a long time) have become increasingly involved in discussions regarding the criteria relevant for cost–benefit and regulatory review exercises, seeing such processes as critical in advancing their agenda (Revesz and Livermore 2008). Similarly, the way in which costs are seen to be inflated (from the view of green-leaning groups) has made impact assessments a key battleground in environmental regulation.

A third methodological problem is an imbalance in terms of the certainty of costs in the short run and the potential uncertainty about long-term benefits. Studies suggest that RIAs suffer from a bias towards cost-overestimation as unanticipated benefits of future developments are not 'monetized'. In general, it can be said that the longer the time-period under consideration, the greater the potential for conflict over discount-rates and scenario-building exercises and their underlying assumptions.

Such problems are particularly pertinent when 'hard-nosed' impact assessment analysis on cost-benefit terms is not confined to a narrow technical problem (should mandatory car tyre pressure indicators be included in every newly constructed vehicle?), but applies to broader policy directions that may require a bundle of subsequent regulatory measures (for example, proposals assessing options on organ donations, see European Commission 2008). In such a context, quantitative cost-benefit analyses are accompanied by a broader 'multiple-criteria analysis' which includes more qualitative analysis and the qualitative scoring of the different options.

A further problem is putting RIAs into operation, in particular in terms of the demands they place on those having to conduct an RIA. One of the most frequent criticisms is that the completion of a particular RIA is little else than a 'box ticking' exercise that hardly qualifies as a 'hard-nosed' or 'deeply reflective' analysis of different options (see annual evaluations by the UK National Audit Office, for example NAO 2001). The quality of an RIA appears to be inversely related to the political salience of a particular measure; there is little appetite to delay the adoption of a ministerial priority through a time-intensive and 'unhelpful' RIA. In contrast, areas where nobody pays any political interest provides for the right environment for a more extensive RIA. More generally, the more extensive or comprehensive the requirements placed on RIAs are, the more likely it is that they will encourage formal compliance responses that hardly go beyond the 'box ticking' stage.

Having to go through the bureaucratic experience of a RIA may also have a direct effect on tool choice and may bias the consideration of initial alternatives in the first place (i.e. which options should we consider in order to reduce the time spent on doing an RIA?). Furthermore, RIAs have been found to be ill-adjusted to complex settings by simply calculating the cost of a single intervention from one single source (Baldwin 2010). Others have argued that the ever-growing demands of RIAs on decision making and other procedural constraints risk 'ossifying' rule-making behaviour by agencies. Such an ossification effect threatens to make agencies less responsive to changes in their environment either in delaying responses or in preventing rule-making outright (for empirical study, see Yackee and Yackee 2006, 2011). In other words, RIAs are shown to provide neither the consistency nor the rigour that enthusiasts of this 'better regulation' tool predicted (although it has been argued that there has been a mild deterrent effect on 'bad' regulation, Hahn and Tetlock 2008).

A related critique is that RIAs are initiated too late in the decision-making process and are hence not effective in influencing regulatory choices. As a consequence, they become *ex post* rationalizations of what has already been decided. The rationale of separating political formulation objectives and analytical search for the best option to meet these objectives breaks down when the selection of a particular course of action is already part of the political and administrative decision-making process. In practice it is more problematic to separate means and ends than the vision of rational policy making suggests (see Lindblom 1979); in particular under conditions of negotiated decision making, agreeing on some course of action is easier than agreeing on the underlying values and hence objectives.

In short, RIAs feature as part of the standard menu on national better regulation agendas. They are advocated by those hoping for a techno-cratic remedy to the political messiness that involves ministerial and regulatory decision making. Others advocate them as a tool to prevent bureaucratic over extension. However, practice suggests a more limited experience: RIAs do offer procedural means to gather information and to consult interests. However, they are unable to remove 'politics' and 'discretion' from the regulatory process. To strengthen the role of RIAs in the regulatory process would require an opening up of the analysis to allow for transparent comparison between the different weightings of values and more extensive examination of different options. However, the inevitable uncertainty regarding future effects, especially in terms of the demands placed on enforcement, means that such extensive exami-nation would inevitably deal with highly unreliable costings.

Cost measurement approaches

The third set of 'better regulation' tools deals with those regulations already in force. Cost measurement exercises have witnessed a 'policy boom' in Europe in the 2000s and, for a time, constituted a rallying point for those who regarded better regulation as being primarily about limit-ing and reducing regulation (Wegrich 2009). Encouraged by the perceived success of the so-called Standard Cost Model (SCM) in the Netherlands in the early Noughties, this measurement model rapidly diffused across national European governments and was endorsed as a key method for EU-level provisions. The SCM seeks to assess the *admin-istrative* costs to business (and also citizens) in complying with informa-tion obligations arising from regulation. It is therefore not about the overall cost of compliance (i.e. the cost of having to change behaviour) or the value of the regulatory objective per se. The aim is to measure the 'total' administrative cost of existing regulation (so called baseline measurement) and then to seek to reduce the total by a set target. Moreover, the SCM approach seeks to constrain policy formulation as the estimated administrative costs of new regulations are added to the 'total stock' of administrative costs of a department. SCM has therefore been integrated into established RIA procedures (and hence deals with the 'stock' of existing and the 'flow' of new regulation).

At the heart of SCM is the quantification of the administrative burden.

Prior to the 'invention' of SCM, the assessment of the actual effects of cutting red tape and administrative simplification exercises proved to be problematic and relied on perceived (or felt) effects. In contrast, SCM introduces a 'management by objectives' approach (the reduction target). The effects of administrative simplification measures are calculated by repeating a simplified baseline measurement exercise at the end of a given time period. The aim is to achieve a particular cost reduction target – most countries set an arbitrary target of 25 per cent. In addition to the encouragement of meeting set targets, SCM is also about encouraging a learning process for those who are involved in standard-setting. One particularly widespread criticism has been that those thus involved pay little attention to the costs of information-gathering. Thus, SCM forces those designing rules and standards to take notice of the administrative burden generated by 'their' regulation. For example, in the German context, the requirement to perform an SCM measurement forced bureaucrats in the federal ministries (some say, for the first time) to consider the actual number of regulatees and the costs imposed on them, something that in the past had remained mostly a concern for those bureaucrats working more closely at the 'coalface', namely at the *Land* (state) and local level.

The key challenge for any cost measurement approach is the choice of 'costs' that are to be included in the measurement exercise. The SCM focuses on a very specific cost dimension, namely the administrative burden. This administrative burden, however, is only a fraction of the overall compliance cost of any regulation. Such a narrow definition of cost is both an advantage and a disadvantage. On the one hand, the limited focus allows for a relatively simple measurement method (largely a time and motion study of individuals having to complete paperwork). This is a task that regulatory and policy bureaucrats should be expected to be able to carry out with some consistency and precision (albeit after some training). Furthermore, such a limited focus eliminates (or avoids) wider political controversies regarding the value of the particular regulatory interventions overall. For example, SCM focuses on the ways in which companies have to report on their emission reduction strategy rather than on the desirability of the emission reduction strategy itself. It therefore seeks to reduce the scope for wider political and administrative conflict by appearing to target administrative costs alone.

On the other hand, the disadvantage of such a narrow approach towards cost is that SCM might only be of limited relevance in addressing the complaints about 'bad regulation'. Administrative costs are only one aspect that businesses face when complying with regulation. A marginal reduction of administrative costs for a large number of businesses may lead to an overall large cost reduction in aggregate, but may be of little relevance to the individual firm (in other words, a time saving of 15 minutes in the completion of some paperwork in its accounting department is unlikely to contribute greatly to a firm's overall productivity). In response, some countries have widened the scope of SCMs to include broader compliance costs. However, such widening comes at the expense of methodological precision.

Another, related, contested issue is whether benefits should be included (and if so how) or not. Some argue that cost assessment only makes sense if observed cost can be compared with observed benefits. European governments have, so far, shied away from adopting such an approach of cost-benefit analysis – mostly because this requires more experience of measurement methods in government, but also because the quantification of benefits is politically contested. A recurring argument is that putting a price tag on environmental benefits is not appropriate and that choices regarding the level of protection should be a matter for political decision making. Another argument, already mentioned, is that the quantification of benefits (and costs) becomes increasingly problematic when broader policy options rather than technical regulations are considered. It is therefore important to consider that the 'harder' cost–benefit analysis approach in the United States applies to agencies, whereas the limited cost measurement exercises and the more qualitative RIAs target ministerial departments in particular.

An attempt to develop SCM towards a broader cost measurement (and management) approach has been to set 'regulatory budgets' for departments and regulators. The key argument in favour of a regulatory budget approach has been that most 'better regulation' tools focus on one individual regulatory proposal. A regulatory budget approach is said to provide a wider and systemic agency wide (or even government wide) perspective on introducing regulations. Regulatory budgets consist of the sum of the compliance costs imposed by any one organization on regulatees (business and/or citizens) – in the same way as the financial budget accounts for all 'expenditures'.

One way to use 'regulatory budgets' is to set an overall target and demand an overall 'reduction', whereas a variant would require that all new or reformed regulatory proposals should remain 'within budget' (Doern 2009). Such an approach, on the one hand, would allow for more oversight over individual departmental and regulatory activities, and might even include the potential benefits of regulatory proposals (which would, however, require a complex and sophisticated administrative machinery). On the other hand, however, a 'regulatory budget' approach quickly turns into a 'deregulation' approach in that it limits the discretion of regulatory agencies to respond to emerging crises, or to externally set agendas (such as those set by international summit meetings). Furthermore, any allowance for major agenda items (such as 'climate change', or 'banking collapse') would quickly lead to any regulatory proposal being classified as addressing climate change- or banking meltdown-related issues. Furthermore, setting budgets for supposedly autonomous agencies might be seen as a major imposition of political control. It is these problems and limitations that led to the abandonment of proposals that would have introduced regulatory budgets in the United Kingdom in 2009.

The most important limitation that affects all cost measurement exercises is that they encourage extensive 'gaming' of data. For example, in the context of SCM, reported gaming includes the inflation of costs during the initial baseline measurement which then makes compliance over time relatively straightforward as reductions can easily be achieved and 'measured'. A related strategy is to dispute the validity of early measurements and claim that those measurements had been incorrectly low. Once the starting position has been belatedly set at a much higher level, cost savings become much less difficult to achieve. Furthermore, small changes in the parameters of the SCM equations, in particular the number of affected companies and the time required to carry out administrative activities can lead to substantial changes in the administrative costs 'measured'. When the trust in the created numbers is low, the system of targets and management by objectives is at risk of losing credibility. This has been the case in the United Kingdom, where reported reductions were not matched by businesses' perceptions of administrative burdens (cf. National Audit Office 2008). As a result, overall interest in SCM declined rapidly.

Sunsetting, one-in, one-out and crowdsourcing

A further set of 'better regulation' provisions focuses on *ex post* evaluation of regulatory activities with the aim to update or terminate particular regulatory provisions. The key regulatory problem to be addressed with these sets of tools is to deal with the 'tombstone' or 'dead-hand' character of much regulation, where rules survive on the rule-book long past their sell-by date. Just like 1980s pop-songs that bemoaned that the sun always shines on TV, the sun supposedly never set on useless or defunct regulation.

To deal with such *mortmain* effect, the idea to introduce so-called *sunset clauses* has been regularly put forward. These clauses set an expiry date on laws, statutes or administrative regulations. This expiry date is said to encourage review and evaluation activities, as well as the mobilization of affected constituencies. Industries mobilize to demand the continuation or the abandonment of particular safety provisions, while consumer groups would also have a focused moment to campaign for or against particular provisions. In the light of these *ex post* considerations, decision makers then take a view as to whether to renew, modify or terminate particular provisions – as a result regulation stays 'forever young'.

Variations on sunsetting, where provisions are terminated until explicitly reinstated, exist. Examples include mandatory review clauses that, however, do not require an explicit commitment towards renewing any particular regulatory provision. One further variant is 'market review' clauses that apply in particular to utility regulators. Every five years or so, a group of experts is obliged to report on the degree of competition within regulated markets and to recommend whether focused regulation should persist or not (i.e. should competitive markets exist, regulation, such as price-setting should be withdrawn). Such a provision allows for an open exchange as to whether markets are competitive or not. However, it also introduces considerable interest-group politics, for example, between those interests that benefit from asymmetric regulation against incumbent providers, and those incumbents who call for relaxations to counter the disadvantages of asymmetric regulation. Such conflicts become even more political where state-owned enterprises are involved.

Sunset clauses emerged in the 1970s in the United States, in particular at the state level. They were used to investigate how agencies had used their legislative mandate for rule making. Over the past three decades, sunsetting has been enthusiastically embraced by various red tape busting exercises across European countries, Australia, New Zealand and Canada. In Europe (and especially in the United Kingdom as part of the 2010 conservative-liberal coalition government) the main focus was on sunsetting primary as well as secondary legislation. The burden of proof was placed on those that wished to prolong the lifetime of the regulation.

Ex post evaluations via sunsetting and equivalent provisions offer politicians and bureaucrats (and interest groups) a 'get out of jail' option should they come to repent earlier regulatory decisions. In contrast, prospective evaluations, for example, through RIAs, are supposed to stop politicians and bureaucrats from regulating in haste and repenting at leisure. The primary emphasis therefore is to stop regulatory provisions from remaining on the statute book regardless of their usefulness. Therefore, if politicians and bureaucrats feel that they need to regulate in order to please public opinion regardless of evidence base, sunset clauses allow them to suggest that 'irrational' regulation will automatically pass away as public opinion moves to other areas.

However, whether sunsetting offers a useful method to evaluate regulatory instruments is more than questionable. In particular, if regulatory review bodies, such as the Amnesian Czar, are confronted by a large number of sunsetting provisions, they may be overwhelmed when faced with concerted special interests and domain-specialists. It is questionable whether Czars (or anyone else) have the time and resources to conduct extensive evaluations, especially as they may also be facing demands to regulate in other first-time domains and to conduct extensive RIAs. Furthermore, it could be argued that sunsetting is likely to worsen regulatory biases instead of addressing them: sunsetting will only mobilize those actors that benefit most or 'hurt most' from particular regulatory interventions (some interests may also have been so fatally wounded by regulatory interventions that they no longer mobilize). In other words, sunsetting benefits those concentrated and highly affected constituencies at the expense of diffuse constituencies that may be unable to mobilize.

Sunsetting, therefore, could be argued to be an excellent recipe for capture – despite its official justification to be able to do just the opposite. In other cases, regulatory sunsetting reviews may not attract any interest whatsoever, leaving domain specialists, such as regulatory agencies, in a position to 'fix' the result. Such a risk can be limited when the criteria and methodological standards for evaluating regulations under a sunsetting regime are set by a 'better regulation unit', such as the Amnesian Czar, in advance. In general, therefore, sunsetting might appear as a convenient tool to remove the dead hand of regulation at set intervals, but overall it hardly removes political processes from shaping which items are on the agenda and in what form.

A second approach, called *one-in, one-out* rules, is aimed to facilitate critical review of regulation and termination. Such rules, enacted in the United Kingdom in 2010, prescribe departments to terminate an existing regulation for every new one that is proposed or to meet the regulatory burden of incoming regulation by the removal of an equivalent burden from those provisions that are currently in force. One-in, one-out provisions are therefore a less ambitious variant to the regulatory budget approach, noted above.

This approach is supposed to operate in two ways. First, it is supposed to suppress the instinct to respond to any pressure to 'do something' with a new regulation. Second, it is supposed to facilitate the cleaning-up of dysfunctional, defunct or poorly designed regulation. Although only limited evidence regarding the practicality of this tool exists, the primary disadvantage is its bluntness. When under pressure, regulators will develop 'creative compliance' means to circumvent the 'one-in, one-out' requirement. A smart regulatory manager will engage in some early planning to set up a stock of older regulations with limited relevance ('zombie regulations') that can be scrapped without hurting anyone or changing the substance of enacted regulations. A similar strategy is to inflate the costs of the 'outgoing' regulation and to minimize the costs of the incoming one. In the United Kingdom, it was said that the calculated costs of outgoing regulation was cut by up to 50 per cent after a review (*Financial Times*, 25 July 2011). Another strategy is to merge rather than terminate regulations, thereby 'cutting' regulation.

A third tool for regulatory review and termination is the use of online consultation to collect proposals from societal actors on how to deal with the existing stock of regulations. Drawing on the popularity of employing 'web 2.0' tools, this approach has been called *crowdsourcing*. Many variations of this idea have been tried out by a number of governments. Across German states (Länder), an online 'bureaucracy censure' (*Bürokratieschelte*) was popular for a short while. Citizens were invited to post complaints about bureaucratic malpractice and government was encouraged to respond. In 2011, the German federal consumer ministry subsidized the launch of a 'citizen reporting portal' that allowed consumers to notify and complain about potentially misleading labelling on food products. More broadly, the UK government has invited online complaints and comments on the quality of regulations. In 2011, the British government took this approach to another level: it posted, at regular intervals, various areas of legislation on a specific website. Anyone was invited to comment on 'what works and what's NOT and what can be simplified and what can be scrapped' (www.redtapechallenge.cabinetoffice.gov.uk/home/index/, 30 January 2012). Government departments were then asked to evaluate the comments received and to develop responses to deal with 'red tape'.

The underlying idea that feeds this attempt to web-ize consultation is to draw on the fashionable idea of the 'wisdom of crowds' (Surowiecki 2004; Howe 2009) to collect evidence about problematic regulations (or to 'test the mood' regarding potential regulatory interventions). Furthermore, the online channel allows supposedly unbiased participation and puts any citizen in the same position as lobby groups with vested interests in the field. However, it is at best questionable how (un-)biased such types of consultations really are. Crowdsourcing might be an approach that offers a 'cheap' alternative to formal consultation exercises. However, it is also faced with considerable limitations: it is more or less impossible to know who the respondents are, attention and responses are driven by newspaper or industry campaigns, the quality of comments is, at best, limited, and it requires constant monitoring of websites for fear of defamatory or other kinds of defacing activity. In other words, a reliance on crowdsourcing and the 'wisdom of the crowds' is problematic on two counts: it remains largely uninformed and ill-targeted regarding 'the crowd' and it is unlikely to generate 'wisdom'.

In other words, all three approaches that were seen to be able to clean out the Augean Stables of left-over, defunct or dysfunctional regulation come with the risk of further side-effects. Such side-effects will become ever more prevalent the more reliance is placed on these approaches. Therefore, these *ex post* evaluations should be used in moderation.

Tool combinations and interaction

As noted, the ambition of the international 'better regulation' agenda is to offer a systemic response to the inherent problem of regulation that imposes costs but adds little overall benefit. This systemic character applies to two aspects. First, it is about setting procedural rules that apply to rule making across organizations and domains. Second, it is about applying various tools across the whole 'life cycle' of regulation (from the well-informed cradle of regulatory initiatives to their well-considered grave).

Various promoters of better regulation claim that only the full-fledged application of the 'better regulation' toolbox will lead to a sustainable improvement in regulatory quality. However, if we consider the logic of the instruments and the underlying objectives they are supposed to realize, we can detect substantial tensions and trade-offs – both across different instruments (discussed in this chapter) and between 'better regulation' instruments on the one hand and other approaches to improving regulation (discussed throughout the volume) on the other hand:

- The general tension between different objectives of better regulation is reflected in particular in the relation between RIA and SCM (and other cost measurement exercises). RIAs have been advocated primarily as a tool for rational decision making and evidence-based regulation. SCM is largely about 'deregulation'. Integrating cost measurement exercises into RIA procedures has therefore created considerable tensions. The SCM *ex ante* measurement requires a substantial amount of departmental attention and resources. This displaces other activities relevant for impact assessment. The rivalry between RIA and SCM objectives has become particularly prominent in the setting of ministerial departments (rather than regulatory agencies) where RIAs have already been well-established and the SCM was 'layered' on top of the existing provisions. Such a 'layering' brought the 'deregulatory' instincts of the SCM agenda into conflict with the dominant view of RIAs as being about enhanced information, *better* regulation and, hence, 'improved rationality'. In addition, tensions within SCM added to the overall confusion. Those who regarded 'administrative burdens' as a first step towards the study of all 'compliance cost' came into conflict with those who purposefully separated administrative cost considerations from wider 'deregulatory' views regarding the need to cut all compliance cost (to business). These multiple compromises – within SCM and between SCM and RIA practices – proved to be short lived, especially as business continued to complain about compliance costs regardless of governmental announcements that praised the achievement of 25 per cent burden reductions. As a consequence, the 'deregulatory' view demanded an expansion of SCM to 'really' target compliance costs more broadly, while those advocating RIAs as a 'technocratic tool' demanded the abandonment of the SCM and the return to a broader and more balanced assessment criteria.

- Further tension emerged between impact assessments and cost-benefit assessments on the one hand and approaches to reform enforcement, that is, risk-based and smart regulation, on the other. The core argument (summarized by Baldwin 2010) is that requirements to conduct all sorts of quantitative assessments place a considerable bureaucratic burden on the policy bureaucrats who have to conduct or commission RIAs and justify regulatory proposals. To reduce the compliance costs caused by the demands of RIAs, officials who are forced to draft regulations and justify them via RIAs, tend to opt for simpler regulatory designs that are easily quantifiable. Those approaches such as complex combinations of state and non-state regulation, that are more difficult to 'cost', are therefore at an inherent disadvantage – although they are seen as 'smart' and preferable by some regulatory observers. Bureaucrats and regulators are therefore inclined to select simple regulatory approaches and limit themselves to minor changes to existing regulations. Such biases conflict with the advice of smart and risk-based regulation to combine various forms of state and self regulation.
- Indeed, it might be argued that RIAs miss the basic insight that most regulation originates from multiple sources, and that the key debate regarding regulatory burdens is often the cumulative effect of multiple regulatory activities, rather than the cost-benefit profile of one single intervention. Furthermore, RIAs assume a 'static' picture of regulatory enforcement (if any), and such a reductionist view conflicts with those who see regulatory enforcement in particular as an interactive and dynamic relationship that requires gradual escalation mechanisms, such as those illustrated by 'responsive regulation'.
- Finally, tensions can be identified between 'administrative simplification' approaches (SCM and related approaches) and risk-based regulation in terms of the role of 'information obligations'. While both approaches are about limiting unnecessary bureaucratic burden, the former defines 'information obligations' as a bureaucratic burden, while for the latter such information constitutes the essential precondition for devising inspection and intervention plans that are targeted according to risk. In short, administrative simplification makes enforcement even more 'low intelligence'.

Such tensions are widely ignored in the 'official' rhetoric of better regulation promoters, but they explain why the regulatory reform agendas vary cross-nationally and why they are volatile over time – reflecting the tensions and trade-offs between different objectives of the 'better regulation' agenda as well as between different tools and their logic of intervention. Managing such tensions is difficult, in particular in the face of competing demands. Whether the Amnesian Better Regulation Czar will be able to steer a clear path through these trade-offs and inherent limitations is therefore more than questionable.

Governing 'better regulation'

The idea to institutionalize a Czar is partly motivated to send a clear signal to business associations that something will be done about regulation. At the same time, doing 'something' requires mechanisms to gather information about the ways in which government departments and regulatory agencies operate 'better regulation' tools and it also requires means to promote compliance with these instruments.

As noted, 'better regulation' relies on procedural devices to steer the behaviour of those making rules in predictable ways. However, there are inherent problems with the imposition of better regulation procedures as such procedures directly interfere with the organizational autonomy of organizations. In other words, imposing regulatory impact assessments or standard cost models on regulatory agencies may be interpreted as a direct assault by central government on agency autonomy. It is therefore unsurprising that better regulation usually receives little but lukewarm (if not chilly) support among regulators and other ministerial departments. Given this inherent disinterest in following procedural requirements (especially when they do not have legal force), our Amnesian Czar requires dedicated structures and mechanisms to govern better regulation.

What are the different options for institutionalizing better regulation within government? A range of organizational solutions have been explored across OECD countries. The Amnesian model that combines a Czar with an expert commission anchored in the Prime Minister's office comes close to the UK model of the Better Regulation Executive (until 2008). A different option would be to establish a commission as an independent watchdog that acts on the basis of statutory jurisdiction and is not directly accountable to any minister or the head of government. Following the Dutch 'Actal' model, Germany, Sweden and the United Kingdom have established such a watchdog unit. Other options are a unit within a ministry or the head of government's office (such as OIRA in the White House's Office of Management and Budget) or within a non-departmental agency (such as in Denmark with respect to the SCM exercise).

All institutional solutions have their strengths and weaknesses (see Table 10.2). While the advantage of a central unit in the prime minister's or president's office shows the direct line of political support from the top (which is why the OECD has been advocating this solution), such top-level political support might be volatile given shifting agendas. Another advantage is that prime ministers' offices already have a responsibility for monitoring departmental policy making and for 'enforcing' a government-wide 'policy-line'. The downside is that such a position might lead to the perception that 'better regulation' tools are little else but attempts at strengthening control from the centre (cf Radaelli and Meuwese 2010).

TABLE 10.2 *Institutionalization of better regulation*

Type of unit	Example	Advantages	Disadvantages
Independent 'watchdog' unit	Dutch 'Actal'; German 'Normenkontrollrat'	Neutral arbiter able to 'speak truth to power'	Dependence on formal intervention powers; decoupling from ministerial departments
Czar and commission at centre of government	UK Better Regulation Executive in the Cabinet Office (until 2007)	Combines 'clout' of experts/ managers with integration in machinery of government	Contested role of non-governmental experts in the machinery of government
Unit in head of government's office	US OMB/OIRA	Direct support from top politicians; control of department's already core business	Dependence on volatile agenda of top politicians
Unit in a ministry	UK Better Regulation Executive in the Department for Business, Innovation and Skills (initially Department for Business, Enterprise and Regulatory Reform) (since 2007)	Alignment of departmental objectives with unit's mission	Limited power of interdepartmental intervention
Agency	Danish Commerce and Companies Agency	Specialization and expertise of staff	Asymmetric relation to ministries, high dependence on ministerial support and formal intervention powers

Opting to establish the Czar as a unit within a particular ministry (such as finance, economics/business, public administration) might encourage a more sustained interest within the department – *if* the better regulation programme is in tune with the traditional policy direction of that department and the current agenda of the minister. The downside is the limited leverage when it comes to intervening in other departments. A minister for agriculture is less likely to accept the demands for better RIAs coming from the minister for business than if this demand comes with the authority of the prime minister.

Establishment as an Independent Watchdog unit would allow the

Czar to play the role of a 'neutral' arbiter of the better regulation mission, without any particular departmental agenda. However, such units quickly become sidelined and detached from the overall governmental agenda, especially when budgetary and other forms of political attention move to different policy areas. Table 10.2 summarizes this discussion. While each institutional set-up brings its own advantages and disadvantages, the key to any successful Czar is to maintain full backing from the very top.

The key governance challenge affecting the Amnesian Czar, however, does not rely on the organizational set-up, or the choice of procedural means to influence ministerial departments or regulatory agencies.

In terms of seeking to secure compliance across ministerial departments, the inherent problem affecting the Czar's effectiveness is linked to the way in which decisions are made within any governmental system. In general, any unit within governmental department enjoys only limited 'programme autonomy'. Units within departments do not develop policies, programmes or regulations in an autonomous way, but need to coordinate with other units in government. The particular unit in government that has primary responsibility for a piece of regulation is usually able to set the agenda by drafting a particular regulation without much direct involvement from other units. However, this initial draft will be checked and moderated in a process of compromise-seeking with other units. This sequential procedure for coordinating policy proposals in which all participants are primarily concerned about their autonomy and organizational 'turf' has been called 'negative coordination' by Scharpf (1994). Such a decision-making process of negative coordination tends to reject any attempt to develop integrated policy solutions to complex problems. Instead it allows the parallel processing of multiple regulatory proposals at the same time on the basis of minimum common denominator decision-making.

Policy-making through negative coordination (or the avoidance of stepping on other unit's jurisdictional turf) does not apply to Better Regulation Czars. Imposing procedural guidelines on ministries is inherently about violating turf and imposing restrictions on autonomy. Furthermore, departments and agencies are in a position to draw on superior expertise and well-organized political support in their regulatory domain to fend-off 'better regulation' oriented interventions. Such information asymmetry problems may be challenged through additional recruitment of staff who 'mirror image' regulatory decision making in departments and agencies. Such a hiring policy would, however, provoke criticisms regarding the supposedly bloated bureaucracy that surrounds 'better regulation'.

In some cases, prime-ministerial or other top-level support can be marshalled to condemn the lack of enthusiasm for adopting 'better regulation' instruments. However, even high-profile Czars will only be able to call on such political favours on rare occasions. For example, a former economics minister in Germany noted how his attempt at introducing an 'anti red tape' programme in the mid-2000s failed because of the daily 'urban warfare' in which all parties fought over single lines and paragraphs. In this particular German example, a list with hundreds of proposals was eventually reduced to a package of about 20 minor regulatory changes (the primary benefactors being those receiving high consultancy fees). In short, any attempt by a 'generalist' better regulation unit to 'fight' the superior expertise and resources of 'specialists' within departments and regulatory agencies is likely to fail. In the wider context, this failure of 'better regulation' units to interfere directly with individual regulatory proposals resembles the criticisms marshalled against 'oversight' or 'police-patrol' control mechanisms, noted in Chapter 2. There it was argued that so-called 'police-patrols' were high-cost devices in that they had to be permanently attentive, but of limited use as enforcement would be highly problematic.

As a result, controlling compliance with 'deck-stacking' is inherently problematic. As noted in Chapter 6 on the problems affecting regulation inside government, seeking to control other departments remains problematic, regardless of whether this control is based on substance or on procedural compliance. The most widely used tool of hierarchical control in the context of better regulation is to grant the Czar and the better regulation unit (or any other administrative arrangement) the power of veto regarding the progress of a draft proposal. If the regulatory proposal has not complied with 'better regulation' requirements, the draft is sent back to the respective departmental unit/agency. For example, in the United Kingdom all regulatory proposals, since 2010, had to be vetted by a 'Regulatory Policy Committee' in terms of the quality of their RIA (RPC 2011). A report in July 2011 noted that 31 per cent of regulatory proposals (a total of 278) had been given a 'red flag' (signifying that the RIA was 'not fit for purpose').

Frequent use of the power to declare RIAs as 'not fit for purpose' comes with considerable political implications, as it might be seen as a direct attack on the ministerial preferences or on the autonomy and quality of decision-making by regulatory agencies. In other words, the higher the status of better regulation within government, the more likely it is that there will be sustained conflict between different objectives within government and the more likely it is that ministerial departments and regulatory agencies will seek to avoid conflict with 'better regulation' provisions by gaming the systems or through other means of creative compliance (such as by fiddling with administrative burden calculations or by carefully designing impact assessment calculations).

Chapter 6 illustrated three alternative modes to hierarchical oversight type controls within government. These alternatives also apply to debates regarding 'better regulation' policies. Mechanisms of *rivalry* are mainly used in the form of naming and shaming of the quality of draft regulations. For example, the European Commission's Impact Assessment Board publishes its opinion on the quality of the Impact Assessments carried out by Directorates General (DG) (European Commission 2010). DGs have made a substantial effort to improve the quality of Impact Assessments to avoid any reputational damage (Tiessen *et al.* 2008). Similarly, the reports by the UK Regulatory Policy Committee, noted above, allowed for a comparison of departmental performance regarding the 'flagging' of RIAs' quality. The units responsible for monitoring the administrative burden measurements by ministerial departments in the Netherlands, Germany and Sweden published their opinions as an attachment to the draft law that goes to Cabinet. The threat of a critical opinion is the most powerful bargaining chip of these units. The incentive to game the data also exists when relying on public naming and shaming or other forms of using competition (such as league tables).

Control through *mutuality*, that is, peer-review and mutual learning, has been given a trial through the creation of a network of better regulation 'satellite' units across government departments. The staff members in the satellite units are supposed to mediate between the central better regulation unit and the policy specialists in the departments, thereby fostering informal exchange and mutual learning. The problem with such a networking strategy is that these satellite units lack 'clout' within the departments; they are not regarded as contributing to core departmental business, and are often staffed with junior people. Career prospects within departments depend on contributing to departmental goals and not on enforcing cross-cutting policies such as better regulation within the departments. Hence, satellite units quickly go native within the department or will be marginalized (this contrasts with 'satellite units' linked to the finance minister, where the budgetary implications of a good relationship are highly pertinent and where the career incentive among staff in satellite units is to return bigger and better outcomes to their 'home' finance department).

Given the limitations of each mode of control, a combination across different modes of control seems appropriate for our Amnesian Better Regulation Czar. Some combinations may be more problematic than others, that is, a strong reliance on competitive forces might undermine the motivation to engage in mutual learning and open discussion of problems and failures. The combination of some hierarchical powers with the careful use of 'naming and shaming' has provided an effective combination of control modes. An element of mutuality, in particular at the working level, between the central unit and the departmental units can been seen as a requirement for effective control.

Finally, the basic problem between better regulation units and those primarily responsible for drafting regulation is inherently one of a lack of common understanding regarding substantive regulatory goals – no procedural device will be able to bridge disputes on competing visions of substantive objectives (or 'the good life'). The so-called econocrats beavering away in better regulation units are likely to have little time for the aesthetic value of ballet or other arts projects.

Conclusion

In general, the better regulation agenda is shaped by two somewhat contradictory forces. On the one hand, better regulation is about controlling all those who regulate, draft regulations and those who call for regulation. A key common thread across better regulation tools has been a reliance on 'analysis' that supposedly counters purely political or bureaucratic ad hoc choices.

On the other hand, the better regulation agenda is based on an appeal to a variety of non-compatible views regarding regulation. Some see better regulation instruments as technocratic tools to improve regulation, others as a means to allow for advanced conversations regarding the purpose and direction of regulation, while others see 'better regulation' as a means to reduce regulation. These differences are reflected in the design of different better regulation tools.

It is therefore difficult to offer any straightforward recommendations as to what our Amnesian Better Regulation Czar is supposed to do. Most of all it is difficult to evaluate the effectiveness of different better regulation tools (although most evaluations point to rather moderate impacts). Any evaluation is limited, given the way in which better regulation seeks to address problems through 'procedure'. Furthermore, any evaluation will be contested as the competing ideals regarding better regulation will come to different judgements as to what a desirable outcome is. Furthermore, whether 'better regulation' is understood in terms of 'enhanced rationality' or in terms of 'cutting red tape', for example, is likely to depend on short-term political moods.

As a result, it is possible to predict three potential futures for the Amnesian Better Regulation Czar. One scenario is that ambitious initiatives will be quickly forgotten as political agendas change. Rather than following through on these initiatives to the stage of nitty-gritty implementation, monitoring and enforcement, 'better regulation' will remain at the stage of ambitious reform announcements with yet a further initiative following the previous one. While such a 'symbolic politics' scenario might serve the purpose of being recognized as a front runner in international reform debates, it will also fuel cynicism regarding the agenda within and outwith the Amnesian government.

A second potential scenario is one of increasing politicization of better regulation. The 'tougher' the Amnesian Prime Minister and the Czar try to shape regulation in departments and agencies, the more 'better regulation' tools will become the subject of power battles. Different constituencies will try to influence the design of 'better regulation' tools so that they support their policy preferences across governmental policy making. Regulators will accuse the Czar of threatening their autonomy. For example, what types of impacts are assessed, and how, will become subject to contestation across advocacy coalitions, for example, between 'deregulators' and 'environmentalists'. Such second order politics will centre around supposedly apolitical and technical aspects of impact assessment, that is, the inclusion/exclusion of assessment criteria and methodological details. Such a development would lead to politics and policy making becoming more complex, rather than increasing transparency and broadening participation. It will favour special interests that are able to play to the tune of the new 'techno-econocracy' of regulation.

A third scenario starts with the acceptance that different regulatory domains are inherently self-referential and will reject external 'top down' advice and are unlikely to pay much attention to 'better regulation' on their own. The Amnesian Czar would seek to embed ideas about regulatory quality as a point of reference in regulatory conversations, in particular in cross-departmental/agency interaction. This requires some tolerance towards rival institutional perspectives and an understanding of potential sources of resistance and reluctance (Peci and Sobral 2011). It also requires a hybrid approach with strong emphasis on facilitating mutual learning and a smart use of 'encouragement' via limited oversight and transparency. The challenge of this approach is that it does not produce quick wins and easily communicable results. It may be normatively the most desirable scenario, but is possibly the most unrealistic.

Chapter 11

Risk and Regulation

The Amnesian food safety authority is considering the licensing of a new type of food. The new food, called Vanessa (after its inventor), promises to be the next 'super food' as it offers high nutritional value and low calories. However, should Vanessa be kept for too long beyond the 'use by' date, it develops into a form of broccoli without any health benefits. Furthermore, in 0.02 per cent of cases, the Vanessa-turned-broccoli has been found to cause severe food poisoning. In an even small number of cases, the transmuted broccoli has been proven to develop aggressive tendencies, jumping out of fridges and knocking unassuming individuals unconscious. Environmentalists are also concerned that introducing Vanessa to the normal food chain will affect 'normal' broccoli production. In addition, the final food production process requires careful handling in order to avoid water pollution, as otherwise fish in neighbouring rivers would be contaminated and killed.

What strategies should the Amnesian regulator adopt regarding Vanessa? First, what key risk regulation strategies exist to assess whether Vanessa should be licensed or not. Second, what risk regulation strategies would you recommend to encourage Vanessa's safe production?

Introduction

How to deal with risks such as the introduction of new kinds of food is at the heart of contemporary regulation (Black 2010). Whether decisions have to be made regarding food safety (BSE, i.e. 'mad cow' disease), EHEC (E.coli), natural disasters (such as flooding causing mass evacuations or volcanic ash disturbing international air traffic) or consumer protection (plastic toys threatening to cause serious illness among children), regulatory activities are at the heart of the way particular risks are handled.

Should the activity or the good be prohibited (if we happen to know about the source of the risk)? Should we allow individuals and companies to take their own decisions; for example, should airlines decide for themselves whether to fly during heightened levels of volcanic ash? Should we advise Amnesian regulators to prohibit Vanessa? Should we rely on extensive labelling? Or should we discount the significance of existing risks and not impose 'burdens' on industry? And how would such an approach towards Vanessa compare with Amnesia's other approaches towards related risks, such as those applying to lemonade, recreational drugs (such as cigarettes), medication (such as painkillers), dangerous dogs or injuries sustained during adventure holidays? Should Vanessa be prohibited while other risks are tolerated (such as those cardiovascular fatalities caused by an overuse of painkillers)? Is the 0.02 per cent likelihood of food poisoning occurring among those who consume Vanessa after its use by date tolerable or not? How seriously should Amnesia take the view of those that argue that any licensing of Vanessa would have serious consequences (in terms of non-reversibility) on 'normal' broccoli production. Finally, how could regulatory strategies motivate the producers of Vanessa to handle the production process carefully enough to minimize the risk of pollution?

Such questions illustrate why risk deserves its own chapter in this volume. In many ways, the regulation of risk could be linked to a range of topics already covered in previous chapters: regulating risks requires standards, it requires an ability to modify behaviour, and it also necessitates a reliable way to gather information. However, risk offers additional dimensions to these generic regulation debates, in particular relating to the inherent contention about what risks are and how they should be assessed and addressed (Hutter 2005).

One key dimension is the contestable nature of the definition of risk. Generally, risk and uncertainty are distinguished in the following way (Knight 1921): *risk* is defined by the possibility of calculating the probability and severity of impact. Thus, risk is the likelihood of a particular adverse effect occurring within a given time period. This contrasts with *uncertainty* where these conditions of calculability do not exist. However, such boundaries between *risk* and *uncertainty* are increasingly blurred and risk has become a term that increasingly spans both 'traditional' risk and uncertainty definitions. This blurring is due to the insight that certain risks are inherently difficult to anticipate (calculate) as ideas regarding probability and predictability become disputed and/or are difficult to process for individual day-to-day decision making (Beck 2009). Such difficulties are compounded by problems in calculating the consequences of one-off events, and the non-linearity of certain processes, given the presence of threshold (tipping points) or sleeper (dormant vulnerability) effects and other types of discontinuities and extreme outliers or 'black swans' (Brooks 1986; Taleb 2007).

In addition, risks are contestable given their inherently varied character. For example, we may wish to distinguish between those risks that are triggered by our own individual actions, and those that arise from other people's activities. In addition, we may wish to distinguish between those risks that are undertaken on a voluntary basis and those that are socially imposed on us. Our advice to Amnesia could therefore be that we should be more preventive when dealing with risks that are involuntarily incurred – we should exercise caution where people have limited or no choice regarding their exposure to particular risks.

Choices in energy generation sources may be seen as one example of a socially imposed and collective risk. For example, if one country has chosen to generate electricity through a reliance on nuclear reactors, the risk of an incident in a nuclear waste dump is a risk that will, should an incident occur, affect a large number of people. Should that incident occur in, say, 200 years when there has been a move to different forms of energy production, then the realization of the nuclear contamination risk will affect individuals who never actively consented to this particular risk during their lifetime. Equally, if this incident occurs in a neighbouring jurisdiction (a 'transboundary risk': Boin 2009) additional issues regarding negative externalities will arise. Similarly, while air transport might be seen as a voluntary choice (we may choose not to travel), individuals are dependent on the airline to operate 'safe' planes (a basic information asymmetry problem). In contrast, the risk of fatally injuring oneself during risky freestyle climbing activities is one that arguably affects only those individuals voluntarily choosing such a lifestyle choice (although there are social costs in terms of bereavement, injury and such like that one may wish to cover via special insurance schemes). The same would hold for those individual and voluntary risks incurred from consuming particular dietary drinks.

These basic two dimensions – voluntariness and information asymmetry – point to differences across types of risks and, consequently, the way they can be approached through regulatory means. These differences, however, blur at the edges when it comes to the wider social impact (or externalities) of individual actions. In addition, these considerations of risk exposure also highlight that the politics of risk regulation cut across conventional understandings of class politics: whereas in the past, the wealthy may have been able to buy themselves out of particular risks (by buying houses in less polluted areas, for example), they are less able to do so in terms of contemporary risks, such as radioactivity contaminating populations or volcanic ash clouds impeding food supplies.

A third area of contestation is the competing treatment of risk across different disciplines and perspectives. Some disciplines treat risk as an 'objective', others as a 'subjective' matter (Renn 2008: 12–45). So-called technical or economic perspectives on risk stress the importance of measurability. Supposedly objective evidence is, according to these perspectives, sought in order to assess risks mathematically. An economic perspective would, in particular, stress the importance of subjective utilities (i.e. taking into account personal preferences or utility functions as well as personal probability distributions) – and such methodologies have proven influential in court proceedings (Renn 2008, see for example the 1980 US Supreme Court ruling *Industrial Union Department v American Petroleum Institute* 448, US 607, which required agencies to conduct scientific assessments in their deliberations on risk regulation).

As noted earlier in our discussion of impact and cost assessment exercises, problems emerge when it comes to estimating particular 'utilities' and in terms of seeking to aggregate diverse individual utilities, the treatment of future costs and benefits, and in the way risks to health and life can be monetized (for 'value of statistical life', see Viscusi 2009). In contrast to these two approaches, psychological and cultural approaches stress the importance of subjectivity. Psychological approaches in particular stress aspects such as personal control (for example, car versus air travel), the degree of catastrophic potential, the risk's visibility and the immediacy of its having an impact. According to such aspects, individuals display 'dread' and other behaviours that may appear, to those believing in 'rational' behaviour, as 'irrational', but they do explain differences in the way risks are addressed.

Sociological approaches stress the importance of taking into account organizational processes. Culturally influenced accounts stress the importance of biases and worldviews. Accordingly, perceptions of risk depend on the values, norms and perceptions of individuals and of groups. Risks are socially amplified through social interactions and institutions, triggering secondary effects that impact on the way in which risks impact on society and the way in which risk regulation is designed and practised (amplification or attenuation; see Kasperson and Kasperson 1996; Rothstein *et al.* 2006). These perspectives also argue that any attempt to 'objectify' risk assessment through instruments (such as cost–benefit analysis) is inherently shaped by distinct worldviews regarding the treatment of particular risks. Any instrument therefore is inherently biased, and therefore debates regarding risk also require debates regarding the underlying assumptions of risk measurement tools (see also Kahan *et al.* 2011).

From these different views there follow different ways of dealing with risks. They reflect fundamental disagreements about their nature, and about the ways in which risks are supposed to be handled. For those who regard risk as something that can be assessed, measured and quantified, there exist 'rational' ways of dealing with risk that avoid over-reaction by acting too hastily, too punitively or too laxly (for an exhibit of such a view, see OECD 2010b). With the 'right' evidence and analytical tools, in particular cost-benefit analysis, and by limiting irrational (political) intervention, recurring problems of risk regulation can be overcome, namely those of irrational amplification of some risks and the ignoring of others. Dealing with risk in a rational way includes acknowledging that there are limits to reducing risks. Hence, regulatory action should be proportionate to the level of risk and therefore needs to be based on systematic risk assessment.

An opposing argument is made by those that suggest that regardless of all attempts at rationalization and quantification, inherent disagreement over risk assessment and appropriate responses to risk remains. At their most extreme, such positions deny the validity of any attempt to 'mitigate' risks and see such attempts as taking a misleadingly benign perspective regarding the state of the world. Accordingly, attempts at assessing risks will only enhance, not reduce contestation. The reason for such a setting of widespread societal 'alarm' about potential dangers is that modern (or 'late modern') society is characterized by a previously unknown level of risk pervasiveness (Beck 1992), which has been generated by individual and societal choices (Luhmann 2004).

The technical capacity of humankind to trigger self-destructive processes, the need for expertise to detect these risks (such as radioactivity, rather than traditional detection by looking outside the window and seeing rain or fire) and a more general scepticism towards authority after a run of technical disasters (such as Bhopal, Chernobyl or Fukushima), combine to a near ungovernable risk regulation challenge. Indeed, a further feature of this modern era of risk regulation is that (many) risks are no longer seen as external to human existence (i.e. water, fire, meteorites), but are increasingly 'man-made' whether because of technological choices (i.e. climate change as a result of industrialization) or because of human errors in applying technology (industrial plant accidents). According to such accounts, attempts to draw distinctions between human, technological and natural risks are also highly problematic, as technologies and technological standards are inherently socially constructed, and human- (or man-made) risks will inevitably occur, as individual and organizational attention fluctuates (Perrow 1984/1999; Vaughan 2005; Lodge 2009).

The growing social scepticism towards expertise has also led to a heightened awareness of risks themselves. Mary Douglas and Aaron Wildavsky (1982) noted that the rise of egalitarianism (and individualism) had led to a growing obsession with risk – in line with Mary Douglas's initial claim that individuals selected risks according to their preferred way of life: harms are seen as harms when they are seen to violate social norms and structures. One example of such changing societal concern with risk is parental fear of skin cancer affecting their young children while playing outside. This has led to a whole new protective clothing industry catering for very young children. Related to this, these parental concerns with exposure to sunlight have given rise to calls for schools to develop mandatory 'sun safety' approaches towards their pupils (*BBC*, 15 July 2011). Equally, the demand for 'risk-free' or 'incident free' areas, such as public swimming pools, has paved the way for the emergence of 'risk approaches' that, for example, allow parents to take only one child at a time to the swimming pool and to require disclaimer statements. In short, the growing concerns with risk have provoked a whole new risk industry that seeks to reduce liability and potential blame through proceduralization and prevention.

These examples highlight the distinct challenge that risk makes to the field of regulation in general. It emerges in the context of technological innovation, changing societal tastes for risk and scepticism towards expertise, and the discovery of risk as manageable rather than as an 'Act of God'. Risk regulation usually touches issues of human identity that give rise to fears and anxieties, if not moral panics. Issues relate to areas such as acid rain, avalanches, collapsing fish stocks, critical infrastructures, nuclear installations, oil platforms or vanishing bee colonies. Such issues, ranging from the general vulnerability of social or natural systems, beliefs in human ability to process risk, to other expressions of 'risk appetite' has generated a range of contradictory approaches towards risk. These differences reveal key disagreements and any system of risk regulation needs to accommodate these rival perspectives. These differences can be summarized in four broad perspectives on the regulation of risk (adapted from Hood *et al.* 2001 and drawing on the argument of Thompson *et al.* 1990). Figure 11.1 summarizes these four perspectives.

From these different worldviews follow different approaches concerning how standards for risk regulation are set and how attention to risk should be institutionalized. For example, there are differences across the four perspectives about the way in which decision making should be open to outside scrutiny, how information should be 'communicated' to those individuals considering 'risky' choices, and how systems engaged in high risk activities maintain an active engagement with the safety of their operation.

Nature as unpredictable *Emphasis*: bounce-back/respond to events *Instrument*: ad hoc/post hoc responses *Goal*: reduce unintended consequences	**Nature as controllable** *Emphasis*: stress on expert forecasting and 'enlightened' management *Instrument*: Stress on expert bodies and committees *Goal*: Anticipative whole-society approaches
Nature as self-regulating *Emphasis*: stress on market and individual choice *Instrument*: reduce distorted price signals and support markets *Goal*: minimize intrusion	**Nature as highly vulnerable** *Emphasis*: stress on encouraging popular participation *Instrument*: Participatory institutions and juries *Goal*: protect or give priority to worst-off

FIGURE 11.1   *Risk regulation and different views of nature*

Source: Adapted from Hood *et al.* (2001: 13).

These approaches also have direct implications for our case of Vanessa in Amnesian food safety.

- Should Amnesia rely on extensive labelling and warnings, so that consumers are well-informed about the potential risks associated with eating Vanessa after its use-by date?
- Should Amnesia ban Vanessa on the basis of the unknown effects of adding Vanessa to the overall food chain?
- Should Amnesia rely on the technical and/or economic assessment of the costs and benefits of introducing Vanessa and rely on expert judgement in allowing Vanessa to be used in general farming? For example, Amnesia may allow the selling of Vanessa if Vanessa was equipped with a special device to contain it safely within the fridge?
- Should Amnesia simply allow Vanessa to be produced and consumed in order to respond subsequently to potential problems as it is impossible to foresee how Vanessa will be consumed and with what effects?

The rest of this chapter considers risk regulation across the three regime dimensions (standard-setting, information-gathering and behaviour-modification). We then turn to competing methods for the management of risk regulation regimes and for the regulation of risk-producing organizations (see Hood and Jones 1996; Hood *et al.* 1999).

Choices in risk regulation regimes

As noted in Chapter 3, the design of rules involves a number of key choices that have a significant impact not just on the way in which regulation is enforced, but also how the target population responds to regulatory interventions. Debates regarding regulatory standard-setting strategy in the area of risk regulation have contrasted those who emphasize the importance of anticipation or precaution, and those who advocate the application of resilience as a strategy. For those emphasizing anticipation, the key idea is to minimize the production or the occurrence of the risk, by, for example, prohibiting or restricting particular production processes, or by building damns to prevent flooding. In contrast, resilience-based strategies operate on the principle of mitigation and 'bouncing back'.

Resilience-based approaches have been articulated in response to the perceived shortcomings of precautionary/anticipatory strategies. In particular, it is said that exercising precaution by preventing particular products from being developed or sold is a costly device that inhibits innovation. Anticipating risks, such as flooding or terrorist acts, is a very costly activity and is likely to fail as the environment is unpredictable and those seeking to cause damage counter-learn. In other words, anticipatory or precautionary methods are accused of incurring high sunk and opportunity costs. Such accusations have been particular vented at the *precautionary principle* that has enjoyed considerable currency in international trade negotiations. The precautionary principle emerged in the context of the German *Vorsorgeprinzip* and, since then, has become part of the European Commission approach towards the licensing of new food products (similarly, it is part of the 1992 Rio Declaration and world trade agreements). The European Commission allows the application of the precautionary principle where there are potential threats of irreversible damage; in other words, the presumption of 'innocent until proven guilty' is reversed in the case where 'scientific evidence is insufficient, inconclusive or uncertain' and where existing scientific evidence raises 'reasonable grounds for concern' (European Commission 2000). Such issues have been regularly raised, for example, in the debates regarding the introduction of genetically-modified crops or of hormone-treated beef (see Majone 2002, 2000). Accordingly, the choice for Amnesia may be to refuse the licensing of Vanessa until further evidence of its toxic and violent properties have been studied in further depth.

As noted, those who emphasize the value of resilience are highly critical of anticipatory or precautionary approaches. They argue that any attempt to prohibit Vanessa until further evidence has been collected would have a number of undesirable effects. Complaints about the potential effect of Vanessa on 'normal' broccoli may be the result of broccoli-farmers' lobbying efforts. In addition, the hyped-up stories regarding Vanessa knocking out very few individuals or causing extreme food poisoning may shift attention away from the great health benefits that the consumption of Vanessa would bring to the population at large. Such arguments are usually backed by the calculation of, for example, so-called DALYs (disability-adjusted life years) or QALYs (quality-adjusted life years; for example, it might be calculated that the estimated consumption of Vanessa leads to the financial equivalent of 56,700 QALYs where one QALY amounting to £30,000 – a not inconsiderable overall health benefit). In other words, prohibiting a 'new' risk does not mean that this is the risk-free option. Therefore, a resilience-based approach would advocate a trial-and-error approach towards the licensing of Vanessa, allowing for subsequent modifications to the licensing regime should side-effects be observed. More generally, a resilience based approach would advocate the use of 'alternatives to regulation', in particular tools such as disclosure, incentive and insurance schemes.

A related debate considers whether risk regulation standards should err on the side of Type I (false positive, or 'false alarm') or Type II (false negative, 'failing to raise an alarm') errors. The choice between these two types of error is not straightforward – for critical technical systems we may wish to impose a bias towards Type I errors (thereby imposing higher costs on production in order to avoid incidents). Similarly in airport security, we may wish to err on the side of preventing weapons being carried on the airplane at the expense of further controls, administrative costs, potential delays and missed flights (Frederickson and LaPorte 2002). In contrast, in criminal justice cases, we may wish to err on the side of Type II errors, as we may prefer to have some guilty individuals to (wrongly) walk free rather than to put innocent people in prison.

In the licensing of new foodstuff, such as Vanessa, we may therefore wish to rely on a Type I rather than a Type II-bias in regulatory decision-making. This suggestion follows Shrader-Frechette's advocacy of 'scientific proceduralism' (1991) which involves the ethical weighting of particular risks (and public deliberation over weighting schemes), alternative risk analyses and evaluations (that shift the emphasis from a Type II to Type I bias), and weighted expert opinions (in which experts are 'scored' on the basis of their previous accuracy). The extent to which scientific proceduralism offers a way to deal with Vanessa is debatable: it would require agreement on the way in which weighting is conducted, disagreements are likely to occur regarding the ease in which different ethical dilemmas can be distilled in various weighting scores, and it is questionable whether the heated atmosphere that generally surrounds debates regarding new foodstuffs would allow such a procedural device in the first place.

In terms of *behaviour modification*, one of the key arguments relates to the extent to which risk regulation should be 'blame oriented' (beyond the more general enforcement debates considered in Chapter 4). In particular, there are differences in opinion between those who see risk regulation as requiring clear assignments of responsibility and blame or whether risk regulation should encourage a blame-free environment that encourages openness and learning. An emphasis on the latter might avoid excessive risk aversion that might come accompany a high-blame regime. Furthermore, differences exist between those approaches that focus on individual responsibility and those that see the source of most problems in terms of organizational conduct, thereby placing an emphasis on collective forms of responsibility. Thus, it is not necessarily the train driver or the pilot who is to blame for poor decision making that led to a fatal incident, but one has to consider the wider organizational 'culture' that might be seen to encourage flawed practices. For example, the sinking of the roll-on/roll-off ferry *Herald of Free Enterprise* in 1987 at the Belgian port of Zeebrugge (killing 193, representing the worst British maritime disaster since the 1912 sinking of the *Titanic*) was not just blamed on the conduct of those seamen who had failed to close the doors, but, more importantly, on poor relationships between ship operators and shore-based managers within an overall company that was accused of being 'infected with the disease of sloppiness' (Department of Transport 1987: 14; in addition, the design of the ship was condemned;

see also McLean and Johnes 2000 for a discussion of the *Titanic* case). Very similar concerns were raised (and blame games exercised) in the aftermath of the sinking of the cruise ship *Costa Concordia* in January 2012 (*BBC*, 24 January 2012). While such an emphasis on blame and responsibility is critical for learning from failures and disasters, too strong an emphasis on blame is likely to lead to perverse effects: a fear of being blamed will lead participants to lose sight of the original objectives in the face of their own fear of having to take responsibility.

In terms of *information gathering*, key choices involve decisions as to whether information should be made available to all interested parties (i.e. everyone) and at what cost or whether information should only be made accessible to experts. Furthermore, in the case of information gathering by regulatory agencies, differences exist between those who make the case for highly intrusive investigations and those that rely on more 'passive' forms (Hood *et al.* 2001: 21). More generally, risk regulation is faced with the inherent problem as to whether a basis of knowledge exists that is able to detect the way in which risk is handled within organizations or how risk evolves in the first place. This raises issues regarding the technologies used for 'detection', what kind of indicators are being used to detect risks, how data, often collected for other purposes, is interpreted, and whether information can be faked or manipulated. Indeed, it raises questions as to how much effort should be involved in 'detecting' risks. As noted in our example of dangerous dogs (Chapter 3), it is inherently difficult to monitor the dog population and dog-related incidents, given limited registration efforts and problems in diagnosing dog breeds and types. Similarly, in the case of Vanessa, this might include active monitoring of Vanessa consumption, or it might simply include a reliance on the monitoring of hospital records, or no active information gathering at all.

Furthermore, questions have been raised as to how participatory such processes of risk information gathering should be (for example, through 'fire-alarm' processes) or whether regulatory agencies should be solely in charge (and then, through what means). Where scientific evidence about risks is inconclusive, a case might be made for involving extended 'peer communities' in the decisions on procedure if the observed patterns do not conform to the desired state of the world as presented in the set standard. However, rival perspectives would argue that any opening up of regulatory processes would lead to the introduction of irrational anxiety and fears into decision making.

Figure 11.2 applies the above discussion to the four different ways in which the request regarding Vanessa could be handled.

A reliance on 'doing nothing' (a resilience based approach) suggests that we should await actual consumer behaviour and cross-pollution before taking any regulatory approaches. This will not only encourage innovation and advance the consumption of healthy foods, but will also

License Vanessa and monitor potential side-effects on an ongoing basis to allow trial-and-error process	License Vanessa after assessment and expert judgement on safety of production
License Vanessa and require producers to take out insurance to deal with side-effects in terms of farming, extensive labelling and disclosure to minimize liabilities regarding food poisoning and physical harm	Prohibit Vanessa on a precautionary basis until clear scientific evidence assuring safety in production is agreed in open participatory process

FIGURE 11.2 *Overview of different risk regulation strategies*

minimize costs to industry and consumers (for example, it does not require industry to develop devices to contain Vanessa in fridges or to sound alarms should Vanessa hit its use-by date and turn into broccoli). A process that relied on liability provisions would combine not just a maximum of consumer choice, but would also rely on the price signal to avoid the side-effects of production. An optimal market-based system would be one where those who wish to grow Vanessa pay compensation to conventional broccoli growers. For those who argue in favour of anticipative solutions, major reliance would be placed on expert judgment, as expressed through risk assessments. All these approaches would find little agreement with those who distrust markets and authorities and who fear that the introduction of Vanessa would lead to irreversible results. In response, a precautionary approach could be applied, preventing the commercial exploitation of Vanessa until more evidence is available and a process of scientific proceduralism has come to a deliberative agreement.

Risk regulation – managing risk assessment and management

The choices involved in licensing new technologies or regulating risk are inherently problematic, as the previous section has shown. In addition, risk regulation is said to be affected by particular properties that affect its 'quality'. As noted, risk regulation is said to be taking place in a social context that is increasingly sceptical and hostile to expert opinion and thus unwilling to accept authority when it comes to issues of prohibition or permission. Parents do not want to be told what they should give their children to eat, while at the same time, they want to have particular technologies forbidden, although experts suggest that these are safe and/or other technologies (that are socially accepted) pose much higher risks (according to the official definition of probability and significance of impact). Such inconsistencies in perceptions of risk are reflected in the inconsistent approaches that characterize different risk regulation (if assessed in terms of actual danger posed) (Meier 1994). For some, such inconsistencies are not particularly problematic, if risk regulation is supposed to be the outcome of processes that reflect public anxieties. However, for others such inconsistencies are inherently problematic, leading to the negative side effects noted by those authors who advocate resilience-based approaches.

In particular, Stephen Breyer (1993) has suggested that 'normal' political institutions systematically produce three types of failures, namely *tunnel vision, random agenda selection* and *inconsistency* in risk assessment. The problem of *tunnel vision* is associated with specialized bureaucrats and politicians focussing on narrow regulatory issues who seek to eliminate all uncertainty and risk and in so doing go 'the final mile' even though the 'final mile' may be disproportionately costly. *Random agenda selection* implies that most issues on the risk regulation agenda are driven by public events and outrages. This leads to the 'risk of the month' phenomenon, in which particular risks are the site of temporary feverish media-feeding frenzies and thus political attention, while other (more fatal) risk remains unnoticed. *Inconsistency* is generated by different agencies using varying methods to calculate the effects of regulation. For example, such differences might be expressed in differences in the way values are attached to the saving of a statistical life. These three inherent problems generate, according to Breyer, a 'vicious cycle' in which politicians are in regulatory heat every time public attention is directed at a particular risk, where public perceptions of risks are likely to differ radically from the 'rational' consensus of subject experts, and where regulators seek to deal with uncertain technologies and therefore tend to deal with highly limited knowledge, data and instruments.

In order to break through this vicious cycle, Breyer advocates two key institutional reforms. One is the creation of a special professional career path for civil servants working in risk regulation areas. This would allow the development of a cohesive body of individuals to apply regulatory principles in a consistent manner. A second is the creation of a separate oversight group that would not just set out overall principles regarding risk regulation but would also, presumably, monitor their application. Such a group, or council, would operate outside the heat of the day-to-day political process and would therefore be in a position to conduct risk assessments and utilize technical and scientific expertise.

The creation of such a special 'risk regulation watchdog' resembles those proposals in the 'better regulation' world that similarly make the case for free-standing and high-profile bodies to influence regulatory quality. Thus, the same potential problem also applies here: such bodies are unlikely to embed themselves in the overall political and administrative process, and are likely to be ignored and to fade out of collective memory unless they are closely connected to high political profiles (i.e. the office of the president/prime minister).

More broadly, the problem with Breyer's suggestions is their belief in the legitimacy (and feasibility) of scientific expertise. In defence, one might argue that such agencies and an emphasis on transparent deliberation of the findings of assessments (so that risk impact studies are just one source for informing decision making rather than the sole decision making criterion) would advance the quality of risk regulation and therefore add both outcome-based (through 'better decisions') and procedural legitimacy. Such a view is also prominent among international organizations (see OECD 2010b), and contemporary administrative doctrine advocates the separation of risk assessment and risk management functions within government. The former (risk assessment) is supposed to provide for the independent, detached and expert view (on the basis of quantitative or qualitative studies as to whether particular goods or products are 'acceptable' or not). Risk management, in contrast, refers to the way in which organizations are supposed to identify and handle the mitigation of risks.

It might be argued that such procedural 'deck-stacking' already advances some interests over others, that a reliance on experts is unlikely to produce better decisions than if there was a reliance on lay persons, and that the distributional implications of deciding on risk regulatory aspects require an open political process and not a reliance on technocratic elites, apart from the obvious costs that such a reliance on extensive risk assessments would bring (in terms of the studies themselves, challenges and the creation of new uncertainties). Indeed, whether attempts to deal with human fears and anxieties can rely on the language of technocratic risk expertise and their procedures may also be doubted, especially as it is likely that politicians will not be able to simply delegate blame to risk-assessing experts in a climate of moral panic.

Indeed, they may not have the time to wait for well-developed expertise. For example, during a severe EHEC (an E.coli strain) outbreak in the early summer of 2011 in Germany, Hamburg's health minister announced that Spanish cucumbers had been identified as the source of infection. This announcement turned out to be based on false information and had to be retracted, after having caused massive economic losses to Spanish cucumber farmers and growing distrust in overall food safety. Dealing with risk during these moments of crisis creates a political trade-off between the need to quickly communicate the source of problems (and the likelihood that such an announcement will turn out to be wrong) and the need for 'sound science' that, however, requires a prolonged period of study that politicians can ill-afford.

At the same time, it has been argued that conflicts regarding particular risk regulatory devices have been successful in addressing disagreement over risks: for example, in 2005, the particularly precautionary measures applied to British beef in the context of BSE were partly lifted (namely not allowing cattle aged over 30 months to enter the food chain) and brought in line with international provisions (which required BSE testing of these older animals) after a study had suggested that the extra costs of these measures stood in no relation to their benefits (also Jensen *et al.* 2005). Indeed, it is noted that bringing different views together through the use of unified procedures and ways of calculating 'value' offers the only way to inform and advance debates about risk regulation, allowing an 'enlightened' assessment as to how to deal with particular risks (Arrow *et al.* 1996; Sunstein 2002).

As noted, one of the key criticisms of Sunstein's (and others) 'cost benefit state' is its belief in the 'objectivity' and 'rationality' of quantitative risk assessment. Criticisms range from methodological and practical problems of cost-benefit analysis and related methods, including hidden value assumptions, the weighing of different dimensions of costs and benefits, to the treatment of uncertainty. It might also be argued that there are certain types of risks where a 'normal' approach is simply unwarranted, namely in those cases that involve catastrophic potential (extermination of all life on planet earth), but are most unlikely to occur. An example of such a catastrophic risk is the risk of planet earth being hit by an asteroid: any risk assessment would suggest that financial resources should be devoted to other causes, given the low probability of such an event, but it might be argued that in cases of 'extermination of all life' the 'significance' of the potential impact is approaching infinity (see Posner 2004).

More generally, regarding risk as inseparable from perception and, hence, cultural worldviews leads to more fundamental doubts regarding centralized decision making based on 'objective' risk assessment. Solutions that take the subjective nature of risk into account include measures to assess ethical concerns, the commissioning of rival risk assessments and the ethical evaluation of risk assessments (Shrader-Frechette 1991). Such a view is supported by the wider literature on the use of knowledge in policy making that highlights the contested nature of knowledge and its inconclusive nature in terms of providing clear direction for action (Cohen and Lindblom 1979; Weiss 1997). Such a view embraces plurality and the subjective dimension in risk assessments is linked to the emphasis on local and discursive styles of decision making. Extensive participation in the formulation of response strategies is said to increase the acceptance of public action (Fischer 2003) and also allows for the 'spanning' of organizational and jurisdictional boundaries.

These discussions are relevant for Amnesia's overall administrative infrastructure regarding the introduction and licensing of food stuffs. However, as noted in the introductory vignette, the production of Vanessa is also risky in the sense of causing potentially harmful pollution. What kind of risk regulatory strategies should be developed to mitigate the potential dangers that emanate from such risk-producing organizations that handle Vanessa before it enters the food-chain? This raises issues that were discussed earlier (under ideas relating to 'enforced self-regulation').

However, as the literature on high reliability organization has highlighted, risk regulation needs to encourage firms to be error-intolerant and 'heedful' (see Weick 1987; LaPorte and Consoline 1991; Weick and Roberts 1993). This means that risk regulation needs to encourage redundancies ('back-up systems') within organizations and the existence of internal 'challenge' functions. These challenge functions could, for example, involve activities that challenge dominant understandings or interpretations of failure and stress the importance of understanding failure not just as a single organizational, but potentially system-wide, feature.

As noted in the case of industrial and other accidents, most man-made errors occur by 'normal' human decision making that 'normalizes' deviance. Diane Vaughan (1996), for example, suggests that one of the key reasons for the *Challenger* tragedy (the US space shuttle that exploded shortly after take-off in 1986) was not that the ultimate cause of the tragedy, an O-ring, had not been detected as a deviating from the norm. Rather, the seemingly safe operation of the space shuttle on previous occasions had meant that the deviation was tolerated and had become an acceptable risk. More generally, the *Challenger* incident pointed to serious issues in the safety culture surrounding NASA. Tragically, the same kind of processes were said to have contributed to the *Columbia* incident (of 2003 when that space ship disintegrated during its descent) (Vaughan 2005, 2006; Boin and Fishbacher-Smith 2011). However, even if risk regulation seeks to motivate firms and other organizations (through, for example, management-based standards) constantly to question their production processes, the safe handling of particularly high vulnerability systems seems to be largely a matter of professional attitudes within organizations rather than the result of regulatory strategies. Indeed, it might be argued that the requirement to add redundancy into an operating system might induce its own risks and uncertainties and therefore become a source of failure in itself.

In contrast to such strategies that emphasize the importance of encouraging highly resourced, error-intolerant 'safety cultures' are those accounts that stress the inevitability of error and accident. As noted by Charles Perrow (1984/1999), accidents in technical systems and organizations are the result of a chain of wrong decisions that often start innocently because of ignorance, omission or 'bad luck' (e.g. a piece of paper covering a warning light). Complex and detailed rules of conduct (e.g. standard operating procedures, decision trees) contribute to a lack of understanding among staff about what is important and what is not. As a result, error is inevitable, and risk regulation should therefore consider the nature of the production process and its likely consequences.

Perrow distinguishes technologies along two dimensions: linearity and coupling. When linear production lines are interrupted, all production is stopped, in contrast, in non-linear systems, processes are ongoing, leading to potential unpredictable effects. In loosely coupled systems, an interruption does not threaten the overall viability of the system, whereas in a tightly coupled system, each component is 'mission critical'. The consequences for risk regulation are that non-linear systems and loosely coupled systems can rely on decentralized risk controlling systems, whereas linear and tightly coupled systems require centralized systems. The key risk regulation 'paradox' emerges among those industries that are both non-linear and tightly coupled, as risk regulation requires both 'decentralized' and 'centralized' risk management devices. For Perrow, the inevitability of something going wrong leads to a question about the potential implications of a disaster or failure, and, therefore, to the suggestion that those industries or types of production that are likely to have a catastrophic impact should simply be prohibited (such as, Perrow suggests, nuclear energy). Another conclusion from Perrow's analysis is to decouple tightly coupled systems when possible, that is, decoupling risky from less risky activities of banks and other financial institutions – so that the impact of some risk materializing on the overall system will be limited (Perrow 1984/1999; Harford 2011). Another potential implication is that dangerous technologies should be exposed to maximum external scrutiny, for example, through the inclusion of laypersons in the monitoring of activities, or even in the assessment of particular risks.

The final contrasting view regarding the way in which risk regulation should handle risky technologies links to those arguments that advocate price signals and insurance markets. If insurance is too costly to cover the potential negative consequences of a particular activity or good, it is unlikely that such an activity or production will continue. If individuals had to take out full cover against all the potential costs of sporting accidents, it is unlikely that they would pursue sports that carried the risk of injury. In other words, firms and consumers should be fully exposed to the costs of their choices (see Freeman and Kunreuther 1997; Kunreuther *et al.* 2009). In particular, it is argued that mandatory insurance markets send populations a signal about the potential catastrophes they are likely to face, as individual decision making is short term and potentially based on optimism bias ('I won't be affected by hurricanes'). In other words, the price signal is used to ensure that the inevitable cost of recurring natural disasters is not aggravated by high concentrations of populations deciding to move into harm's way (rather than away from it) (see Kunreuther *et al.* 2009).

So what does this all mean for the production of Vanessa? How can risk regulation succeed in encouraging its safe production? We may, in

Normal accidents	High reliability organizations
Abandon too risky technologies	Rely on mechanisms that encourage highly resourced redundancy within production systems and high degree of error-intolerant professionalism
Insurance markets	**Local accountability**
Rely on price signal and insurance markets to make firms 'pay' for the potential consequences of their production	Rely on mechanisms of local accountability to monitor production

FIGURE 11.3   *Competing risk regulations strategies to make Vanessa safe*

line with the previous paragraph, rely on insurance markets and therefore require those wishing to produce Vanessa to insure themselves against all potential risks. For those inspired by Perrow, the question becomes one of catastrophic potential: what are the consequences of Vanessa contaminating the overall broccoli farming sector and what is the impact on the overall river environment from potential contamination? Vanessa is arguably a process that involves both non-linearity and tight coupling; however, it might be said that the contamination risk is largely a local one. For those who believe in the possibility of high reliability organizations, a major emphasis needs to be placed on creating redundancy and a strong culture of 'professionalism' that is intolerant of error. Finally, for those who are highly sceptical of such 'military-type' organizations, the introduction of local accountability structures will become one key demand, such as the inclusion of laypeople in the monitoring of local production facilities. Figure 11.3 summarizes this debate.

Conclusion: regulating risks

Risk has become a central aspect in any public policy debate. Much has been made of the competing ideas and perceptions that make any decision making problematic. If one agrees with the diagnosis that contemporary societies (especially in the developed world) are less willing to accept authority and more distrustful of experts or corporations telling that things are safe, then risk regulation becomes more than just a matter of finding the 'right' set of instruments in terms of standard setting, information gathering and behaviour modification. Instead, the public management of risk regulation now becomes a process of 'boundary spanning' in a number of dimensions. First, it requires a form of boundary spanning that links expert and lay opinions. It also requires an understanding of competing worldviews and analytical perspectives. Second, it requires boundary spanning in identifying and bringing together different perspectives to allow a discussion of (potentially competing) risk assessments. Third, it requires boundary spanning capacities in the sense of needing to deal with the potentially tragic consequences when things do go 'wrong', but also the need to communicate about risk.

Chapter 12

What is Good Regulation?

The various regulatory debates confronting Amnesia have created considerable unhappiness with the state of regulation in the country. It is said that Amnesia's regulatory state is in crisis. This general discontent has encouraged the Amnesian government to ask for one concluding meeting with you. It wants to know how to ensure 'good regulation' in the future. What key dimensions should underline 'good regulation'? What strategies should be used to achieve 'good regulation'? What are the key themes that will continue to influence the regulatory state in Amnesia (and elsewhere)?

Introduction

A regulatory analysis perspective emphasizes the importance of theoretical and methodological openness to different perspectives and approaches. It is therefore not associated with any one perspective or recipe. Instead, the regulatory analysis angle suggests that any discussion regarding regulation needs to consider the plurality of diagnoses of the problem and the related competing solutions. Regulatory analysis, therefore, is about identifying the implicit assumptions and essential prerequisites that characterize regulatory proposals. In addition, it is essential to understand whether particular prerequisites are obtainable or too demanding within a given context. In other words, regulatory analysis is about embracing the variety of perspectives on regulatory regimes, seeking to provide a systematic approach towards utilizing these diverse approaches and avoiding the potential trap of listening to 'easy answers'. Regulatory problems are not easy or technical problems but require adaptive capacity to deal with complex circumstances (see Heifetz 1994).

Is this all we can say about 'good regulation' from a viewpoint of regulatory analysis? What broader general lessons can we draw from the various insights that have emerged over the previous chapters? What are the key issues that regulatory analysis-inspired students and practitioners of regulation should consider?

Orthodox answers – and questions

Orthodox responses to the question 'What is good regulation?' point to the legal and efficient use of regulatory powers. Across the previous chapters, we have considered how regulation can go 'bad', whether in terms of 'regulatory failures' (see Chapter 2), the inability to use formal enforcement tools (see Chapter 6) or the failure to design regulatory institutions that address the 'commitment problem' (see Chapter 8). Similarly, heavy-handed or too light-touch enforcement practices are said to constitute 'bad regulation'. Thus, it might be easy to say when regulation is 'bad', but how would we recognize 'good' regulation? There is, unfortunately, no easy answer, as different perspectives (and academic disciplines) give different responses, ranging from the maximization of social utility or wealth to procedural justice. Nevertheless, if one wanted to create a standard checklist (see Baldwin *et al.* 2012: ch. 3) for the Amnesian government, it would include the following requirements for good regulation:

- *Regulation is performed within the legislative mandate and intent*: It might seem to be obvious, but good regulation requires all the parties involved act according to their appropriate roles. In particular, regulators who operate outside their legislative mandate pose problems of legitimacy, as usually regulators have no direct democratic or political mandate. Furthermore, regulation outside the legislative mandate and intent may also be seen as an example of the commitment problem – regardless of whether this 'acting outside the mandate' is due to political or regulatory decisions. The theoretical literature on 'drift' has noted how shirking can be seen as a result of self-interest that violates public interest considerations. If investors and other parties cannot predict the broad thrust of regulatory activity, they will respond accordingly, namely by withdrawing their own resources.
- *Regulation follows 'due process'*: Regulation that follows procedures provides not only for predictability, it also allows sufficient time and space for consultation and the consideration of particular affected constituencies. Due process provides for a means of 'deck-stacking' (in the widest sense): it facilitates accessibility, participation and accountability, therefore potentially checking against 'drift'. Hence procedures safeguard against political or industry pressure, as well as force self-interested regulators to undertake particular tasks they would otherwise choose to neglect. Thus, due process provides a means of 'equality before the law' in that it grants involved parties particular rights and obligations. Due process is also important for those who argue that regulation cannot be evaluated on its outputs or outcomes, and therefore it is procedural rationality that matters. In other words, following due process is not just an expression of control, it also has

more far-reaching implications regarding the overall legitimacy of the regulatory regime in question.

- *Regulation reflects expertise*: It seems relatively uncontroversial to suggest that regulation should be informed and that regulatory decisions should reflect the outcome of rigorous analysis. Again, the application of expertise should provide a degree of predictability and reduce the scope for arbitrary regulatory decisions. Regulatory decision making is enhanced because of the subject expertise that regulators are supposed to bring to particular regulatory decisions, whether it is the subject expertise of the economist whose analysis of markets is required, or the legal analysis of rights and obligations, or other expertise in terms of engineering, veterinary science (in food) or environmental health.

- *Regulation is efficient*: This claim refers to two key aspects. One is that regulatory procedures are 'efficient' in the sense of being conducted with minimal 'wastage' and in a timely manner. The second aspect is that regulation is efficient in the sense of minimizing the distortion of market transactions and reducing the compliance burden on regulatees for a given regulatory objective.

Amnesia's government might be delighted to be handed such a list of conventional and uncontroversial requirements. One may add a few ingredients from the 'better regulation' toolbox (see Chapter 10) by insisting on, for example, the use of *ex ante* and *ex post* evaluation instruments (such as Regulatory Impact Assessments), coordination bodies to facilitate capacity building within subnational governments and across domains, as well as a commitment towards risk-based enforcement (see OECD 2011: 5). Such broad commitments would certainly make Amnesia appear fashionable in international 'regulatocracy' circles.

However, the above five aspects of good regulation do not present straightforward instructions and are therefore unlikely to reduce the criticism facing the Amnesian government. First, legislative intent is usually vague and ambiguous – as debates about judicial activism would suggest (it might also be argued that regulatory decisions should go beyond regulatory intent in cases where the initial legislation is seen as insufficient or flawed). How regulators interpret mandatory objectives that require them to consider, for example, 'competition', 'social impact' and 'environmental sustainability', is hardly uncontroversial. Such terms are (possibly intentionally) vague and potentially contradictory. For some, one objective should enjoy primacy over the others. For example, competition may lead to the elimination of wasteful and inefficient services (thereby complying with all three objectives). For others, the abandonment of inefficient services may be seen as socially problematic. Others may argue that inefficient industries that however produce less emissions than 'efficient' ones should be promoted, as the price signal is distorted (by not costing in pollution) or as, in the long-term, costs are likely to decline. In other words, as Chapter 3 suggested, mandates are unlikely to be clear and precise enough to allow uncontroversial judgements as to whether particular regulatory activities have been within the regulatory mandate and intent or not (and, indeed, much of transnational regulation occurs outside any form of *legislative* mandates). Even where regulatory standards seem to be highly technical, for example, by prescribing specific technical standards (that are 'best available technology'-type standards) and are not of a 'principles'-based nature (e.g. 'do not harm'), actual enforcement and monitoring will require interpretation, especially when it comes to transition periods and the need to analyze whether the actual equipment fully complies with the prescribed standards or what to do in case of temporary technical failures.

Second, even if regulation follows due process, it is not clear whether this makes for good regulation. The deck may be stacked in favour of particular interests rather than others (thereby violating the principle of facilitating access and procedural justice). Similarly, the importance of consulting legitimate societal interests is hardly controversial. However, *who* is a legitimate societal interest is highly controversial, as noted in the discussion of the regulation of risk (Chapter 11). Moreover, consultation requires choices to be made, whether to treat 'new' market entrants in the same way as the established and incumbent, or whether to promote new entrants' interests to facilitate competition. Similarly, one may debate whether small enterprises should be treated in the same way as big ones. At the same time, one may wish to differentiate between those interests that are genuinely 'small' and/or domestic and those 'small' organizations that are subsidiaries of powerful and resourceful industries in other domains and/or countries. Furthermore, what are appropriate forms of accountability is also highly contested. For some, accountability is about promoting 'choice' options, for others it is about maximum disclosure, while for another set of perspectives, accountability is about systematic monitoring and requiring to report by special oversight bodies (see Lodge and Stirton 2010; Koop 2011).

Similar controversy exists when it comes to expertise. As noted throughout this volume, what counts as expertise is a matter of controversy. Competing views about regulatory problems will rely on different sources of knowledge and it is difficult to claim that one expertise is inherently 'more informed' than the other, as scientific knowledge is uncertain or disputed. We do not suggest that relative scientific certainty cannot exist, but it is always open to challenge and falsification. Indeed, some regulatory problems may be of a 'trans-scientific nature' (questions that can be phrased in scientific terms, but are not answerable in 'pure' science terms, see Weinberg 1972), that is, standard setting will inevitably take place within a battlefield of conflicting epistemologies, methodologies and research traditions (Majone 1984: 15). The expertise of engineers is not inferior to the expertise of lawyers or that of economists – but it is not clear which expertise should 'win' in cases of disagreement (even if economists, lawyers and engineers happened to agree among themselves).

It is therefore not clear how expertise on its own can offer a guiding criterion for good regulation. Instead, what counts as expertise will be shaped by those professions that dominate regulatory proceedings within any one domain. Similarly, scientific expertise may conflict with other sources of expertise (such as laypeople) and may also be closely linked to industry interests, thus hardly representing a 'neutral' position. How, therefore, regulators encourage an exchange between different opinions and options is therefore a critical challenge for any process. This may include the commissioning of studies that assess and discuss controversies, or the establishment of 'round tables' to bring together different and competing interests and perspectives.

However, such devices that seek to reduce conflict are hardly efficient in the sense of allowing speedy decisions, and are also potentially difficult or 'unhelpful' in a political sense (when, for example, consultation exercises reveal that the minister's preferred option lacks any support or is ill-conceived). When the going gets tough and public/media opinion demands action, it is extremely difficult for any regulator or politician to establish an 'inquiry' to develop proposals before acting. Such reasons point to the limitations of the 'efficiency' criterion for 'good regulation'. Procedural devices that encourage participation and deliberation between different perspectives are not necessarily efficient in that they require time and resources. One may even wish to challenge the efficiency criterion head-on and suggest that ideas of fairness or redundancy are more important than efficiency, or at least of equal status. Thus, it is not clear how our different dimensions should be assessed or prioritized in the light of potential conflicts. At what point is consultation under due process no longer efficient and who should decide when consultation options have been exhausted?

In sum, the basic answers as to what 'good regulation' is raise even more questions than they provide answers. This does not mean that the above 'checklist' is inherently useless. It is hard to argue that ignorance, violation of procedures, and disregard for legislative mandates offer a recipe for successful regulation. However, good regulation is about asking the tough questions that underlie the checklists. Furthermore, such checklists usually focus on the activities of regulatory agencies. They are less useful in fragmented regulatory regimes (where different bodies, often at various levels of government are involved in standard setting, information gathering and behaviour modification). As argued in the context of 'better regulation' (Chapter 10), it is often the cumulative effect of diverse actors operating within a fragmented regulatory regime that causes the complaints about 'bad regulation', not the activity of one single organization itself. Therefore, a regulatory analysis perspective is about asking difficult questions and not about offering seemingly easy answers that are oblivious to the real-life complexity of regulation, such as the decentred nature of regulatory regimes.

Moving beyond criteria for the evaluation of specific regulatory activities, what else can we say about good regulation, especially regarding choice of regulatory strategies and instruments? The academic literature on regulation offers some key insights (see Gunningham and Grabosky 1998). One key argument has been that mixed strategies are preferable to single-type approaches. Such mixed strategies come in many forms: they rely on mixtures in standard-setting strategies (for example relying on management-based and performance-based strategies), they rely on enforcement pyramids that offer initial cooperation, backed by the threat of sanctions, and they generally rely on an emphasis on responsibility, persuasion and discretion, thereby leaving coercion and deterrence as means of last resort.

In addition, to reduce the difficulties for regulators to monitor the conduct of regulatees, the use of third parties as 'fire-alarms' is recommended. Such third parties could include affected industries, local populations and/or other kind of public interest groups (see Ayres and Braithwaite 1992). Finally, and similarly intended to reduce the 'burden' on the regulator, there has been an emphasis on using incentives to shift regulatee behaviour towards the production of the desired outcome (i.e. the use of incentive-based regulation to reduce emissions or to enhance efficiency). All of these instruments can be seen as facing up to the inherent limitations of regulation through hierarchical oversight: they seek to address, to some extent at least, the inherent information asymmetry that shapes the relationship between regulator and regulatee.

An emphasis on mixes is said to be advantageous for a number of reasons. First, as noted throughout the volume, regulatory settings are inherently complex. Therefore, a reliance on complex tools is likely to offer far more variation in tool application than a regulatory strategy that relies on merely one instrument. Such variation is also reflected in the diagnosis that motivations and capabilities for compliance vary. Second, a monocultural use of a single instrument is also more likely to be prone to exploitation. If regulatees can predict the way in which regulation is going to be applied, they will respond accordingly. A mixed approach provides regulators with more options to respond to attempts at strategic behaviour, both in information gathering and in behaviour modification strategies. Similarly, if regulatees are encouraged to develop their own responses to regulatory objectives, this not only treats them as responsible citizens but also reduces potential problems that come with prescriptive approaches, namely confrontation and disagreement.

Finally, relying on regulatory mixes is also said to provide for overall stability. This stability is generated by the reduced ability of those hostile to the regulatory intent to game the system, while it also stems from the inbuilt variability of regulatory strategies and the reliance on redundant channels of communication (Scott 2000). Thus, a strategy that relies on multiple sources for information gathering, for example, is less likely to be captured than one that relies on one single channel, such as a regulatory agency.

As promising as these mixed strategies are, they are, however, for a number of reasons hard to apply in practice. One reason is that these mixed strategies are very difficult to sustain over time. Regulatees demand certainty and consistency and therefore demand clarification when they should be demanding discretion. Regulated organizations are therefore often found to be making contradictory demands, advocating reduced regulatory burdens and more 'discretion' in general, but also more prescriptive and clear regulation in particular (see Chapter 3). Of course, demands for regulatory prescription also offers industry one way to reduce threats of market entry, as capture-theorists would suggest. However, this form of 'regulatory creep' is mostly guided by the risk-averse behaviour of regulatees who seek to eliminate sources of potential challenge and unpredictability. Similarly, regulators, especially those at street-level, are said to be hostile to discretionary approaches as they require interpretative judgement and are therefore likely to be open to challenge and accusations of inconsistent application (see Chapters 3 and 4; also Lodge and Wegrich 2011b).

In addition, regulation does not take place within a value-free space. Instruments represent value choices and seek to develop particular outcomes. As noted by Christopher Hood (1991), *public* policy and administration is inherently about achieving three fundamental values: efficiency, fairness and resilience. The same applies to regulation (as noted above). We prefer to use a minimum amount of resources to achieve particular regulatory outcomes, but we also wish to have provisions that safeguard fairness (or public service obligations) and spare capacity (such as in network and generation capacity in energy). However, it is impossible to address all three values at the same time to an equal extent – they are in mutual tension rather than in a mutually reinforcing relationship. It is impossible to have efficient regulation that places a similarly strong emphasis on resilience and/or fairness (efficient outcomes would not allow subsidized public services to enter remote areas of Amnesia and/or maintain considerable idle standby capacity). Similarly, a maximum emphasis on resilience and back-up capacity is costly – having an impact on the objective of fairness as it raises costs to consumers (it also affects the value of efficiency). In other words, regulation is faced with inherent trade-offs between values. In a good regulation setting, such choices between values require transparency and a commitment towards making underlying assumptions explicit. In other words, regulatory choices are political in that they are value choices which are inherently contested, involve sensitive trade-offs, and raise opposition.

The final challenge for mixed and smart regulatory design is regulation's intrinsically political character. Accounts suggesting that one can intelligently design oneself out of any regulatory quagmire are likely to be disappointing. Regulatory strategies are required to adjust to the political considerations characterizing particular settings. In addition, regulation takes place in a political context where scandals and accidents happen, politicians seek to promote their pet topics, interest groups demand favourable treatment (couched, of course, in public-interest justifications) and public opinion demands responses. It is therefore important to realize (and to persuade Amnesia's government) that regulation cannot function in a technocratic and politics-free zone. Good regulation considers the political and administrative feasibility of particular strategies within a given context. Given the inherent trade-offs of any regulatory decision, the weightings that are accorded to any one decision criteria should be openly considered (see also Baldwin *et al.* 2012: 39).

Contested routes towards good regulation

As noted, the values that regulation seeks to achieve are inherently contested. However, contestation does not stop there. Strategies to achieve particular values are also contested. A key contribution of the regulatory analysis perspective is not to offer uncontroversial checklists, but to contrast different reform strategies that are built on different perspectives and contrasting underlying assumptions. Figure 12.1 points to four different strategies that can be said to constitute good regulation in order to achieve good regulatory values.

We do not wish to suggest that all regulation can be designed by applying a (mix of) four strategies to achieve a (mix of) three regulatory values. But, we suggest that this perspective captures a broad range of possible different strategies and highlights underlying assumptions (that often remain unspoken in 'regulatocracy speak'). Figure 12.1 suggests that there are clear differences between the various routes towards whatever is defined as the key regulatory objective. While some mixing of different strategies is possible, a simple mixing everything together is likely to end in a volatile and hardly palatable cocktail of regulatory strategies. These four strategies are in competition with each other and have their own distinct advantages and disadvantages.

For those emphasizing the importance of strengthened predictability, the importance of sustained and well-informed oversight is central

Strengthen adaptability	Strengthen predictability
Emphasis on unpredictable elements in terms of standards, information gathering, and behaviour modification, thereby facilitating flexibility	Emphasis on non-negotiable rules, reporting duties and legal sanctions
Strengthen incentives	**Strengthen participation**
Emphasis on self-interest and rivalry-based standards and yardstick-type information revelation	Emphasis on consultation and close relational distance for information gathering, emphasis on persuasion and 'responsive regulation'

FIGURE 12.1   *Strategies for good regulation*

Source: Adapted from Hood *et al.* (1999: 49).

to any regulatory regime. This contrasts with those that advocate a strengthening of participation, by involving so-called stakeholders and various professional communities in deliberations about regulation, and by bringing third parties into the application of dynamic enforcement systems (such as 'responsive regulation' or 'really responsive regulation'; Ayres and Braithwaite 1992; Baldwin and Black 2008). Those who stress the importance of adaptability highlight the genuine uncertainty and potential for strategic behaviour across all aspects of regulation. It is therefore argued that more uncertainty and variability needs to be introduced into regulatory processes. This gives reduced scope for gaming, and allows a continued 'alertness' when it comes to the gathering of information (or, to use the language of organizational psychologist Karl Weick (1995) such strategies allow for a state of 'arousal' in sense-making activities that is vital for the interpretation and processing of information). Finally, those advocating a strengthening of incentives would argue that regulation will fail if it is not aligned with the self-interest of regulated organizations and of regulators themselves.

Each one of these strategies has its disadvantages, whether this relates to problems, for example, of participatory stalemate, a blind trust in authority, the development of highly distrustful relations due to unpredictability, or the emergence of highly competitive organizations that in their ambition to be 'best in class' focus on individual performance rather than system-wide effects. We may therefore wish to mix these different strategies. However, whether there can be anything more than an uneasy compromise between different strategies, for example, between those demanding more participation and those demanding more adaptability and surprise, is a matter for debate (Hood 1998; Lodge and Wegrich 2005b).

Regulatory state deficits and debates

Much has been said about the claim that we are living in the age of the regulatory state (as noted in Chapter 1). Much has also been said about the challenges to (if not limitations of) the regulatory state in addressing contemporary problems, whether these relate to the oversight of financial institutions, the capacity to address environmental questions or the capability to address transnational issues. Others have noted that a focus on the regulatory state fails to account for the extensive nature of non-state regulation, whether this relates to the extent to which domestic regulation is characterized by co- or self-regulation (see Chapter 5), or the extent to which transnational regulation is organized through private interests (see Chapter 7).

Without claiming to offer an exhaustive account, four central diagnosed deficits can be identified that are at the heart of contemporary debates and that draw on the four perspectives outlined above (Figure 12.1). Debates regarding the failings of contemporary (state and non-state based) regulation have been widespread, as the discussions regarding the regulatory failures surrounding the financial crisis have shown (whether in the United Kingdom, the United States, Iceland, Ireland or Germany) (Lodge and Wegrich 2011a). Similarly, conflicts about what lessons one can draw from food scandals or environmental disasters, such as oil spills or nuclear accidents, have revealed how contested the regulatory terrain has become (Lodge 2011). The habitat of regulation has dramatically changed in the past decade, but the four deficits outlined below continue to recur in different shapes (and will continue to do so).

Accordingly, we can diagnose that contemporary regulation suffers from:

- *An oversight deficit*: one of the key arguments in contemporary discussions has been the lack of consistency across different regulatory domains. A second key criticism has been that individual regulatory bodies lack the resources (financially and staff-wise) to engage in information-gathering and behaviour-modification activities. Thus, a good regulation agenda should seek to check the fragmentation of regulatory experiences by developing centralized guidance mechanisms or organizations (see Black 2007). Such problems may be addressed at the domestic level (through central regulatory oversight mechanisms) but are likely to face resistance as any attempt at centralizing regulation will be challenged by pointing to the threat to the autonomy of particular regulatory regimes. Furthermore, the ability to oversee the growth in transnational private regulation also challenges the notion of centralizing regulatory principles. More broadly, the continued rise of transnational production chains challenges any notion of centralized regulatory oversight over any one particular product or service.

Similarly, the argument for a better resourced regulatory infrastructure raises issues of recruitment, careers and expertise. It raises the question whether a close relational distance between industry and regulators should be encouraged or not (for example, by 'revolving door' career patterns). In other words, if a lack of oversight is seen as the fundamental problem in contemporary regulation, then one way of addressing this deficit is to demand a higher degree of prescriptiveness in terms of procedural conduct (at least) and greater separation between regulators and regulatees. It also includes considerable resource commitments in order to enhance the capacity of those who practise regulatory oversight. Such proposals are hardly novel: they regularly feature in campaigns that seek to establish public structures that counteract the supposedly corrupting forces of the market place. However, they face considerable challenge in an age of transnational regulation, often of a non-state nature. They, furthermore, face continued challenges in the context of enforcement, in industrialized and industrializing countries.

- *A participation deficit*: a second key argument has been that contemporary regulatory discussion is too focused on the relationship between agencies and the regulated industries while ignoring the wider context of, and excluding, other affected parties (such as citizens). In addition, transnational regulation has been accused of lacking openness and legitimacy as regimes emerge without the consent of elected politicians or affected citizens. Therefore, it can be argued that regulation is not sufficiently participatory and open to third parties. As noted, 'smart' and responsive regulation accounts have emphasized the role of third parties in supporting information-gathering activities. It might also be argued that self-regulatory activities require greater external validation by including outside interests. Web 2.0 (or other real-time) enthusiasts would argue that we are only at the beginning of exploiting the potential of digitalization for including 'citizen regulators' in achieving regulatory objectives. Furthermore, as our discussion of risk regulation has noted (Chapter 11), bringing more diverse perspectives into the deliberation of regulatory conversations challenges dominant, but possibly 'wrong', arguments. In other words, advancing participation is not just about enhanced legitimacy by including further interests in the decision-making process. It is also about enhancing the knowledge base that informs regulatory activities.
- *An adaptability deficit*: a third argument is that regulatory activities have become too predictable and lack the capability of imagining different types of failures. Regulators have followed the rule book (as they are risk averse and unwilling to be accused of arbitrary activities).

Furthermore, regulatory regimes have developed dominant under-standings of how regulated processes are supposed to work, thereby ignoring potential warning signs in other parts of the system that may lead to catastrophic failure. Finally, the failure of financial regulation has also been said to be a result of a lack of system-wide adaptability: whereas individual firms were encouraged to be adaptable by taking a portfolio-approach (instead of relying on a single source of invest-ment), these portfolios were similar, therefore aggravating the losses once the financial crisis broke. Thus, regulatory activities need to establish system-wide diversity to encourage stability (Haldane and May 2011).

In other words, regulatory activities have proven incapable of deal-ing with strategic actors, of anticipating the inevitable occurrence of unintended consequences, and of being able to address system-wide rather than organization-specific stability. One way to enhance adapt-ability is to reduce the opportunities for strategic behaviour; for exam-ple, by making inspections less predictable, by regularly altering benchmarks and by rotating regulatory staff across domains and activities. Reducing the capability of systems to be 'routinized' is therefore a key factor in advancing the 'adaptability' of regulatory systems, especially as it provides an inbuilt challenge function in the way in which information is processed. It also means that regulatory enforcement will not rely on a sole emphasis on close and iterative relationships that may be reluctant to escalate enforcement strategies. In short, advocating more adaptability means being in favour of build-ing unpredictability and challenge functions into regulatory regimes that focus on system-wide effects.

- *An incentive deficit*: the fourth and final argument is that regulatory regimes lack sufficient incentives to encourage 'performance'. A lack of incentives can be diagnosed on a number of fronts. First, the perfor-mance of regulators is hardly ever benchmarked, in contrast to the popularity of using yardsticks and benchmarks in assessing the behav-iour of regulatees. Of course, it might be argued that the regulation of prisons is fundamentally different to the regulation of food hygiene or the regulation of trade flows of diamonds from conflict zones. However, it is still possible to envisage ways of comparing regulatory regimes, if only in terms of procedural performance (for example, the comparison of resource input in taking decisions).

  Second, despite decades of incentive-based regulation (for example, price-setting formulas in infrastructure industries), it might be argued that attention to actual individual behaviours has only recently emerged on the regulatory agenda with the 'discovery' of behavioural economics and so-called 'nudging' approaches (Thaler and Sunstein 2008; see also Chapter 5). A greater focus on incentives would facili-tate our understanding of how simple design choices could manipulate individual choices in desirable ways and at low cost. However, we are still in a phase of developing our understanding of how to incentivize behaviour within regulatees' organizations, for example, between headquarters and subsidiaries of firms, rather than merely focusing on the individual behavioural responses to particular regulatory interventions. Furthermore, a focus on incentives also requires a greater emphasis on the behaviours of those doing the regulation rather than focusing solely on the targets of regulation. In sum, the incentive deficit is said to be prominent in two ways: first, in a lack of rivalry and performance assessment between regulatory agencies, and, second, in the way in which regulatory regimes have paid insufficient attention to the actual individual and organizational responses to rules.

Cutting across these debates are larger philosophical battles, for example, regarding the extent to which market failures are likely, and how such market failures (when left unaddressed) are balanced out by potential 'government/regulatory failure' that occurs if regulatory action is taken. Another cross-cutting debate concerns the capability of individuals to undertake informed individual decisions, or whether individual choice needs to be curtailed for the wider good (i.e. because of the complexity of information requirements, the timescale involved and the like).

Such debates produce no easy answers and reflect the fundamental philosophical arguments that have shaped the regulatory debates which further illustrate that good regulation is about being willing to confront these questions openly rather than viewing regulation through any fixed prism or against any paradigm.

The value of regulatory analysis

Giving advice on 'good regulation' is not about advising on 'best in world' options. It is about highlighting the inherent tensions and conflicts that emerge when choosing one particular (mixed) approach rather than another. It is not possible to combine all approaches at the same time – such a regime would collapse under its own contradictions. Ultimately good regulation is about legitimate regulation and any debate as to what is legitimate is likely to cause controversy. However, legitimate regulation is about the acceptance of the rules of the game (in terms of explicit rules and implicit understandings). Without such an acceptance or embeddedness, any regulatory regime is likely to face adversarial relations, the need to resort to coercive rather than cooperative approaches, and, inevitably, attempts to undermine the overall regulatory regime.

So what can regulatory analysis contribute to 'good' or legitimate regulation? Regulatory analysis, as noted in the Introduction, is about thinking like a regulator who acts within an inherently political (i.e. contestable) environment. The acceptance that the environment is contestable (and therefore political) is one that may be hard to swallow for those enthusiasts who regard regulation as a technocratic tool that promises to take uncertainty, volatility and 'politics' out of politics and public policy.

Robert Goodin once argued that a 'well-designed institution … is both internally consistent and in harmony with the rest of the social order in which it is set' (1996: 34). A regulatory analysis perspective does not deny the importance of a regulatory regime's fit with the particular social order. This would, for example, have considerable implications on the feasibility of management-based standards, on the creation of supposedly independent regulatory agencies, or on the utilization of particular alternatives to regulation. However, a regulatory analysis perspective would disagree with an argument of a well-designed institution that placed its emphasis on 'harmony'. Any regulatory choice is fundamentally about trade-offs and therefore choosing one subset of the social order over another. A goodness of fit criterion, therefore, makes little sense – as any regulatory regime will be supported by some, but opposed by others (Lodge 2002b: 178). Opposition towards, and criticism of, particular regulatory measures (and regulation in general) will always be prominent and is unavoidable. Similarly, as our earlier discussion of mixed strategies suggested, it is also contested whether 'internally consistent' regulatory strategies offer benevolent outcomes. It appears that regimes that seek to hold somewhat contradictory components together offer a less vulnerable approach towards exploitation and other side effects that might undermine regulatory intentions (Hood 1998: 240).

A regulatory analysis perspective therefore emphasizes the importance of accepting discretion and interpretation in all regulatory activities. To build regulatory capacity and therefore to facilitate good regulation is to endorse and encourage the open discussion of different problem definitions and solutions. Contestation – as noted already in the Introduction – does neither mean that 'nothing works', nor that 'it all depends'. The field of regulation has developed critical insights about the feasibility of various strategies in different contexts. It has also advanced an increasingly sophisticated awareness of the limitations of different strategies. For those practicing regulatory analysis, this means that the core task is, first of all, to distil actual regulatory problems to the key analytical concerns and to develop different potential solutions. In a second step, then, these insights need to be considered in the light of the actual institutional and political opportunities and constraints.

Combining an understanding of contestation (and hence politics) with a discursive approach to solving problems is inherently challenging, and possibly goes against the grain of appropriate behaviour in the world of regulators that emphasizes technocratic rule following. However, it is also a key to avoiding falling into the trap of cheap expert advice. Such a strategy would require two key steps for any regulatory analyst:

1. Keep a critical mind on one's own biases and implicit assumptions about particular situations. Good regulation is about understanding the advantages and limitations of particular approaches, and the way we go about regulation, in terms of the basic interactions between regulators and regulatees, in terms of favouring particular regulatory arrangements over others, and in terms of the kind of standard operating procedures that govern particular regimes.
2. Pluralize the deliberation regarding regulatory options. As noted throughout this book, all potential solutions to particular regulatory problems are inherently contestable and limited. This does not mean that we should just accept our limitations or become cynical about them, as we stressed in the Introduction. In contrast, it places a considerable responsibility on regulatory analysts: it requires the ability to be aware, to understand, to communicate and to apply contrasting regulatory recipes that are often linked to very different constituencies. Such demands also have implications for the kind of competencies that are in demand for a regulatory analyst. They go beyond the demands for technocratic and judge-type subject expertise (in whatever relevant discipline or interdisciplinary field), and extend to so-called boundary-spanning skills, namely the skills of being able to pick expertise, to access these different sources of expertise and to translate that expertise to particular contexts. It also requires considerable sage-type skills, as it requires an understanding of the political and administrative feasibility of particular strategies in a given context. In other words, regulatory analysts do not know all the answers, but they know (some of) the questions and, importantly, they also know who to ask and how to communicate with different constituencies.

If this book has offered some encouragement towards bringing regulatory analysis to life for the benefit not just of Amnesia but also of 'real people' we will have succeeded.

Bibliography

Abbott, K.W., Keohane, R.O., Moravcsik, A., Slaughter, A.-M., and Snidal, D. (2000) 'The concept of legalization', *International Organization*, 54(3): 519–48.

Abbott, K. and Snidal, D. (2009) 'Strengthening international regulation through transnational new governance', *Vanderbilt Journal of Transnational Law*, 42: 501–78.

Affuso, L. and Newbery, D. (2000) 'Investment, reprocurement and franchise contract length in the british railway industry' *CEPR Discussion papers* no. 2619, www.cepr.org/pubs/dps/DP2619.asp (last accessed 6 March 2012).

Akerlof, R. (1970) 'The market for "lemons": quality uncertainty and the market mechanism', *Quarterly Journal of Economics*, 84(3): 488–500.

Althingi (2010) *Skýrsla rannsóknarnefndar Alþingis* [Report of the Special Investigation Commission], Iceland, Alþingis, http://sic.althingi.is/ (last accessed 4 September 2011).

Armstrong, M., Cowan, S. and Vickers, J. (1994) *Regulatory Reform: Economic Analysis and British Experience*, Cambridge, MA, MIT Press.

Arrow, K., Cropper, M., Eads, G., Hahn, R., Lave, L., Noll, R., Portney, P., Russell, M., Schmalensee, R., Smith, V.K. and Stavins, R. (1996) 'Is there a role for benefit-cost analysis in environmental, health, and safety regulation?', *Science*, 272 (12 April): 221–2.

Atlas, M. (2007) 'Enforcement principles and environmental agencies: principal-agent relationships in a delegated environmental program', *Law & Society Review*, 41(4): 939–80.

Ayres, I. and Braithwaite, J. (1992) *Responsive Regulation*, Oxford, Oxford University Press.

Baccaro, L. and Mele, V. (2011) 'For lack of anything better? International organizations and global corporate codes', *Public Administration*, 89(2): 451–70.

Baldwin, R. (1990) 'Why rules don't work', *Modern Law Review*, 53(3): 321–37.

Baldwin, R. (1995) *Rules and Government*, Oxford, Clarendon Press.

Baldwin, R. (1997) 'Regulation: after command and control', in D. Harris and K. Hawkins (ed.) *The Human Face of Law*, Oxford, Oxford University Press.

Baldwin, R. (2004) 'The new punitive regulation', *Modern Law Review*, 67: 351–83.

Baldwin, R. (2008) 'Regulation lite: the rise of emission trading', *Regulation & Governance*, 2(2): 193–215.

Baldwin, R. (2010) 'Better regulation: the search and the struggle', in R. Baldwin, M. Cave and M. Lodge (eds) *Oxford Handbook of Regulation*, Oxford, Oxford University Press.

Baldwin, R. and Black, J. (2008) 'Really responsive regulation', *Modern Law Review*, 71(1): 59–94.

Baldwin, R., Cave, M. and Lodge, M. (eds) (2010) *Oxford Handbook of Regulation*, Oxford, Oxford University Press.

Baldwin, R. Cave, M. and Lodge, M. (2012) *Understanding Regulation*, Oxford, Oxford University Press.

Barber, M. (2007) *Instruction to Deliver*, London, Politico.

Bardach, E. (2004) 'The extrapolation problem: how can we learn from the experience of others?', *Journal of Policy Analysis and Management*, 23(2): 205–20.

Bardach, E. and Kagan, R. (1982) *Going by the Book*, Philadelphia, Temple University Press.

Bartley, T. (2011) 'Certification as a mode of social regulation', in D. Levi-Faur, D (ed.) *Handbook of the Politics of Regulation*, Cheltenham, Edward Elgar.

Barzelay, M. (2007) 'Learning from second-hand experience: methodology for extrapolation-oriented research', *Governance*, 20(3): 521–43.

Baumol, W.J., Panzar, J. and Willig, R. (1982) *Contestable Markets and the Theory of Industry Structure*, Fort Worth, TX, Saunders College Publishing/Harcourt Brace.

BBC, 8 September 2009; 'Samoa switches to driving on the left', http://news.bbc.co.uk/1/hi/8243110.stm (last accessed 19 January 2012).

BBC, 5 January 2011; 'German dioxin scandal', www.bbc.co.uk/news/world-europe–12120321 (last accessed 21 January 2012).

BBC, 4 March 2011; 'Lords debate "dogbo" sanctions for pet owners', www.bbc.co.uk/news/uk-politics–12645088 (last accessed 19 January 2012).

BBC, 15 July 2011; 'Mandatory "sun safety" policies for schools are needed', www.bbc.co.uk/news/health–14104524 (last accessed 28 January 2012).

BBC, 5 December 2011; 'Global Witness leaves Kimberley Process diamond scheme', www.bbc.co.uk/news/business–16027011 (last accessed 23 January 2012).

BBC, 24 January 2012; 'Costa Concordia disaster', www.bbc.co.uk/news/world-europe–16563562 (last accessed 28 January 2012).

Beck, U. (1992) *The Risk Society*, London, Sage.

Beck, U. (2009) *World at Risk*, Cambridge, Polity Press.

Becker, G. (1968) 'The optimum enforcement of laws', *Journal of Political Economy*, 76(2): 169–217.

Becker, G. (1983) 'A theory of competition among pressure groups for political influence', *Quarterly Journal of Economics*, 98: 371–400.

Bernheim, B.D. and Whinston, M.D. (1986) 'Menu Auctions, resource allocation, and economic influence', *Quarterly Journal of Economics*, 101(1): 1–32.

Bernstein, M. (1955) *Regulating Business by Independent Commission*, Princeton, Princeton University Press.

Bevan, G. and Hood, C. (2006) 'What's measured is what matters: targets and gaming in the English public health care system', *Public Administration*, 84(3): 517–38.

Bild, 20 November 2008; 'Immer mehr Schwarzfahrer in Berlin', www.bild.de/regional/berlin/berlin/immer-mehr-zahlen-nicht-fuer-ihr-ticket–6524450.bild.html (last accessed 21 January 2012).

Black, D. (1976) *The Behavior of Law*, New York, Academic Press.

Black, J. (1997) *Rules and Regulators*, Oxford, Oxford University Press.

Black, J. (2000) 'Proceduralizing regulation: part 1', *Oxford Journal of Legal Studies*, 20(4): 591–614.

Black, J. (2001) 'Proceduralizing regulation: part 2', *Oxford Journal of Legal Studies*, 21(1): 33–58.

Black, J. (2002a) 'Critical reflections on regulation', *CARR Discussion Paper*, no. 4, London, London School of Economics.

Black, J. (2002b) 'Regulatory conversations', *Journal of Law and Society*, 29: 163–96.

Black, J. (2002c) 'Decentring regulation: understanding the role of regulation and self-regulation in a "post-regulatory" world', *Current Legal Problems*, 54: 103–46.

Black, J. (2005) 'The emergence of risk-based regulation and the New Public Management in the UK', *Public Law*, 512–49.

Black, J. (2007) 'Tensions in the regulatory state', *Public Law* 58–73.

Black, J. (2010) 'The role of risk in regulatory processes', in R. Baldwin, M. Cave and M. Lodge (eds) *Oxford Handbook of Regulation*, Oxford, Oxford University Press.

Black, J. and Baldwin, R. (2010) 'Really responsive risk-based regulation', *Law and Policy*, 32(2): 181–213.

Bloor, M., Datta, R., Gilinsky, Y. and Horlick-Jones, T. (2006) 'Unicorn among the cedars: on the possibility of effective "smart regulation" of the globalised shipping industry', *Social & Legal Studies*, 15(4): 534–51.

Bó, E.D. (2006) 'Regulatory capture: a review', *Oxford Review of Economic Policy*, 22(2): 203–25.

Boin, A. (2009) 'The new world of crises and crisis management', *Review of Policy Research*, 26(4): 367–77.

Boin, A. and Fishbacher-Smith, D. (2011) 'The importance of failure theories in assessing crisis management', *Policy and Society*, 30: 77–87.

Börzel, T. (2010) 'European governance: negotiation and competition in the shadow of hierarchy', *Journal of Common Market Studies*, 48(2): 191–219.

Boyer, R. and Saillard, Y. (eds) (2002/1995) *Regulation Theory: The State of the Art*, London, Taylor & Francis.

Braithwaite, J. (2000) 'The new regulatory state and the transformation of criminology', *British Journal of Criminology*, 40(2): 222–38.

Braithwaite, J. (2002) 'Rules and principles: a theory of legal certainty', *Australian Journal of Legal Philosophy*, 27: 47–82.

Braithwaite, J. (2008) *Regulatory Capitalism. How it Works, Ideas for Making it Work Better*, Cheltenham: Edward Elgar.

Braithwaite, J. and Drahos, P. (2000) *Global Business Regulation*, Cambridge, Cambridge University Press.

Braithwaite, J., Walker, J. and Grabosky, P. (1987) 'An enforcement taxonomy of regulatory agencies', *Law & Policy*, 9: 322–51.

Braithwaite, V. (2007) 'Responsive regulation and taxation', *Law and Policy*, 29(1): 3–10.

Brandsen, T., Boogers, M. and Tops, P. (2006) 'Soft governance, hard consequences: the ambiguous status of unofficial guidelines', *Public Administration Review*, 66(4): 546–53.

Breidenich, C., Magraw, D., Rowley, A. and Rubin, J.W. (1998) 'The Kyoto Protocol to the United Nations Framework Convention on Climate Change', *American Journal of International Law*, 92(2): 315–31.

Breyer, S. (1982) *Regulation and its Reform*, Cambridge, MA, Harvard University Press.

Breyer, S. (1993) *Breaking the Vicious Circle*, Cambridge, MA, Harvard University Press.

Brooks, H. (1986) 'The typology of surprises in technology, institutions and development', in W.C. Clark and R.E. Munn (eds) *Sustainable Development of the Biosphere*, Cambridge, Cambridge University Press.

Brown, K. (2001) 'Cut and run? Evolving institutions for global forest governance', *Journal of International Development*, 13(7): 893–905.

BRTF (Better Regulation Task Force) (2000) *Alternatives to State Regulation*, London, Better Regulation Task Force, http://webarchive.nationalarchives. gov.uk/20100807034701/http://archive.cabinetoffice.gov.uk/brc/ upload/assets/www.brc.gov.uk/stateregulation.pdf (last accessed 11 June 2011).

BRTF (Better Regulation Task Force) (2003) *Imaginative Thinking for Better Regulation*, London, Better Regulation Task Force, http://webarchive. nationalarchives.gov.uk/20100807034701/http://archive.cabinetoffice.gov.uk/ brc/upload/assets/www.brc.gov.uk/imaginativeregulation.pdf (last accessed 11 June 2011).

BRTF (Better Regulation Task Force) (2004) *Avoiding Regulatory Creep*, London, Cabinet Office.

BRTF (Better Regulation Task Force) (2005) *Regulation – Less is More*, London, BRTF.

Brütsch, C. and Lehmkuhl, D. (eds) (2007) *Law and Legalization in Transnational Relations*, London, Routledge.

Button, K. and Weyman-Jones, Y. (1993) 'X-inefficiency and regulatory regime shift in the UK', *Journal of Evolutionary Economics*, 3: 269–84.

Carpenter, D.P. (2010) *Reputation and Power*, Princeton, Princeton University Press.

Carrigan, C. and Coglianese, C. (2011) 'The politics of regulation: from new institutionalism to new governance', *Annual Review of Political Science*, 14: 107–29.

Cashore, B. (2002) 'Legitimization and the privatization of environmental governance', *Governance*, 15(4): 503–29.

Cave Review (2009) *Competition and Innovation in Water Markets*, http://archive.defra.gov.uk/environment/quality/water/industry/cavereview/ (last accessed 8 September 2011).

Chadwick, E. (1859) 'Research of different principles of legislation and administration in Europe of competition for the field as compared with competition within the field of service', *Journal of the Royal Statistical Society*, 22(3): 381–420.

Chalmers, D., Davies, G. and Monti, G. (2010) *EU Law*, Cambridge, Cambridge University Press.

Clune, W.H. (1992) 'Implementation as autopoietic interaction of autopoietic organizations' in G. Teubner and A. Febbrajo (eds) *State, Law and Economy as Autopoietic Systems – Regulation and Autonomy in New Perspective*, Milan, Guiffre.

Coglianese, C. and Lazer, D. (2003) 'Management based regulation: prescribing private management to achieve public goals', *Law & Society Review*, 37: 691–730.

Coglianese, C. and Mendelsohn, E. (2010) 'Meta-regulation and self-regulation', in R. Baldwin, M. Cave and M. Lodge (eds) *Oxford Handbook of Regulation*, Oxford, Oxford University Press.

Cohen, D. and Lindblom, C. (1979) *Usable Knowledge*, New Haven, Yale University Press.

Courville, S. (2003) 'Social accountability audits: challenging or defending democratic governance?', *Law and Policy*, 25(3) 269–97.

Croley, S.P. (2008) *Regulation and Public Interest: The Possibility of Good Regulatory Government*, Princeton and Oxford: Princeton University Press.

Dean, M. (1999) *Governmentality*, London, Sage.

Demortain, D. (2010) 'The many meanings of "standard": the politics of the international standard for food risk analysis', *CARR Discussion Paper 58*, London, LSE.

Demsetz, H. (1968) 'Why regulate utilities', *Journal of Law and Economics*, 11(1): 55–65.

Demsetz, H. (1971) 'On the regulation of industry: a reply', *Journal of Political Economy*, 79(2): 356–63.

Department of Transport (1987) *The Merchant Shipping Act 1894, MV Herald of Free Enterprise*, report of Court No. 8074 (Sheen Report), London, HMSO.

Department of Treasury and Finance (2007) *Victorian Guide to Regulation*, Department of Treasury and Finance, Melbourne, www.dtf.vic.gov.au/ CA25713E0002EF43/WebObj/VictorianGuidetoRegulation2007/$File/ Victorian%20Guide%20to%20Regulation%202007.pdf (last accessed 11 June 2011).

Derthick, M. and Quirk, P. (1985) *The Politics of Deregulation*, Washington DC, Brookings.

Diver, C.S. (1983) 'The optimal precision of administrative rules', *Yale Law Journal* 93: 65–109.

Doern, G.B. (2009) 'A regulatory budget and a strategic regulatory agenda', manuscript, http://papers.ssrn.com/sol3/papers.cfm?abstract_id=1532412 (last accessed 6 March 2012).

Döhler, M. and Wegrich, K. (2010) 'Regulierung als Konzept und Instrument moderner Staatlichkeit', *der moderne staat*, 3(1) 31–52.

Dominion Post, 23 January 2012; 'Stalled dog laws review to get bite', www.stuff.co.nz/dominion-post/news/6297407/Stalled-dog-laws-review-to-get-bite (last accessed 24 January 2012).

Dominion Post, 5 April 2011; 'Leaky homes: acrisis with no end in sight', www.stuff.co.nz/national/politics/4847027/Leaky-homes-A-crisis-with-no-end-in-sight (last accessed 19 January 2012).

Doron, G. (1979) 'Administrative regulation of an industry: the cigarette case', *Public Administration Review*, 39: 163–70.

Douglas, M. (1986) *How Institutions Think*, London, Routledge.

Douglas, M. (1992) *Risk and Blame*, London, Routledge.

Douglas, M. and Wildavsky, A. (1982) *Divided We Stand*, Berkeley, University of California Press.

Downer, J. (2007) 'When the chick hits the fan', *Social Studies of Science*, 31: 7–26.

Downs, A. (1967) *Inside Bureaucracy*, Boston, Little, Brown.

Drauth, C. (2010) *Closing Global Governance Gaps Through Corporate Social Responsibility*, Berlin, Hertie School of Governance Working Papers, No. 54, August 2010 (http://www.hertie-school.org/fileadmin/images/Downloads/working_papers/54.pdf, last accessed 11 March 2012).

Economist, 7 July 2011; 'Indonesian schools: more cheating, or else!' www.economist.com/node/18929180 (last accessed 23 January 2012).

Eden, L. and Kudrle, R. (2005) 'Tax havens: renegade states in the international tax regime', *Law & Policy*, 27(1): 100–27.

Ekelund, R. and Ford, G. (1997) 'Nineteenth century urban market failure? Chadwick on funeral industry regulation' *Journal of Regulatory Economics*, 12(1): 27–51.

Ellis, R., Wildavsky, A. and Thompson, M. (1991) *Cultural Theory*, Boulder, Westview.

Estache, A. and Wren-Lewis, L. (2010) 'On the theory and evidence on regulation of network industries', in R. Baldwin, M. Cave and M. Lodge (eds) *Oxford Handbook of Regulation*, Oxford, Oxford University Press.

European Commission (2000) 'Communication on the precautionary principle', COM (2000)1.

European Commission (2008) 'Impact assessment on the standards of quality and safety of human organs intended for transplantation', SEC/2008/2956.

European Commission (2010) 'Impact Assessment Board report for 2009', SEC/2009/1728.

European Court of Auditors (2009) 'Impact assessments in the EU institutions: do they support decision making?', Special Report No. 3/2010.

Fairman, R. and Yapp, C. (2005) 'Enforced self-regulation, prescription and conceptions of compliance within small businesses', *Law and Policy*, 27(4): 491–519.

Falkner, G., Treib, O., Hartlapp, M. and Leiber, S. (2005) *Complying with Europe*, Cambridge, Cambridge University Press.

Feintuck, M. (2010) 'Regulatory rationales beyond the economic: in search of the public interest', in R. Baldwin, M. Cave and M. Lodge (eds) *Oxford Handbook of Regulation*, Oxford, Oxford University Press.

Feldman, M. and Khademian, A. (2007) 'The role of the public manager in inclusion', *Governance*, 20(2): 305–24.

Financial Times, 7 January 2012; 'Plastic surgery worries fuel broader debate over provision', London edn, p. 2

Financial Times, 15 June 2010; 'Groups slam scheme on "blood diamonds"', www.ft.com/cms/s/0/6b861a28–76f6–11df-ba79-00144feabdc0.html (last accessed 23 January 2012).

Financial Times, 31 May 2011; 'Inspectors doubt ability to protect residents', London edn, p. 3.

Financial Times, 11 June 2011; 'Alarm over access to credit' FT weekend Money Supplement, London edn, p. 32.

Financial Times, 25 July 2011; 'Whitehall sheds some red tape', London edn, p. 2.

Financial Times, 10 September 2011; 'Coppers and robbers in battle of iron wills', www.ft.com/cms/s/0/84c0078a-d580–11e0–9133-00144feab49a.html#axzz1kMqWnCWW (last accessed 25 January 2012).

Finer, S.E. (1950) *A Primer in Public Administration*, London, Frederick Muller.

Fiorina, M (1982) 'Legislative Choice of Regulatory Forms', *Public Choice*, 39(1): 33–66.

Fischer, F. (2003) *Reframing Public Policy*, Oxford, Oxford University Press.

Foster, C. (1992) *Privatization, Public Ownership, and the Regulation of Natural Monopoly*, Oxford, Blackwell.

Foucault, M. (1991) 'Governmentality' in G. Burchell, C. Gordon, and P. Miller (eds) *The Faucault Effect: Studies in Governmentality*, Chicago, Chicago University Press.

Frederickson, H.G. and LaPorte, T.R. (2002) 'Airport security, high reliability and the problem of problem of rationality' *Public Administration Review*, 62: 33–43.

Freeman, P. and Kunreuther, H. (1997) *Managing Environmental Risk through Insurance*, Dordrecht, Kluwer.

FSA (Financial Services Authority) (2011) *The Failure of the Royal Bank of Scotland*, London, FSA, www.fsa.gov.uk/pubs/other/rbs.pdf (last accessed 18 January 2012).

FSA (Financial Services Authority) (2009) *The Turner Review: a Regulatory Response to the Global Banking Crisis*, London, FSA.

Fung, A., Graham, M. and Weil, D. (2007) *Full Disclosure. The Perils and Promise of Transparency*, Cambridge: Cambridge University Press.

Gilardi, F. (2002) 'Policy credibility and delegation to independent regulatory agencies', *Journal of European Public Policy*, 9(6): 873–93.

Government of Canada (2011) 'Order amending Schedule 1 to the Species at Risk Act' *Canada Gazette*, 2 July, 145(27), www.gazette.gc.ca/rp-pr/p1/2011/2011-07-02/html/reg6-eng.html (last accessed 6 March 2012).

Grabosky, P. (1995a) 'Counterproductive regulation', *International Journal of the Sociology of Law*, 23: 347–69.

Grabosky, P. (1995b) 'Regulation by reward: on the use of incentives as regulatory instruments', *Law and Policy*, 17(3): 257–82.

Grabosky, P. (1995c) 'Using non-governmental resources to foster regulatory compliance', *Governance*, 8: 527–50.

Graham, C. and Prosser, T. (1991) *Privatizing Public Enterprises*, Oxford, Clarendon Press.

Gilad, S. (2010) 'It runs in the family: meta-regulation and its siblings', *Regulation & Governance*, 4(4): 485–506.

Gómez-Ibáñez, J.A. (2003) *Regulating Infrastructure*, Cambridge, MA, Harvard University Press.

Goodin, R. (1996) *Theory of Institutional Design*, Cambridge, Cambridge University Press.

Gormley, W.T. (1988) 'Regulatory enforcement styles', *Political Research Quarterly*, 51: 363–83.

Grabosky, P. and Braithwaite, J. (1986) *Of Matters Gentle*, Melbourne, Oxford University Press.

Gray, J. (2009) 'Is it time to highlight the limits of risk-based financial regulation', *Capital Markets Law Journal*, 4(1): 50–62.

Guasch, J.L., Laffont, J.J. and Straub, S. (2008) 'Renegotiation of concession contracts in Latin America', *International Journal of Industrial Organization*, 26: 421–42.

Gunningham, N. (1995) 'Enforcement, self-regulation and the chemical industry', *Law & Policy*, 17(1): 57–107.

Gunningham, N. (1997) 'Negotiated non-compliance: acase study of regulatory failure', *Law & Policy*, 9(1): 69–96.

Gunningham, N. (2007) 'Corporate environmental responsibility, law and the LIMITS of voluntarism', in D. McBarnett, A. Voicelescu and T. Campbell (eds) *The New Corporate Accountability: Corporate Social Responsibility and the Law*, Cambridge University Press.

Gunningham, N. (2010) 'Enforcement and compliance strategies', in R. Baldwin, M. Cave and M. Lodge (eds) *Oxford Handbook of Regulation*, Oxford, Oxford University Press.

Gunningham, N. and Grabosky, P. (1998) *Smart Regulation: Designing Environmental Policy*, Oxford, Clarendon Press.

Gunningham, I. and Sinclair, D. (2009) 'Organizational trust and the limits of management-based regulation', *Law & Society Review*, 43(4): 865–900.

Gunningham, N., Thornton, D. and Kagan, R.A. (2005) 'Motivating management: corporate compliance in environmental protection', *Law & Policy*, 27(2): 289–316.

Haas, P.M. (1992) 'Introduction: epistemic communities and international policy coordination', *International Organization*, 46(1): 1–35.

Hahn, R. and Sunstein, C. (2002) 'A new executive order for improving federal regulation? Deeper and wider cost–benefit analysis', *University of Chicago Law & Economics* Olin Working Paper No 150, http://papers.ssrn.com/sol3/papers.cfm?abstract_id=309754 (last accessed 6 March 2012).

Hahn, R. and Tetlock, P.C. (2008) 'Has economic analysis improved regulatory decisions?', *Journal of Economic Perspectives*, 22(1): 67–84.

Haines, F. (1997) *Corporate Regulation: Beyond 'Punish or Persuade'*, Oxford, Clarendon Press.

Haldane, A. and May, R. (2011) 'Systemic risk in banking ecosystems', *Nature*, 469: 351–5.

Hall, C., Scott, C. and Hood, C. (2000) *Telecommunications Regulation*, London, Routledge.

Hall, P.A. (1993) 'Policy paradigms, social learning, and the state', *Comparative Politics* 25: 275–96.

Hall, P.A. and Soskice, D. (2001) 'An introduction to varieties of capitalism', in P.A. Hall and D. Soskice (eds) *Varieties of Capitalism: The Institutional Foundations of Comparative Advantage*, Oxford, Oxford University Press.

Hammond, T.H. and Knott, J.H. (1988) 'The deregulatory snowball: explaining deregulation in the financial industry', *Journal of Politics*, 50: 3–30.

Hampton, P. (2005) *Assessing Our Regulatory System*, London, Department of Business Innovation and Skills, http://webarchive.nationalarchives.gov.uk/+/http://www.bis.gov.uk/policies/better-regulation/improving-regulatory-delivery/assessing-our-regulatory-system (last accessed 21 January 2012).

Hancher, L. (1998) 'Community, state and market', in P. Craig and G. de Burca (eds) *The Evolution of EU Law*, Oxford, Oxford University Press.

Hancher, L. and Moran, M. (1989) 'Organizing regulatory space', in L. Hancher and M. Morgan (eds) *Capitalism, Culture and Economic Regulation*, Oxford, Oxford University Press.

Hanretty, C. and Koop, C. (2011) 'Measuring the formal independence of regulatory agencies', *Journal of European Public Policy*, 19(2): 198–216.

Hardin, G. (1968) 'The tragedy of the commons', *Science*, 162: 1243–8.

Harford, T. (2011) *Adapt: Why Success Always Starts With Failure*, New York, Farrar, Straus and Giroux.

Hawkins, K. (1984) *Environment and Enforcement*, Oxford, Clarendon Press.

Heclo, H. and Wildavsky, A. (1974) *The Private Government of Public Money*, London, Macmillan.

Heifetz, R. (1994) *Leadership without Easy Answers*, Cambridge, MA, Harvard University Press.

Helm, D. and Tindall, T. (2009) 'The evolution of infrastructure and utility ownership and its implications', *Oxford Review of Economic Policy*, 32(3): 411–34.

Heritier, A. (2001) 'Market integration and social cohesion', *Journal of European Public Policy*, 8(5): 825–52.

Hindmoor, A. (2010) 'The banking crisis: grid, group and the state of the debate', *Australian Journal of Public Administration*, 69(4): 442–56.

Honohan, P. (2010) *The Irish Banking Crisis: regulatory and Financial Stability Policy 2003–2008*, www.bankinginquiry.gov.ie/Preliminary_Reports.aspx (last accessed 6 March 2012).

Hood, C. (1974) 'Administrative diseases: some types of dysfunctionality in administration', *Public Administration*, 52(4): 439–54.

Hood, C. (1986) *Administrative Analysis*, Hemel Hempstead, Harvester Wheatsheaf.

Hood, C. (1991) 'A public management for all seasons?', *Public Administration*, 69(1): 3–19.

Hood, C. (1994) *Explaining Economic Policy Reversals*, Buckingham, Open University Press.

Hood, C. (1998) *The Art of the State*, Oxford, Oxford University Press.

Hood, C. (2006) 'Gaming in targetworld: the target approach to managing British public services', *Public Administration Review*, 66(4): 515–20.

Hood, C. (2010) 'Can we? Administrative limits revisited', *Public Administration Review*, 70(4): 527–34.

Hood, C. (2011) *The Blame Game*, Princeton, Princeton University Press.

Hood, C., James, O., Peters, G.B. and Scott, C. (eds) (2004) *Controlling Modern Government*, Cheltenham, Edward Elgar.

Hood, C. and Jones, D. (eds) (1996) *Accident and Design*, London, UCL Press.

Hood, C. and Lodge, M. (2005) 'Pavlovian innovation, pet solutions and economizing on rationality?', in J. Black, M. Lodge and M. Thatcher (eds) *Regulatory Innovation*, Cheltenham, Edward Elgar.

Hood, C. and Peters, B.G. (2004) 'The middle ageing of new public management: into the age of paradox?', *Journal of Public Administration Theory and Research*, 14(3): 267–82.

Hood, C., Rothstein, H. and Baldwin, R. (2001) *The Government of Risk*, Oxford, Oxford University Press.

Hood, C., Scott, C., James, O., Jones, G. and Travers, T. (1999) *Regulation Inside Government*, Oxford, Oxford University Press.

Horn, M. (1995) *Political Economy of Public Administration*, Cambridge, Cambridge University Press.

Howe, J. (2009) *Crowdsourcing*, New York, Random House.

Huntington, S.P. (1952) 'The marasmus of the ICC: the commission, the railroads and the public interest', *Yale Law Journal*, 61: 467–509.

Hutter, B.M. (1988) *The Reasonable Arm of the Law? The Law Enforcement Procedures of Environmental Health Officers*, Oxford, Clarendon Press.

Hutter, B.M. (1997) *Compliance*, Oxford, Clarendon Press.

Hutter, B. (2005) 'The attractions of risk-based regulation' *CARR Discussion Paper 33*, London, LSE.

Independent Farming Regulation Task Force (2011) *Striking a Balance: Reducing Burdens; Increasing Responsibility; Earning Recognition*, London, DEFRA, www.defra.gov.uk/publications/files/pb13527-farm-reg-task-report.pdf (last accessed 21 January 2012).

Industrial Union Department v American Petroleum Institute, 448 US 607, see: http://supreme.justia.com/cases/federal/us/448/607/ (last accessed 28 January 2012).

Jennings, W. and Lodge, M. (2011) 'Governing mega-events', *Government & Opposition*, 46(2): 192–222.

Jensen, K., Lassen, J., Robinson, P. and Sandøo, P. (2005) 'Lay and expert perceptions of zoonitic risks', *International Journal of Food Microbiology*, 99(3): 245–55.

Jessop, B. (1997) 'Capitalism and its future: remarks on regulation, government and governance', *Review of International Political Economy*, 4(3): 561–81.

Jojarth, C. (2009) *Crime, War, and Global Trafficking*, Cambridge, Cambridge University Press.

Kagan, R.A. (1994) 'Regulatory enforcement', in D.H. Rosenbloom and R.D. Schwartz (eds) *Handbook of Regulation and Administrative Law*, New York, Marcel Dekker.

Kagan, R.A. (2001) *Adversarial Legalism*, Cambridge, MA, Harvard University Press.

Kagan, R. and Scholz, J. (1984) 'The "criminology of the corporation" and regulatory enforcement strategies', in K. Hawkins and J.M. Thomas (eds) *Enforcing Regulation*, Boston, MA, Kluwer-Nijhoff.

Kahan, D., Jenkins-Smith, H. and Braman, D. (2011) 'Cultural cognition of scientific consensus', *Journal of Risk Research*, 14(2): 147–74.

Kahnemann, D. (2003) 'A perspective on judgement and choice', *American Psychologist*, 58(9): 697–720.

Kasperson, R.E. and Kasperson, J.X. (1996) 'The social amplification and attenuation of risk', *ANNALS of the American Academy of Political and Social Science*, 545(1): 95–105.

Kaufman, H. (1967) *The Forest Ranger*, Baltimore, Johns Hopkins University Press.

Kaufman, H. (1971) *The Limits of Organizational Change*, Tuscaloosa, University of Alabama Press.

Keeler, T. (1984) 'Theories of regulation and deregulation', *Public Choice*, 44: 103–45.

Kelman, S (1981) *Regulating America, Regulating Sweden*, Cambridge, MA, MIT Press.

Kelman, S. and Friedman, J.N. (2009) 'Performance improvement and performance dysfunction', *Journal of Public Administration Research and Theory*, 19(4): 917–46.

Khademian, A. (2009) 'A public administration moment: forging an agenda for financial regulatory reform', *Public Administration Review*, 69(4): 595–602.

Kimmitt, R.M. (2008) 'Public footprints in private markets', *Foreign Affairs*, January/February 2008, www.foreignaffairs.com/articles/63053/robert-m-kimmitt/public-footprints-in-private-markets (last accessed 6 March 2012).

Klein, M. (1998) 'Network industries', in D. Helm and T. Jenkinson (eds) *Competition in Regulated Industries*, Oxford, Oxford University Press.

Klemperer, P. (1999) 'Auction theory: a guide to the literature', *Journal of Economic Surveys*, 13(3): 227–86.

Klemperer, P. (2002) 'What really matters in auction design', *Journal of Economic Perspectives*, 16: 169–89.

Knight, F. (1921) *Risk, Uncertainty, and Profit*, Boston, MA, Hart, Schaffner & Marx.

Koenig-Archibugi, M. (2010) 'Global regulation', in R. Baldwin, M. Cave and M. Lodge (eds) *Oxford Handbook of Regulation*, Oxford, Oxford University Press.

Kolko, G. (1965) *Railroads and Regulation 1877–1916*, Cambridge, MA, Harvard University Press.

Koop, C. (2011) 'Explaining the accountability of independent agencies', *Journal of Public Policy*, 31(2): 209–34.

Koremenos, B., Lipson, C. and Snidal, D. (2001) 'The rational design of international institutions', *International Organization*, 55(2): 289–325.

Krasner, S.D. (1982) 'Structural causes and regime consequences', *International Organization*, 36: 185–205.

Kunreuther, H., Michel-Kerjan, E., Heller, C., Doherty, N., Grace, M., Klein, R. and Pauly, M. (2009) *At War with the Weather*, Cambridge, MA, Harvard University Press.

Laffont, J. and Tirole, J. (1988) 'Repeated auctions of incentive contracts, investment and bidding parity with an application to takeovers', *RAND Journal of Economics*, 19(4): 516–37.

Lanchester, J. (2010) *Whoops: Why Everyone Owes Everyone and No One Can Pay*, London, Allen Lane.

LaPorte, T. (2007) 'Anticipating rude surprises', in L. Jones (ed) *Communicable Crises*, Amsterdam, Elsevier.

LaPorte, T. and Consolini, P. (1991) 'Working in practice but not in theory: theoretical challenges of "high reliability organizations"', *Journal of Public Administration Research and Theory*, 1: 19–47.

Law, M. (2006) 'How do enforcers regulate?', *Journal of Law, Economics and Organization*, 22(2): 459–89.

Lehmkuhl, D. (2008) 'Control modes in the age of transnational governance', *Law & Policy*, 30(3): 336–63.

Lessig, L. (2000) *Code and Other Laws of Cyberspace*, New York, Basic Books.

Levi-Faur, D. (2006) 'Varieties of regulatory capitalism', *Governance*, 19(3): 367–82.

Levine, M.E. and Forrence, J.L. (1990) 'Regulatory capture, public interest and the public agenda: towards synthesis', *Journal of Law, Economics and Organization*, 6: 167–98.

Levy, B. and Spiller, P. (1994) 'The institutional foundations of regulatory commitment: a comparative study of telecommunications regulation', *Journal of Law, Economics and Organisation*, 10(2): 201–46.

Levy, B. and Spiller, P. (1996) *Regulation, Institutions and Commitment*, Cambridge, Cambridge University Press.

Light, J. (2010) 'Public choice: a critical reassessment', in E.J. Balleisen and D.A. Moss (eds) *Government and Markets*, Cambridge, Cambridge University Press.

Lin, A.C. (2000) *Reform in the Making*, Princeton, Princeton University Press.

Lindblom, C.E. (1979) 'Still muddling, not yet through', *Public Administration Review*, 39: 517–26.

Lodge, M. (1999) 'Competing approaches to regulation', in K. Eliassen and M. Sjovaag (eds) *European Telecommunications Liberalisation*, London, Routledge.

Lodge, M. (2002a) '"The wrong type of regulation?" Regulatory failure and the railways in Britain and Germany', *Journal of Public Policy*, 22(3): 271–97.

Lodge, M. (2002b) *On Different Tracks*, Westport, CT, Praeger.

Lodge, M. (2004) 'Germany', in C. Hood, O. James, G.B. Peters and C. Scott (eds) *Controlling Modern Government*, Cheltenham, Edward Elgar.

Lodge, M. (2005) 'The importance of being modern', *Journal of European Public Policy*, 12(4): 649–67.

Lodge, M. (2007) 'Comparing non-hierarchical governance in action', *Journal of Common Market Studies*, 45(2): 343–65.

Lodge, M. (2008) 'Regulation and the regulatory state', *West European Politics*, 30(1): 280–301.

Lodge, M. (2009) 'The public management of risk', *Review of Policy Research*, 26(4): 395–408.

Lodge, M. (2011) 'Risk, regulation and crisis', *Journal of Public Policy*, 31(1): 25–50.

Lodge, M. and Hood, C. (2010) 'Regulation inside government', *Oxford Handbook of Regulation*, Oxford, Oxford University Press.

Lodge, M. and Scott, C. (2003) 'Administrative simplification in the United Kingdom', in P. Ladegaard, C. Córdova-Novion, R. Alter, P. Czaga, J.S. Lubbers, and R. Deighton-Smith (eds) *From Red Tape to Smart Tape: Administrative Simplification in OECD Countries*, Paris, OECD: pp. 195–216.

Lodge, M. and Stirton, L. (2006) 'Withering in the heat? The regulatory state and reform in Jamaica and Trinidad & Tobago', *Governance*, 19(3): 465–95.

Lodge, M. and Stirton, L. (2010) 'Accountability in the regulatory state', in R. Baldwin, M. Cave and M. Lodge (eds) *Oxford Handbook of Regulation*, Oxford, Oxford University Press.

Lodge, M. and Wegrich, K. (2005a) 'Governing multi-level governance: domain dynamics in German prisons and building administration', *Public Administration*, 83(2): 417–42.

Lodge, M. and Wegrich, K. (2005b) 'Control over government: institutional isomorphism and governance dynamics in German public administration', *Policy Studies Journal*, 33(2): 213–33.

Lodge, M. and Wegrich, K. (2009) 'High quality regulation: its popularity, its tools and its future', *Public Money and Management*, 29(3): 145–52.

Lodge, M. and Wegrich, K. (2010) 'Letter to the Editor of *Public Administration Review* in response to a recent symposium on financial regulatory reform', *Public Administration Review*, 70(2) 336–41.

Lodge, M. and Wegrich, K. (2011a) 'Arguing about financial regulation', *PS: Political Science*, 44(4): 726–30.

Lodge, M. and Wegrich, K. (2011b) 'Governance as contested logics of control', *Journal of European Public Policy*, 18(1): 90–105.

Lodge, M., Wegrich, K. and McElroy, G. (2010) 'Dodgy kebabs everywhere? Variety of worldviews and regulatory change', *Public Administration*, 88(1): 247–66.

Loeb, M. and Magat, W. (1979) 'A decentralized method for utility regulation', *Journal of Law and Economics*, 22(2): 399–404.

Luhmann, N. (2004) *Law as a Social System*, Oxford, Oxford University Press.

Macey, J.R. (1992) 'Organizational design and political control of administrative agencies', *Journal of Law, Economics and Organization*, 8(1): 93–110.

Mahoney, J. and Thelen, K. (2010) 'A theory of gradual institutional change', in J. Mahoney and K. Thelen (eds) *Explaining Institutional Change*, Cambridge, Cambridge University Press.

Majone, G. (1984) 'Science and trans-science in standard setting', *Science, Technology & Human Values*, 9(1): 15–22.

Majone, G. (1989) *Evidence, Argument & Persuasion in the Policy Process*, New Haven, Yale University Press.

Majone, G. (1994) 'The rise of the regulatory state in Europe', *West European Politics*, 17(3): 77–101.

Majone, G. (1997) 'From the positive to the regulatory state: causes and consequences of changes in the mode of governance', *Journal of Public Policy*, 17(2): 139–68.

Majone, G. (2000) 'The credibility crisis of community regulation', *Journal of Common Market Studies*, 38(2): 273–302.

Majone, G. (2002) 'What price safety? The precautionary principle and its policy implications', *Journal of Common Market Studies*, 40(1): 89–109.

Makkai, T. and Braithwaite, J. (1992) 'In and out of the revolving door', *Journal of Public Policy*, 12: 61–78.

Maor, M. (2007) 'A scientific standard and an agency's legal independence', *Public Administration*, 85(4): 961–78.

Maor, M. (2010) 'Organizational reputation and jurisdictional claims', *Governance*, 23(1): 133–59.

Mashaw, J. (1983) *Bureaucratic Justice*, New Haven, Yale University Press.

Mattli, W. and Buethe, T. (2003) 'Setting international standards', *World Politics*, 56: 1–42.

May, P. (2003) 'Performance-based regulation and regulatory regimes: the saga of leaky buildings', *Law & Policy*, 25(4): 381–401.

May, P. and Winter, S. (2000) 'Reconsidering styles of regulatory enforcement', *Law & Policy*, 22: 143–73.

Mayntz, R. (2010a) 'Global structures: markets, organizations, networks – and communities?, in M.-L. Djelic and S. Quack (eds) *Transnational Communities: Global Economic Governance*, Cambridge, Cambridge University Press.

Mayntz, R. (2010b) 'Legitimacy and compliance in transnational governance', *MPIfG Working Paper* 10/5, Cologne, Max Planck Institute www.mpifg.de/pu/workpap/wp10–5.pdf (last accessed 3 November 2011).

McAllister, L. (2010) 'Dimensions of enforcement style: factoring in regulatory autonomy and capacity', *Law and Policy*, 32(1): 61–78.

McBarnet, D. and Whelan, C. (1991) 'The elusive spirit of the law: formalism and the struggle for legal control', *Modern Law Review*, 54: 848–73.

McCubbins, M., Noll, R.G. and Weingast, B.R. (1987) 'Administrative procedures as instruments of political control', *Journal of Law, Economics and Organisation*, 3(2): 243–86.

McGarity, T. (1990) *Reinventing Rationality*, Cambridge, Cambridge University Press.

McLean, I. (2004) 'The history of regulation in the United Kingdom: three case studies in search of a theory', in J. Jordana and D. Levi-Faur (eds) *The Politics of Regulation*, Cheltenham, Edward Elgar.

McLean, I. and Johnes, M. (2000) '"Regulation run mad": the Board of Trade and the loss of the *Titanic*', *Public Administration*, 78(4): 729–49.

Meidinger, E. (2007) 'Beyond Westphalia', in C. Brütsch and D. Lehmkuhl (eds) *Law and Legalization in Transnational Relations*, London, Routledge.

Meier, K. (1994) *Politics of Sin*, Armonk, NY, M.E. Sharpe.

Merton, R. (1936) 'The unintended effects of purposive social action', *American Sociological Review*, 1(6): 894–904.

Miller, P. and Rose, N. (2008) *Governing the Present*, Cambridge, Polity Press.

Moran, M. (1986) 'Theories of regulation and changes in regulation', *Political Studies*, 34(2): 185–201.

Moran, M. (2003) *The British Regulatory State*, Oxford, Oxford University Press.

Morgan, B. and Yeung, K. (2007) *An Introduction to Law and Regulation*, Cambridge, Cambridge University Press.

Mossell (Jamaica) Limited v Office of Utilities Regulation Cable & Wireless Jamaica Limited and Centennial Jamaica Limited, see: www.jcpc.gov.uk/decided-cases/docs/JCPC_2009_0079_Judgment.pdf (last accessed 28 January 2012).

National Audit Office (2001) *Better Regulation: Making Good Use of Regulatory Impact Assessments*, HC 329 2001–2, 15 November 2001, http://www.nao.org.uk/publications/0102/better_regulation_making_good.aspx (last accessed 11 March 2012).

National Audit Office (2008) *The Administrative Burdens Reduction Programme*, London, National Audit Office, HC: 944 2007–2008.

National Audit Office (2009) *HM Treasury: The Nationalisation of Northern Rock*, HC 298 2008/9, 20 March 2009, www.nao.org.uk/publications/0809/northern_rock.aspx (last accessed 6 March 2012).

Newbury, D. (1999) *Privatization, Restructuring, and Regulation of Network Utilities*, Cambridge, MA, MIT Press.

Newsweek, 13 February 2011; 'Are dogs steeling our jobs?' www.the dailybeast.com/newsweek/2011/02/13/are-dogs-stealing-our-jobs.html (last accessed 19 January 2012).

Nickson, A. and Vargas, C. (2002) 'The limitations of water regulation: the failure of the Cochabamba concession', *Bulletin of Latin American Research*, 21(1): 99–120.

Noll, R.G. (1989) 'Economic perspectives on the politics of regulation', in R. Schmalensee and R.D. Willig (eds) *Handbook of Industrial Organisation*, Amsterdam, Elsevier.

OECD (2002) *Regulatory Policies in OECD Countries: From Interventionism to Regulatory Governance*, Paris, OECD.

OECD (2010a) *Obesity and the Economics of Prevention*, Paris, OECD.

OECD (2010b) *Risk and Regulatory Policy: Improving the Governance of Risk*, Paris, OECD.

OECD (2011) *Draft Recommendation on Regulatory Policy and Governance*, Paris, OECD, www.oecd.org/dataoecd/49/43/48087250.pdf (last accessed 1 September 2011).

Ogus, A. (1994) *Regulation*, Oxford, Oxford University Press.

Olson, M. (1965) *The Logic of Collective Action*, Cambridge, MA, Harvard University Press.

O'Rourke, D. (2003) 'Outsourcing regulation: analysing nongovernmental systems of labor standards and monitoring', *Policy Studies Journal*, 31(1): 1–29.

Ostrom, E. (1990) *Governing the Commons*, Cambridge, Cambridge University Press.

Parker, C. (1999) 'Compliance professionalism and regulatory community', *Journal of Law and Society*, 26(2): 215–39.

Parker, C. (2002) *The Open Corporation*, Cambridge, Cambridge University Press.

Parker, C. (2003) 'Regulator-required corporate compliance program audits', *Law and Policy*, 25(3): 221–44.

Pattberg, P. (2003) 'Private governance and the South: lessons from global forest politics', *Third World Politics*, 27(4): 579–93.

Peci, A. and Sobral, F. (2011) 'Regulatory impact assessment: how political and organizational forces influence its diffusion in a developing country', *Regulation & Governance*, 5: 204–20.

Peltzman, S. (1976) 'Toward a more general theory of regulation', *Journal of Law and Economics*, 19: 211–40.

Peltzman, S. (1989) 'The economic theory of regulation after a decade of deregulation', *Brookings Papers on Economic Activity (Microeconomics)*: 1–44.

Perrow, C. (1984/1999) *Normal Accidents*, New York, Basic Books.

Pires, R.R. (2011) 'Beyond the fear of discretion: flexibility, performance, and accountability in the management of regulatory bureaucracies', *Regulation & Governance*, 5(1): 43–69.

Polinsky, M. and Shavell, S. (2000) 'The economic theory of public enforcement of law', *Journal of Economic Literature*, 38: 45–76.

Pollack, M. (1997) 'Delegation, agency, and agenda setting in the European Community', *International Organization*, 51: 99–134.

Pollitt, C., Girre, X., Lonsdale, J., Mul, R., Summa, H. and Waerness, M. (1999) *Performance or Compliance? Performance Audit and Public Management in Five Countries*, Oxford, Oxford University Press.

Posner, R. (1972) 'The appropriate scope of regulation in the cable television industry', *Bell Journal of Economics and Management Science*, 3(1): 98–129.

Posner, R. (2004) *Catastrophe*, New York, Oxford University Press.

Posner, R. (2009) *A Failure of Regulation*, Cambridge MA, Harvard University Press.

Power, M. (1997) *The Audit Society*, Oxford, Oxford University Press.

Power, M. (2007) *Organized Uncertainty*, Oxford, Oxford University Press.

Prosser, T. (1986) *Nationalised Industries and Public Control*, Oxford, Blackwell.

Prosser, T. (1999) 'Theorising utility regulation', *Modern Law Review*, 62(2): 196–217.

Prosser, T. (2006) 'Regulation and social solidarity', *Journal of Law and Society*, 33(3): 364–87.

Prosser, T. (2010) *The Regulatory Enterprise: Government, Regulation and Legitimacy*, Oxford, Oxford University Press.

Radaelli, C. and Meuwese, A.C.M. (2010) 'Hard questions, hard solutions', *West European Politics*, 33(1): 136–53.

Reason, J. (2008) *The Human Contribution*, Farnham, Ashgate.

Regling, K. and Watson, M. (2010) *A preliminary report on the Sources of Ireland's Banking Crisis*, www.bankinginquiry.gov.ie/Preliminary_Reports. aspx (last accessed 6 September 2011).

Regulatory Policy Committee (2011) *Rating Regulation*, London, RPC http://regulatorypolicycommittee.independent.gov.uk/wp-content/ uploads/2011/07/Rating-Regulation-July–2011-FINAL-two-blank-pages.pdf (last accessed 6 March 2012).

Renn, O. (2008) *Risk Governance*, London, Earthscan.

Revesz, R. and Livermore, M. (2008) *Retaking Rationality: How Cost Benefit Analysis Can Better Protect the Environment and Our Health*, Oxford: Oxford University Press.

Ritchey, M. and Nicholson-Crotty, S. (2011) 'Deterrence theory and the implementation of speed limits in the American states', *Policy Studies Journal*, 39(2): 329–42.

Roberts, A. (2010) *The Logic of Discipline*, Oxford, Oxford University Press.

Robson, W.A. (1960) *Nationalized Industry and Public Ownership*, London, Allen & Unwin.

Rose, N. (1999) *Powers of Freedom*, Cambridge, Cambridge University Press.

Rostein, T. (2010) 'Self-regulatory authority, markets, and the ideology of professionalism', in R. Baldwin, M. Cave and M. Lodge (eds) *Oxford Handbook of Regulation*, Oxford, Oxford University Press.

Rothstein, H., Huber, M. and Gaskell, G. (2006) 'A theory of risk colonisation' *Economy and Society*, 35(1): 91–112.

Scharpf, F.W. (1994) 'Games real actors could play: positive and negative coordination in embedded negotiations', *Journal of Theoretical Politics*, 6(1): 27–53.

Scharpf, F.W. (1996) 'Negative and positive integration in the political economy of European welfare states', in G. Marks, F.W. Scharpf, P.C. Schmitter and W. Streeck (eds) *Governance in the European Union*, London, Sage.

Scholz, J.T. (1984) 'Cooperation, deterrence and the ecology of regulatory enforcement', *Law & Society Review*, 18: 601–46.

Schwintowski, H.-P. (2003) 'The common good, public subsistence and the functions of public undertakings in the European internal market', *European Business Organization Law Review*, 4(3): 353–82.

Scott, C. (2000) 'Accountability in the regulatory state', *Journal of Law and Society*, 27(1): 38–60

Scott, C. (2001) 'Analysing regulatory space: fragmented resources and institutional design', *Public Law*, summer: 329–53.

Scoular, J. (2010) 'What's law got to do with it? How and why law matters in the regulation of sexwork', *Journal of Law and Society*, 37(1): 12–39.

Schrader-Frechette, K.S. (1991) *Risk and Rationality*, Berkeley, CA, University of California Press.

Selznick, P. (1985) 'Focusing organizational research on regulation', in R. Noll (ed.) *Regulatory Policy and the Social Sciences*, Berkeley, University of California Press.

Shapiro, S. (2011) 'The evolution of cost–benefit analysis in U.S regulatory decisionmaking', in D. Levi-Faur (ed.) *Handbook of the Politics of Regulation*, Cheltenham/Northampton: Edward Elgar.

Shapiro, S. and Rabinowitz, R. (1997) 'Punishment versus cooperation in regulatory enforcement: acase study of the OSHA', *Administrative Law Review*, 14: 713–62.

Shavell, S. (1993) 'The optimal structure of law enforcement', *Journal of Law and Economics*, 36: 255–87.

Sieber, S. (1981) 'Regressive intervention in contemporary theory and research', in *Fatal Remedies: The Ironies of Social Intervention*, New York, Plenum Press.

Simmons, B. (2001) 'The international politics of harmonization', *International Organization*, 55(3): 589–620.

Simon, H. (1947) *Administrative Behavior*, New York, Free Press (4th edn 1997).

Simpson, S. (2002) *Corporate Crime and Social Control*, Cambridge, Cambridge University Press.

Sparrow, C. (2000) *Regulatory Craft*, Washington, DC, Brookings.

Stern, J. (2009) 'The relationship between regulation and contracts in infrastructure industries', *CCRP Working Paper*, February 2009.

Stigler, G. (1970) 'The optimum enforcement of laws', *Journal of Political Economy*, 78(3): 526–36.

Stigler, G. (1971) 'The theory of economic regulation', *Bell Journal of Economics and Management Science*, 2(3): 3–21.

Sunstein, C. (1990) 'Paradoxes of the regulatory state', *University of Chicago Law Review*, 57: 407–41.

Sunstein, C. (2002) *Risk and Reason*, Cambridge, Cambridge University Press.

Surowiecki, J. (2004) *The Wisdom of Crowds*, London, Little Brown.

Tagesspiegel, 25 April 2011; 'Stunk in der WG', www.tagesspiegel.de/meinung/die-stadt-und-der-muell-stunk-in-der-wg/4096358.html (last accessed 21 January 2012).

Taleb, N.M. (2007) *Black Swans*, London, Penguin.

Telser, L.G. (1969) 'On the regulation of industry: a note', *Journal of Political Economy*, 77(6): 937–52.

Tett, G. (2009) *Fools Gold*, London, Little, Brown.

Teubner, G. (1986) *Dilemmas of Law in the Welfare State*, London, Walter de Gruyter.

Teubner, G. (1993) *Law as an Autopoietic System*, London, Blackwell.

Teubner, G. (1998) 'Legal irritants: good faith in British law or how unifying law ends up in new divergences', *Modern Law Review*, 61(1): 11–32.

Thaler, R. and Sunstein, C. (2008) *Nudge*, London, Penguin.

Thatcher, M. (1998) 'Regulating the regulators: the regulatory regime for the British privatised utilities', *Parliamentary Affairs*, 51(2): 209–22.

Thatcher, M. (2005) 'Sale of the century: 3G mobile phone licensing in Europe', in J. Black, M. Lodge and M. Thatcher (eds) *Regulatory Innovation*, Cheltenham, Edward Elgar.

Thomas, C.R., Soule, A.B. and Davis, T.B. (2011) 'Special interest capture of regulatory agencies', *Policy Studies Journal*, 38(1): 447–64.

Thompson, M., Ellis, R., and Wildavksy, A. (1990) *Cultural Theory*, Boulder, CO, Westview Press.

Tiebout, C. (1956) 'A pure theory of local expenditures', *Journal of Political Economy*, 64(5): 416–24.

Tiessen, J., Stolk, C. van, Brutscher, P.-B., Drauth, C., Hallsworth, M. and Ling, T. (2008) *Evaluation of DG SANCO's Impact Assessments*, Cambridge: RAND Europe.

Time, 21 January 2011; 'Swiss village to dog owners: pay your taxes, or poochie does', http://newsfeed.time.com/2011/01/11/swiss-village-to-dog-owners-pay-your-taxes-or-poochie-dies/ (last accessed 21 January 2011).

Tivey, L. (1982) 'Nationalised industries as organised interests', *Public Administration*, 60: 42–55.

US Senate (2011) *Wall Street and the Finance Crisis: Anatomy of a Financial Collapse*, US Senate, Permanent Subcommittee on Investigations.

Vaughan, D. (1996) *The Challenger Launch Decision*, Chicago, Chicago University Press.

Vaughan, D. (2005) 'Organizational rituals and error' in B. Hutter and M. Power (eds) *Organizational Encounters with Risk*, Cambridge, Cambridge University Press.

Vaughan, D. (2006) 'NASA revisited: theory, analogy, and public sociology', *American Journal of Sociology*, 112(2): 353–93.

Verweij, M., Douglas, M., Ellis, R., Engel, C., Hendricks, F., Lohmann, S., Ney, S., Rayner, S. and Thompson, M. (2006) 'The case for clumsiness', in M. Verweij and M. Thompson (eds) *Clumsy Solutions for a Complex World*, Basingstoke, Palgrave Macmillan.

Viscusi, W.K. (2009) 'The devaluation of life', *Regulation & Governance*, 3(2): 103–27.

Viscusi, W.K., Harrington, J.E. and Vernon, J.W. (2005) *Economics of Regulation and Antitrust*, Cambridge, MS, MIT Press.

Vogel, D. (1995) *Trading Up – Consumer and Environmental Regulation in a Global Economy*, Cambridge, MA, Harvard University Press.

Wagener, F. (1979) 'Der öffentliche Dienst im Staat der Gegenwart', *Veröffentlichungen der Vereinigung der deutschen Staatsrechtslehrer*, 37: 216–66, Berlin Walter de Gruyter.

Weber, M. (1956) *Wirtschaft und Gesellschaft*, Tübingen, Mohr Sieback.

Wegrich, K. (2009) 'The administrative burden reduction policy in Europe', *CARR discussion paper 52*, London, LSE.

Wegrich, K. (2011) *Das Leitbild 'Better Regulation': Ziele, Instrumente, Wirkungsweise*, Berlin: Edition sigma.

Weick, K. (1987) 'Organizational culture as a source of high reliability', *Californian Management Review*, 29: 1–27.

Weick, K. (1995) *Sensemaking in Organizations*, London, Sage.

Weick, K. and Roberts, K.H. (1993) 'Collective mind in organizations', *Administrative Science Quarterly*, 38: 357–81.

Weinberg, A.M. (1972) 'Science and trans-science', *Minerva*, 10: 209–22.

Weiss, C. (1997) *Evaluation* (2nd edn), Upper Saddle River, NJ, Prentice-Hall.

Wenger, E. (1998) *Communities of Practice*, Cambridge, Cambridge University Press.

Werle, R. (1995) 'Staat und standards', in R. Mayntz and F.W. Scharpf (eds) *Gesellschaftliche Selbstregelung und politische Steuerung*, Frankfurt am Main, Campus.

Wildavsky, A. (1987) 'Choosing preferences by constructing institutions', *American Political Science Review*, 81(1): 3–21.

Wildavsky, A. (1988) *Searching for Safety*, New Brunswick, Transaction Publishers

Williams, R.J. (1976) 'Politics and the ecology of regulation', *Public Administration*, 54(2): 319–31.

Williamson, O. (1976) 'Franchise bidding for natural monopolies', *Bell Journal of Economics*, 7(1): 73–104.

Willke, H. (1995) *Systemtheorie III: Steuerungstheorie*, Stuttgart, Gustav Fischer.

Wilson, G. (1989) 'Social regulation and explanations for regulatory failure', *Political Studies*, 32(2): 203–25.

Wilson, J.Q. (1980) 'The politics of regulation', in J.Q. Wilson (ed.) *The Politics of Regulation*, New York, Basic Books.

Wilson, J.Q. (1989) *Bureaucracy*, New York, Basic Books.

Wilson, J.Q. and Rachal, P. (1977) 'Can the government regulate itself?', *The Public Interest*, 46: 3–14.

Yackee, S.W. (2006) 'Assessing inter-institutional attention to and influence on the bureaucracy', *British Journal of Political Science*, 36: 723–44.

Yackee, J.W. and Yackee, S.W. (2006) 'A bias towards business? Assessing interest group influence on the bureaucracy', *Journal of Politics*, 68: 128–39.

Yackee, J.W. and Yackee, S.W. (2011) 'Administrative procedures and bureaucratic performance: is federal rule-making "ossified"?', *Journal of Public Administration Research and Theory*, 20: 261–82.

Yandle, B. (2011) 'Bootleggers and Baptists in the theory of regulation', in D. Levi-Faur (ed.) *Handbook on the Politics of Regulation*, Cheltenham, Edward Elgar.

Yeung, K. (2004) *Securing Compliance*, Oxford, Hart.

Yeung, K. (2005) 'Government by publicity management: sunlight or spin?', *Public Law*, 360–83.

Zupan, M. (1989) 'The efficacy of franchise bidding schemes in the case of cable television', *Journal of Law and Economics*, 32: 401–56.

Index